And They Dreamt of A Kingdom

Biblical Studies in Discipleship And The Kingdom of God
Volume 1

By Maurice Smith

I0135451

RISING
RIVER
MEDIA

Other Titles Available From Rising River Media

All Dogs Go To Heaven, Don't They?
Biblical Reflections On Christian Universalism and Ultimate Reconciliation

River Houses Rising
The Rise of Safe Houses Of Hope And Prayer

Safe Houses of Hope And Prayer
Your Practical Guide To Organic Church In Your House

Secret Church
Your Invitation To The Coming Underground Church

The Inextinguishable Blaze
God's Call to Holiness, Repentance, Intimacy and Spiritual Awakening

The Least of These
The Role of Good Deeds In A Jesus-Shaped Spirituality

When Jesus Visits His Church
A Study In The Seven Churches of Asia (Revelation 2-3)

All titles are available on our website at
www.risingrivermedia.org

Table of Contents

From The Author
Preface To The Revised Edition

While working on the second Volume in this series, I decided to use the opportunity to review and update this first Volume. Updates to this Volume include: some formatting changes, a map of 1st Century Israel during the time of Jesus, the inclusion of an additional Lesson (*"25 - Two Sabbath Confrontations"*), the conversion from "Footnotes" to "Endnotes" (along with additional and updated notes), an Appendix listing Scripture passages for each lesson along with an improved Chronology, and the general clean-up of several lessons. Otherwise, the overall book is the same as the original print edition. Just better.

The Question That Started It All

"Would you disciple us?"

Those were the fateful words which generated this book. It was a Saturday evening and I was facilitating an area-wide organic house church gathering. I had asked two young men if they would video the evening's session. Up to this point these two young men had not expressed any particular interest in organic house church. But on that particular night, during which I talked on the importance of personal discipleship to organic house church, their question posed a very real and practical challenge. How do we intentionally disciple those who are seeking to become disciples of the Kingdom? This book is my personal answer to the challenge and the question.

My wife and I have spent the past decade (or so) laboring in the organic house church movement. I believe that one of the enduring legacies of the organic house church movement will be an emphasis upon returning to "basics," a genuine focus upon the biblical essentials of what it means to "be the Church" (as expressed in the saying *"We don't go to church; we ARE the Church"*) apart from centuries of institutional trappings. This focus upon basics includes a willingness to question long-standing traditions and to ask, *"Where do we find that in Scripture?"*

Short of becoming complete "iconoclasts,"[1] there is an ever present danger in asking such questions for the simple reason that you and I might be surprised by the answer we get. My own journey into organic house church and its roots in Scripture eventually forced me to ask (and answer) a fundamental question that every believer should confront at some point in their spiritual journey. This question has three basic components: 1) What is the Kingdom of God, 2) What is the relationship of the Kingdom to the Church, and 3) What does it mean for us to be disciples of that Kingdom? The first two components of this question are theological in nature. The third component is personal, and asks the practical question of what it means to take the truths of the Kingdom of God as taught by Jesus and to live them out in our daily walk with God and with one another. What does it mean to live on a daily basis as a disciple of the Kingdom? These are the three questions which this book seeks to address. How well we have done so will be determined by you, the reader.

Ed Stetzer of Lifeway Research has written about the "subversive" nature of the Kingdom of God.[2] He is right, of course, although I don't think he has gone quite far enough. I believe that the contemporary church of the early 21st Century is in trouble. It has departed so far from the biblical understanding and teaching concerning the Kingdom of God that any genuine teaching on the subject of the Kingdom would be subversive to the church itself, challenging our structures, questioning our programs, overturning our values and generally "wreaking havoc in Zion." And nowhere would the havoc be more profound than in our understanding of what constitutes "discipleship."

"Come to me, all who labor and are heavy laden, and I will give you rest. Take my yoke upon you, and learn from me, for I am gentle and lowly in heart, and you will find rest for your souls. For my yoke is easy, and my burden is light." (Matthew 11:28-30)

As these words of Jesus suggest, discipleship is relational as opposed to informational or even educational. You and I don't become disciples of Jesus by taking a class, reading a book (including this one), memorizing Bible verses or completing some "Ten Steps" curriculum (none of which are bad in and of themselves). There is no "Certificate of Completion" to prove that you are an official disciple. In the Kingdom of God, discipleship isn't about what you know or even how much you know. It is about Who you know . . . and Who knows you. As practiced and modeled by Jesus Himself, discipleship is first and foremost a relationship between a student-learner and a master-teacher which results in the impartation of Kingdom values and life, not religious knowledge.

Discipleship is about accepting Jesus' yoke of obedience to the call of the Kingdom and following that yoke wherever He and it lead us. Jesus yoked His disciples to Himself, and refused to release them until their religion-shaped spirituality had given way and been replaced with a Jesus-shaped spirituality. Jesus challenged their understanding of religion until He embodied their understanding of religion. He challenged their understanding of the Sabbath and the Law until He embodied their understanding of the Sabbath and the Law. He challenged their understanding of spirituality until He embodied their understanding of spirituality. And He challenged their understanding of the Kingdom of God until He, and He alone, embodied their understanding of the Kingdom. And that is how He wants to challenge and transform each of us.

Too much of what passes for discipleship in the organized church today represents an attempt on someone's part to define discipleship as participation in their particular church programs. We take surveys to determine self-perceived needs, create programs to meet those perceived needs, and then label participation in those programs as "discipleship." As a result, our efforts to produce disciples reflect the perceived needs of our set of survey respondents or the perceived needs of our particular church or organization more than they reflect the clear teachings of Jesus and Scripture.

Another common approach is to begin with a particular desired result (i.e., "missions") and then proceed to create a "discipleship curriculum" which we believe will produce that result. We assume a conclusion and then reverse-engineer a program to produce that conclusion. When the process is done, we have produced something which reflects our survey, our agenda or the values of our organization. But have we produced disciples of the Kingdom who embody the values of the Kingdom and manifest a genuine Jesus-shaped spirituality? All too often, the answer is "No."

Who Is This Book For?

This book is intended for those who want to understand Jesus' message of the Kingdom of God and what it means to be a disciple of that Kingdom. It is intended for those who harbor the secret hope that biblical Christianity consists of more than four points and a prayer followed by a lifetime of participation in programs organized by survey-takers. This book is intended for those willing to dream that the "place" Jesus is preparing for His people is, in fact, a Kingdom, the perfection of which beggars all human attempts to describe it. As Paul told those early Corinthian believers, *"What no eye has seen, nor ear heard, nor the heart of man imagined, what God has prepared for those who love him - these things God has revealed to us through the Spirit."* (1 Corinthians 2:9-10) Whether you are a curious searcher who makes no profession of biblical faith, or a professing believer in Jesus with years of experience in the church, this book is intended to challenge you to re-examine your understanding of biblical faith and discipleship and what it means to respond to the call of Jesus to *"deny yourself, take up your cross and follow Me."*

How To Best Use This Book

The last command which Jesus gave to His disciples before His return to the Father was quite simple: *"make disciples of all nations . . . . teaching them to observe all that I have commanded you.* This book, along with its companion volumes, has been written to challenge the reader with those same discipleship lessons which Jesus taught His disciples. Jesus took roughly three-and-a-half years to impart the truths of these lessons, to free His disciples from the religion-shaped spirituality given to them by 1st century Judaism and to re-mold them, like clay on the Potter's wheel, into a spirituality fashioned and shaped around Jesus Himself. The point here is simple. The discipleship of Jesus requires truth embodied over time. There is no quick path or easy short-cut to biblical discipleship.

This book is organized to offer the reader bite-sized pieces of truth, and to challenge the reader to reflect on what he (or she) has read. It is not the goal or plan of this book to spoon feed the reader with pre-digested conclusions and applications. Far too many professing believers today demonstrate little or no ability to "think beyond the spoon." The goal of this book is to take the reader on a journey of discovery into the Kingdom of God along side Jesus and His disciples. We need to see what they saw. To learn what they learned. To be challenged as they were challenged. To be transformed, just as they were. And to eventually emerge from the journey as fully committed disciples of that Kingdom.

I have attempted to design this book in such a way that it offers lessons which can be used either for personal study or as lessons for a group discipleship gathering. Most importantly, I have designed it for anyone who is serious about understanding biblical discipleship as practiced by Jesus and His disciples. This means that whether it is used individually as a devotional/discipleship guide, or as a guide in a group discipleship setting, the burden is on you, the reader. You must make the serious effort to read the Scripture passages cited without bringing preconceived notions or interpretations as to what it might mean. That will be difficult for some of you. You must allow yourself the freedom to wrestle with both the Scripture being examined and the discipleship truth being offered by each lesson. An unwillingness to wrestle with the lesson and to reflect on its application to your own life will render any further "discipleship study" fruitless. And there are enough fruitless believers in the church today. You really don't need to add your name to their ranks.

Prolegomena

A few words are in order about this book as we begin. This book originated

And They Dreamt Of A Kingdom

in a study I was doing on the Kingdom of God. That study raised the question of how our discipleship as professing believers relates to the Kingdom, and what it means to be a "disciple of the Kingdom." The Jesus message of the Kingdom of God represents the dominant message of this book.

After the process of writing was underway and I had written some twenty lessons, it became apparent that a clear chronology of Jesus' ministry was indispensable for an accurate understanding of Jesus' work with His disciples. For example, a clear chronology of Jesus' ministry reveals that for the first year or so of His ministry, Jesus called only six disciples (as we will talk about later). For this reason I have worked to present Jesus' discipleship lessons in chronological order, using a "harmony of the Gospels" as a guide. I would strongly encourage the reader, and any serious student of the Gospels and the ministry of Jesus, to secure a copy of a good "Harmony." I personally recommend the harmony of the Gospels by Thomas and Gundry cited below.[3]

The use of a harmony along with an attempt to place the teachings of Jesus into a chronology necessitated a decision as to dates in order to address such issues as the year in which Jesus began His public ministry or how much time had passed before the commissioning of the twelve or the sending out of the seventy-two, etc. Following the conclusions of Thomas and Gundry (along with numerous other New Testament Scholars), I have adopted a chronology/time-line which places the beginning of Jesus' ministry in mid-to-late A.D. 26, and culminating just over three years later in His crucifixion and resurrection in the Spring of A.D. 30.[4] The reader will find a chart of Scripture passages and a more detailed chronology in the *Appendix* of this book. We will also make other chronology observations along the way as Lessons progress. Our basic chronology of Jesus' ministry is as follows:

6/5 B.C.	Jesus Birth
4 B.C.	Death of Herod
A.D. 26 (Spring/Summer)	Beginning of Jesus' Ministry
A.D. 27 (Spring)	First Passover (John 2:13)
A.D. 28 (Spring)	Second Passover (Unrecorded)
A.D. 28 (Fall)	Feast of Booths (John 5:1)
A.D. 29 (Spring)	Third Passover (John 6:4)
A.D. 29 (Fall)	Feast of Booths (John 7-8)
A.D. 30 (Winter)	Feast of Dedication (John 10:22)
A.D. 30 (Spring)	Final Passover (John 11:55)
A.D. 30 (Spring/Passover)	Crucifixion

Before we leave this introduction, a word is probably in order concerning repetition. At some point in our study of Jesus' dealings with His disciples, someone is going to notice a certain degree of repetition. Simply put, Jesus frequently repeated Himself. He taught similar lessons more than once. As a result, so will we. The reason behind this repetition, both then and now, is tied to human nature. Even after Jesus dispels our spiritual blindness and our faith in Him begins to grow, we struggle with our own "dullness." Like the disciples on the road to Emmaus, even with Jesus in our midst we remain "foolish and slow of heart" when it comes to embracing truth which is right in front of us. Jesus knew that the dullness of our hearts and minds requires that we hear, see and experience truth more than once. Repetition is a key to our learning, both then and now. For this reason alone, Jesus repeated Himself. And so will we.

Dedication

For Brock and David, whose question that fateful evening, started me on the journey which became this book. Thank you.

For Nick, whose many encouragements along our journey helped make this book possible.

And They Dreamt Of A Kingdom

1 - October Tomatoes And The Kingdom of God

"The most difficult subjects can be explained to the most slow-witted man if he has not formed any idea of them already; but the simplest thing cannot be made clear to the most intelligent man if he is firmly persuaded that he knows already, without a shadow of doubt, what is laid before him." -Leo Tolstoy, **The Kingdom of God is Within You**

"There is nothing in the world more powerful than an idea. No weapon can destroy it; no power can conquer it, except the power of another idea." - Albert Einstein, 1879-1955

"I can find in my undergraduate classes, bright students who do not know that the stars rise and set at night, or even that the Sun is a star." -The late Carl Sagan, astronomer

I have a confession to make. I love tomatoes, and nearly everything made with them. As a result I have often found it necessary to grow my own during the summer. Most store-bought tomatoes are picked green and allowed to "ripen" while in transit. All too often the net result is something resembling a tomato, but whose taste and texture more closely resemble the box they were shipped in than the whole-bodied flavor God intended and I enjoy on a sandwich, or in a Greek salad with generous amounts of Feta cheese. In northern latitudes where I live, a couple hours south of the U.S.-Canadian border, the mild summers make for slow growing and slow ripening tomatoes. It is usually late August or early September before tomatoes achieve that deep red richness of color and flavor which reward the months of tending, pruning and watering that must be invested in their growth. All too soon the first frosts of late September bring an end to this summer delight. But occasionally, if the plants haven't been cleared out and the frosts have been mild or late, you may find yourself treated to an out-of-season delight. October tomatoes.

In case you're wondering, this is not a book on horticulture or on growing tomatoes. It is a book about life. It is a book about the Kingdom of God. And more specifically it is a book about what it means to be a disciple of the Kingdom of God. Life sometimes offers us important lessons out of due season. Some of the most meaningful lessons in the Christian life come to us by surprise, like October Tomatoes. Truths which should have fully ripened and been enjoyed earlier in the spiritual seasons of life come to us late, but not too late to be either deeply meaningful or fully appreciated. In my own life and Christian experience the truth of the Kingdom of God has come like October tomatoes, ripening only after a long growing season.

This new-found appreciation for the truths of the Kingdom of God is somewhat embarrassing. To place it in perspective, for a Christian to not understand the Kingdom of God is on the same embarrassing level as Carl Sagan's undergraduate student who doesn't know that the stars rise and set at night, or that the Sun is a star. Now, please don't misunderstand me. It wasn't that I was a complete stranger to the concept of the Kingdom. During my seminary days I studied the idea of the Kingdom both in Scripture and in systematic theology. But all of that was simply knowledge, rather than understanding. It's one thing to know that Rudolph Bultman or Adolf Harnack or Oscar Cullman wrote books about the Kingdom of God. It's quite another to understand and to wrap one's life around the truth that the Kingdom of God in all its fullness is the central message of the New Testament, indeed, of the Bible itself.

And They Dreamt Of A Kingdom

The difference between such knowledge and genuine understanding is like . . . well, being able to name the stars in the sky, but not knowing that they rise and set at night, or that our own Sun is, in fact, a star.

I am hopeful that as we unfold this study on discipleship and the Kingdom of God, at least two things will happen. First, I am hopeful that you can and will successfully avoid the trap of Tolstoy's intelligent man who was firmly persuaded that he already knew, without a shadow of doubt, the truth of the matter at hand. This may (and probably will) require you to temporarily set aside what you think you already know about the Kingdom of God. In suggesting that you set aside what you already know, I am not asking you to suspend any discernment, only that you set aside any preconception you may have. Sometimes the greatest enemy of learning . . . is knowledge. If you

> *. . . the Kingdom of God is that 'idea' which could challenge and transform the barren spiritual landscape of our Postmodern generation.*

can avoid the "frost" of existing knowledge which wilts some things while freezing and killing others, you may yet be surprised by October tomatoes - a fresh understanding of the Kingdom of God and your role as a disciple of that Kingdom. Secondly, I am hopeful that in the process you will discover what Einstein understood - the power of an idea. I am convinced that, properly understood and fully embraced, the Kingdom of God is that "idea" which could challenge and transform the barren spiritual landscape of our Postmodern generation.

The Lost Kingdom

Let's begin our consideration of the Kingdom with a friendly little wager. I would be willing to wager a modest Starbucks gift card that if you and I asked a typical evangelical Christian in a typical American church about their particular church they could - and probably would - engage us in a prolonged conversation. Perhaps they would tell us about their pastor and his wonderful messages. Or perhaps they would tell us about their Sunday School class and the gifted Bible teacher who leads it, the various wonderful programs the church offers, the dynamic youth director, the recent mission trip to another neighborhood, city or country, and more. If they were really involved they might offer us a quick history of their church; maybe even some denominational background (or an animated explanation for why they aren't part of ANY denomination). In other words, this could quickly turn into a lengthy conversation requiring a visit to a local Starbucks and a large cup of coffee (hence, the wager for a modest Starbucks gift card - emphasis upon modest!).

But what if we were to ask that same evangelical believer to share with us their understanding of the Kingdom of God, what Jesus taught about the Kingdom, its relationship to the Church, and what it means on a practical level for us to be disciples of that Kingdom? My wager is that our conversation would be short, and that my Starbucks gift card would remain safely tucked away in my wallet, awaiting the next challenge. Like Carl Sagan's undergraduate student who didn't know that the stars rise and set at night, or that the Sun itself is a star, I think I could very safely wager that many (if not most) evangelical believers today are blissfully unaware of the Kingdom of God, what Jesus taught about the Kingdom, its relationship to their church, its impact upon their lives or what it means to be a disciple of that Kingdom.

Why? Well, I'm sure we could come up with any number of reasons, not the least of which would be a lack of competent teaching on the subject in most Churches. On the occasion of his 80th birthday, theologian J.I. Packer was asked what he regarded as the pressing need of the church today. *"The Church needs to catechize itself,"* he replied, *"Christians today do not know what they believe."* Packer was right, of course, and no where is this more evident than in the lack of biblical teaching concerning discipleship and the Kingdom of God.

Regardless of the reasons for this theological and practical illiteracy, at the end of the day we are confronted with a stark truth. Simply stated, the church of our generation has substituted church for the Kingdom of God, and in the process we have lost our sense of the majesty of the Kingdom, our sense of the grand sweep of God's plan for the ages, and our own sense of where we fit in God's plan. But it gets worse. We have also lost the interest and imagination of our Postmodern culture which is no longer enamored with our slickly produced worship services. It is my opinion - and the underlying thesis of this book - that if the church of our generation is ever to ignite a spiritual fire and recapture the hearts and minds of our lost Postmodern culture, we must once again become a people who *"speak of the glory of Thy Kingdom, and talk of Thy power; to make known to the sons of men Thy mighty acts, and the glory of the majesty of Thy Kingdom."* (Psalm 145:11-12)

And that is where our journey needs to go next.

And They Dreamt Of A Kingdom

2 - The Kingdom

The Kingdom of God has always existed.

During ages long enough for mountains to crumble and for stars to burn cold in the heavens, had they existed, but short enough to seem like a hand full of days had God chosen to record them, the Kingdom of God stretched like a seamless canvas through eternity past. Before there was time, before the worlds were created and the morning stars sang together, the Kingdom of God had existed. It existed in the person of the King, the triune God - Father, Son and Holy Spirit - Who among themselves exercised kingly power, dominion and rule within the God-head. Like a boundless, limitless and undisturbed ocean of divine Presence, the God-head existed in perfection of beauty, love, glory, honor, blessing, power and dominion. Kingship exists in the ability to exercise kingly dominion and rule over oneself, and this the Lord God, the Almighty, the One-in-Three and Three-in-One, did with that perfection of holiness and beauty which belongs to Him alone. Then, from within that perfection of self-dominion, and for reasons we are never given, He spoke those words which would forever change all that followed.

"Let there be light," were the simple words uttered by the Most High. And there was light, for in Him is no darkness at all. Now, like mixed fabrics upon a weavers loom, the time of men and angels intruded upon the eternity of God. Worlds came into being by the power of His word, and the Lord God, the Almighty, wore His creation like a newly spun garment perfectly befitting the Kingly wearer. Like a traveler inhabiting a spacious tent, God's kingly Presence inhabited His freshly created universe where newly created beings attended Him and experienced His kingly power and dominion. Myriads times myriads upon countless myriads of angels, perfect and incorporeal in their being, now worshiped the One Who called them into existence and Who now called them to serve His Kingdom purposes with spiritual power which reflected their maker. They would be His emissaries, servants and messengers to bear His Name and to do His bidding in this newly created universe which would soon be populated by another created being.

In the midst of countless galaxies, and stars without number, spread over unimaginable light-years of time and space, spanning little more than their Maker's handbreadth, hung a world of unique significance. The Lord God had spoken existence, order and life into empty space. But now the music and power of His spoken word focused upon this tiny blue globe, turning chaos into order, darkness into light and a formless void into timeless beauty. At His command, empty sea-beds filled with water and dry land called "earth" appeared. He spoke and this once-barren world brought forth vegetation of every kind. He spoke again and the music of His spoken word caused living creatures to appear in the sea, in the air and on the land.

Then, on the sixth and final day of His creative song, the Lord God created a being different from all the rest. This one He created without a word. While angelic majesties watched in wonder, the Lord God fashioned this one with His own hands from the dust of His newly created world. And with His own mouth He breathed life into this creature of clay and spittle. Unlike the angels or any other created being, this one - this "Ish" and his "Isha," this man and this woman - together would bear the very image of their Creator, a free will and moral agency unknown by any other creature. In His kingly dominion, the Lord God would now rule a realm inhabited not just by angels but also by men and women created in his own image. They would be His unique creatures and He would pursue a unique and intimate relationship with them.

And They Dreamt Of A Kingdom

They would walk together, God and man, in the beauty of this newly created world. Together they would experience the morning dews, the glorious days and the indescribable sunsets. God and man would experience the joy of one another's company - a unique fellowship of creature and Creator, of subject and King. His Kingdom would come and His kingly will would be done on this newly created world, and these two - the man and the woman - would be the beginning of a Kingly rule which would know no end.

But then it happened. No one knows exactly when, but it began among the angelic host. One of their number, Lucifer, the "Light Bearer" and "star of the morning," who stood, worshiped and served in the very Presence of the Lord God as the greatest of all the angelic beings, chose pride rather than humility and rebellion rather than obedience. *"I will make myself like the Most High,"* he declared. And with that declaration Lucifer led a third of the numberless angelic host in rebellion against the King of Heaven. But like the pot rebelling against the potter, the creatures were no match for their Creator. The heavens shook as angels battled angels, but with one stroke of His mighty right arm the Lord God gave Himself the victory, vanquishing all opposition and banishing them forever from His Presence. Creatures which had once enjoyed the light of God's Presence now fell into a darkness of their own making. And a creation which had been brought forth in perfection now experienced the first bitter taste of corruption. Where there had once been only a single Kingdom of light, ruled by the Lord God as King, a new, lesser domain now arose. A domain of darkness, rebellion and corruption ruled by one who was more than a man but less than a god. From the seed of that angelic rebellion, watered by the bitter moisture of unimaginable hatred, emerged the Adversary, the Serpent - Satan - along with his demonic host of fallen angels. He who once bore the light of God's Presence now ruled a domain of darkness. Together, Satan and his demonic hordes would devote themselves to the destruction of everything the Lord God loved. The creature would challenge the Creator. And he would begin that challenge with that unique creature who inhabited that world of the Lord God's special attention.

Rebellion breeds rebellion. Fueled and driven by an unbounded hatred of the Lord God and everything He loved, Lucifer now devised a plan to destroy God's Kingdom rule and dominion over His newly created world. He would work tirelessly to bring unimaginable pain, suffering and misery to the race of men. Diabolically methodical in his planning, Lucifer - the Serpent - was more crafty than any beast of the field which the Lord God had made. He who had once been "the Light Bearer" now plotted to spread spiritual darkness. He would attack God's creation at its most vulnerable point by questioning the words and the goodness of the Most High. Lucifer would raise the dark cloud of doubt. And he would begin with the woman. *"And he said to the woman, 'Indeed, has God said, 'You shall not eat from any tree of the garden'?"* The approach of the Serpent was both dark and clever. *"That isn't really what God said, is it?"* he whispered into the heart of one who had never before entertained a doubt. The approach had been made. The seed of doubt had been sown in uncorrupted soil. But if it was to sprout and bear its terrible fruit, then it must be watered.

"And the woman said to the serpent, 'From the fruit of the trees of the garden we may eat; but from the fruit of the tree which is in the middle of the garden, God has said, 'You shall not eat from it or touch it, lest you die'" (3:2-3).

Eve's understanding of God's instructions was faulty. God never said anything about touching the fruit, only that they were not to eat it. Here was the opportunity the Serpent had planned and waited for. He knew that Eve would not die if she touched the fruit. So, to win this argument all he needed to do was to get her to touch it. The weight of a faulty understanding of the Most High would do the rest. It was time to water the seed of doubt and to reap the fruit of dis-trust. *"And the serpent said to the woman, 'You surely shall not die! For God knows that in the day you eat from it your eyes will be opened, and you will be like God, knowing good and evil.'"* The battle over doubt and dis-trust was now underway. *"Not only are you not going to die,"* the Serpent argued, *"but God is holding out on you! The fruit of this tree is beautiful. And its good for food. Why wouldn't He want you to eat it? Why wouldn't he want your eyes to be open? Why wouldn't He want you to have this knowledge? I think you've misunderstood what He said, or at least what He meant! If he loves you He couldn't possibly be so unreasonable about a simple piece of fruit!"*

A critical moment had arrived for Eve. Her argument with Satan had momentarily cracked open a previously closed door. She now saw the situation surrounding the tree and its fruit differently. Why wouldn't God want her and the man to have this food (after all, they needed to eat)? Why wouldn't He want them to have something that is such a delight to look at. After all, wasn't it part of this beautiful garden He had given them to tend? And why wouldn't God want them to be wise? After all, wisdom is a good thing, isn't it?

"When the woman saw that the tree was good for food, and that it was a delight to the eyes, and that the tree was desirable to make one wise, she took from its fruit and ate; and she gave also to her husband with her, and he ate" (Genesis 3:6).

We can only wonder what thoughts must have raced through Eve's mind when she touched the fruit for the first time and did not die. Wrong beliefs poorly applied give birth to doubt, disappointment and confusion. In time they lead to wrong conclusions about ourselves and God. *"The Serpent was right!,"* she must have thought to herself in that moment. *"And if he was right about that, then he must be right about all the other things, too. God is being unfair to withhold this lovely fruit from us."* An emboldened Eve, who had not died when she touched the forbidden fruit, now found encouragement to distrust the other words of her Creator. Eve now took the fateful step and, along with the man, ate the forbidden fruit.

It was done. Satan, the Serpent, appearing as an "angel of light," had won. All creation fell into sin and darkness that fateful day. And in the darkness of that moment, Eve discovered the awful truth. The "angel of light" she had trusted was, in truth, the darkest of demons. And with his cunning deception he had killed her. She had died, just as God had warned. In that moment, she and the man, who joined her in open disobedience, died to God's Kingdom and to everything it offered. It was a death far worse than anything they could have imagined or would ever experience in their long lives. Darkness fell. And in the darkness of that moment the man and the woman saw their own nakedness. For the first time since the Lord God had breathed life into them and placed them in the Garden, they knew sin, guilt and shame. Not only had they sinned, but they now knew they had sinned, a knowledge which was almost unbearable.

No words can adequately express the moral and spiritual catastrophe which befell both the creature and the creation. The Lord God still ruled as King, but He now ruled over a world in rebellion. In His Kingly authority He banished the man and the woman from the Garden He had created for them. And with that banishment came the

And They Dreamt Of A Kingdom

spreading corruption of sin which now replaced willful submission with bitter rebellion. A realm of darkness once unknown now fell upon the world of men. Like a drop of India ink falling into clear water, sin and its spreading corruption now tainted God's creation. And creation itself groaned beneath the weight of the spreading corruption. Fear replaced fellowship. Fig leaves replaced intimacy. Innocence gave way to shame and concupiscence. An earth which once offered up its fruit willingly, now offered up the first fruit of its corruption; thorns and thistles. Unrestrained by submission to their King and Creator, fallen and rebellious creatures now warred with one another. Brother against brother. Men against men. Until rebellion, sin and darkness ruled the world of men.

But the Lord God of all creation was also the God of all hope. He Who had planned creation's beginnings from eternity past now unfolded His plan for its redemption. Man's rebellion had taken a mere handful of days to unfold. Man's redemption would require much longer. He who banished the man and the woman from the Garden as punishment for their rebellion now offered them a promise of a future redemption. A future day would come when one of their offspring would mortally "bruise the head" of the Serpent who had betrayed them. But that day now lay shrouded in a future which only the Lord God Himself could see.

And so it began, the spiritual battle for man's redemption and restoration to the Kingdom of God. No shadow of doubt clouded the heart of the Triune God concerning the outcome. His Kingdom would come, and His Kingly will would be done on this world of His special favor. Kingdoms of men would rise and fall as God prepared His promised redemption. Generations of men would move forward in their new-found freedom, rebellion and self-worship, building towers, cities and even empires as monuments to their own pseudo-greatness. And through it all the Lord God would search the earth for those individuals to whom He could reveal Himself, those willing to walk in faith and obedience and to experience His favor as they walked in submission to His Kingly rule.

From among all these sons of Adam and daughters of Eve another man and woman would be chosen. Promises would be given to them to guide their journey and to anchor their hope and their faith. A son of promise and laughter would be given to this childless barren couple. And from their offspring a people would be born who would become a great nation. That people and that nation would be set apart from all the people and nations of the earth as the Lord God's special possession. They would enter into a covenant together. He would be their God, and they would be His people, the sheep of His pasture. He would rule over them as King, and they would learn what it means to be the people of the King of Kings. To them the Lord God would entrust His Laws in order to teach them how to live and not be destroyed with a Holy God dwelling in their midst. Those Laws would teach them that all sin and rebellion against God's kingly rule must be unflinchingly punished. Over time the people of God would discover the true purpose of the Law, to serve as a tutor and to teach them their need for the promised coming Savior and deliverer from rebellion, sin and death.

But fallen, wayward hearts tend to wander over time. So, the Lord God would raise up messengers to remind, warn and admonish His people. These "prophets" would highlight the sin and disobedience of God's people, calling them to repent, warning them of the dire consequences which lay in store if they refused, and reminding them of the blessings which lay in store for those willing to walk in faith and obedience. And the prophets would remind God's people of a coming day when the Kingdom of God would fill the earth, when the knowledge of God would cover the earth as the waters cover the sea, and when the Lord God, through His Messiah, would rule the nations with a scepter of righteousness. The call of God's prophets represented an on-going call to God's people to repent, to believe the good news of the coming Kingdom, and to believe in a coming day when the Lord God would make a "new" covenant with them. It would not be like the "old" covenant of outward obedience and conformity to laws written on stone tablets, an old covenant which they and their fathers had broken countless times throughout their generations. The Lord God Himself would make a "new" covenant with all who believed the message of the Kingdom. He would write His Law upon their hearts, and would remember their sin and rebellion no more.

And so the centuries of men would roll forward in their unfolding generations. Kingdoms of men would rise and fall, serving as unknowing instruments in the hands of the Lord God to achieve His Kingdom purposes. Conquerors and oppressors would come and go, because that is what fallen, sinful men do to one another. God's prophetic voice would fall silent for nearly 400 years as the Lord God quietly worked all things together for His Kingdom purposes and to move all things toward the fullness of His appointed time. Hope of any future Kingdom would grow dim in the hearts of God's people. But through it all the Lord God would remain faithful to His people and His promises. For though God's promises may seem slow, as men measure such things, yet they await God's appointed time. Indeed, God's promises do not lie, but hasten to their appointed end. Though they seem slow in coming, men must wait for them. They will surely come and will not delay. But as they await the fullness of His promises, the righteous must live by faith, and believe in a Kingdom that is yet to come and which they cannot yet see, except through a glass dimly, or as in a dream.

And then it happened. In the fullness of God's time the voice of a promised forerunner was heard crying in the wilderness. A prophetic message silent for some 400 years rang out with fresh power and authority, *"Repent, for the Kingdom of God is at hand."* (Mark 1:15) The Lord God had remembered both His people and His promises. All His promises of redemption and the coming of His Kingdom now came to be manifested as the Word Who had spoken creation into existence became flesh and dwelt among men. The Kingdom had arrived in the person of the Messiah-King, Who called upon all men to repent of their sin and rebellion and to embrace His Kingly rule and authority. Now, the hopes, the fears and the desires of all the ages came to rest upon the shoulders of a carpenter's son from Nazareth - an itinerant Rabbi - and the unlikely band of disciples He now called to walk alongside Him in radical faith and radical obedience. His message was profoundly simple, and rang with eternal truth.

"The Kingdom of God is at hand. Repent, and believe the good news!"

And They Dreamt Of A Kingdom

3 - The Kingdom As God's Plan

The story of the Kingdom is your story and my story. It is the story of human history. It is the story recorded for us in the Old and New Testament Scriptures of the Bible. And it is to those Scriptures that we now want to turn in order to more fully understand that Kingdom.

The prophetic Scriptures of the Old Testament, books like Daniel, have always given secular historians head aches. The reason is quite simple. If the Scriptures are true and were indeed written hundreds of years before the events they describe, then they confront us with two unavoidable realities. First, they confront us with the reality that history has a purpose, as opposed to being random or driven by the whims of men. To use a fancier word, history is "teleological" in nature. It is moving in an orderly manner toward a pre-determined end and purpose. And this leads us to the second unavoidable reality which confronts us. God exists and He - not men - controls history. The story of the Kingdom of God dictates the flow of history and NOT the other way around.

> *The story of the Kingdom is your story and my story. It is the story of human history.*

Let's pause and reflect on this reality for just a moment. If the Scriptures are true (and they are), then the flow of history is not determined by politicians, generals, diplomats, economists or other "notables" who briefly blossom on the stage of history but who quickly wither and fade like grass. While God may and does use all of these people to accomplish His ultimate purposes, He rules them with or without their active obedience and laughs at their on-going revolts against His Kingly reign, *"Why do the nations rage and the peoples plot in vain? The kings of the earth set themselves, and the rulers take counsel together, against the LORD and against his Anointed, saying, 'Let us burst their bonds apart and cast away their cords from us.' He who sits in the heavens laughs; the Lord holds them in derision."* (Psalm 2:1-4)

The Scriptures continually remind us, teach us and encourage us that God is in control; actively at work throughout history fulfilling His Kingdom plan and purposes.

Two Paramount Questions

If God is, indeed, in control of history and if He has a plan for how history will unfold and how His purposes will be accomplished, then it only makes sense that you and I would want to know at least two things. *First,* it only makes sense that we would want to know something about His plan. *Second,* it only makes sense that we would want to know where we fit in His plan. These are the two paramount questions you and I need to answer. What is God's plan? What role do you and I play in His plan?

Let's begin with an overview of God's plan. In order to do this, and at the risk of stretching your attention for a moment, I need to engage in a quick lesson in biblical history. Not the *"Who were the Hittites and why should I care?"* kind of history (as interesting as that might be!). No, I want to talk about something bigger than that. I want to talk briefly about God's plan for history, what the Bible refers to as the "ages."

At the risk of over-simplifying things and seriously irritating detail oriented theological types, here's the "big picture" when it comes to history. The Bible divides all of human history into two "ages" (Greek: *aion*). Jesus Himself referred to these two ages in Matthew 12:32 when he said, *"And whoever speaks a word against the Son of Man will be forgiven, but whoever speaks against the Holy Spirit will not be forgiven,*

And They Dreamt Of A Kingdom

*either in **this age** or in **the age to come**."* The first "age" (which Scripture refers to as *"this age"* or the *"present evil age,"* see Galatians 1:4)[5] began at creation and will last until Jesus returns at what Jesus Himself referred to as *"the end of the age."*[6] At *"the end of the age"* Jesus will return, send forth His angels to harvest His spiritual wheat and pull down the curtain on human history as we have known it. This *"present evil age"* will be over. At this point Jesus Himself will initiate the second "age" of human history, what Scripture refers to as *"the age to come."*[7] This second "age," this *"age to come,"* has another name: *"The Kingdom of God."*

God's plan throughout *"this age"* I profoundly simple. His plan is to quell man's rebellion against His Kingdom rule and dominion, to provide a means by which God's justice could be satisfied and man could be redeemed from the moral catastrophe of his rebellion and fall into sin, and to re-establish His Kingly rule over both His creation and His creature. In short, God's plan is to establish His Kingdom on earth. And the history of *"this age"* (i.e., from Creation until Jesus returns) is nothing less than the unfolding in space and time of God's great plan to establish His Kingdom among men, a Kingdom which will **only** be fully manifested in *"the age to come,"* beginning with the Millennial reign of Christ on earth and continuing into the New Heavens and the New Earth.[8]

Let's take a look at our role in God's plan for the ages to establish His Kingdom. What is our role - yours and mine - in this "plan for the ages"? Our role - our calling - is to respond in repentance, faith and obedience to the gospel of the Kingdom, *"Jesus came into Galilee, proclaiming **the good news** of God, and saying, 'The time is fulfilled, and the kingdom of God is at hand; repent and believe in **the good news**'"* (Mark 1:14-15).

This passage from the Gospel of Mark tells us that Jesus began His public ministry by proclaiming "good news." Many translations render the phrase "good news" simply as "gospel." While "gospel" is an accurate translation, in our day and culture the term "gospel" has lost much of its original Middle English meaning of "good news." In Classical Greek, the underlying Greek word, *euaggelion*, originally referred to the reward given to a messenger who brought good news. As time went by and usage progressed it came to refer to the good news itself. Biblically speaking, the "gospel" is simply "good news."

According to the Gospel of Mark, Jesus began His ministry in Galilee by proclaiming *"God's good news."* What exactly was the "good news" that Jesus proclaimed? That the long awaited rule and reign of God - the Kingdom of God - had finally arrived in the person of the Messiah-King, Jesus. Now, men and women, Jews and Gentiles, who had lived their lives as rebellious subjects were being called to renounce their rebellion, to repent of their sin and to believe the good news of the Kingdom's arrival by submitting their hearts and their lives to the rule and reign of the King. They were now being called upon to become disciples of the Kingdom and to live a life of radical discipleship expressed through radical faith and radical obedience.

That same simple message of the Kingdom of God is our message today, both to believe and to proclaim. Through that message God calls each of us to cease from our rebellion against the King, to repent of our sins against His Holiness and to submit our will to His in personal faith and obedience. As a result of that act of faith, a radical, inward, spiritual transformation takes place in us as He delivers us from *"the domain of darkness"* and transfers us to *"the kingdom of his beloved Son, in whom we have redemption, the forgiveness of sins"* (Colossians 1:13-14). That act of faith transforms us from rebellious subjects to "citizens in good standing" in the Kingdom of God. But there's more.

Ambassadors Of The Kingdom

"All this is from God, who through Christ reconciled us to himself and gave us the ministry of reconciliation; that is, in Christ God was reconciling the world to himself, not counting their trespasses against them, and entrusting to us the message of reconciliation. Therefore, we are ambassadors for Christ, God making his appeal through us. We implore you on behalf of Christ, be reconciled to God. For our sake he made him to be sin who knew no sin, so that in him we might become the righteousness of God." (2 Corinthians 5:18-21)

By common agreement and definition, an "ambassador" is *"an accredited diplomat sent by a country as its official representative to a foreign country."* The significance of Paul's declaration in the above passage should not be missed. As disciples of the Kingdom, walking in radical faith and obedience, not only are we forgiven rebels and citizens in good standing in the Kingdom of God, but King Jesus has appointed us as official representatives of His Kingdom. We have the

> *The flow of history is now in the hands of disciples of the Kingdom.*

privilege and the responsibility of speaking on His behalf. Like any ambassador, we are not free to make up whatever message suits us. Our responsibility is to faithfully deliver the message He has entrusted to us, *"We implore you on behalf of Christ, be reconciled to God. For our sake he made him to be sin who knew no sin, so that in him we might become the righteousness of God."*

No longer rebels against the King, but now disciples of His Kingdom. No longer rebellious subjects, but "citizens in good standing." Now proclaiming to others that same message which He proclaimed to us. Now serving as ambassadors of the King Himself. Now appealing to and imploring our former fellow-rebels to be reconciled to the King. What an incredible truth! Former rebels against the King, walking in faith and obedience as disciples of His Kingdom, now hold the fate of this *"present evil age"* in their hands. Since that day when Jesus ascended into heaven to take His seat at the right hand of His Father, the flow of history favors the faithful. The flow of history is now in the hands of disciples of the Kingdom. His Kingdom will come and His will be done, on earth as it is in heaven. And it is to a better understanding of that Kingdom that we now want to turn our attention.

And They Dreamt Of A Kingdom

Questions For Reflection

How has God spoken to you through this Lesson regarding His plan for the Kingdom and your role in it?

Read Psalm 2 and Isaiah 8:11-15. How does God respond to the plans and conspiracies of men who seek to control history and to thwart His purposes?

Returning to the "two paramount questions" of this Lesson: 1) How would you summarize God's plan for the ages? 2) How do you see yourself as a part of God's plan for the ages?

Describe how you see yourself as a disciple and an Ambassador for the Kingdom of God? Why would you NOT want to trust your life to a loving God Who is able to show you your place in His plan?

Key Thought

God is in control of history and He has a plan for how His Kingdom purposes will unfold and be accomplished both in the world and in our individual lives as disciples.

---

4 - The Kingdom of God In Four Stages

The chances are good that you've never heard of Jean-François Lyotard. And yet Lyotard - along with those who share his philosophical perspective - has had a profound impact upon you, your church and upon our collective ability to communicate the good news of the Kingdom of God to our generation. The cultural impact of Lyotard and the philosophical school of Postmodernism which he championed has been so profound that you and I see and experience its after-effects every day without ever recognizing, knowing or understanding it.

Postmodernism And The Kingdom

We experience the moral effects of Postmodernism every time we watch a news story about same-sex marriage or watch a "sitcom" which portrays sexual immorality and family dysfunctionality as the new normal. We experience the effects of Postmodern existentialism every time we hear a talk show host attempt to wax eloquent about the need to discover your "personal truth." We experience the effects of Postmodernism's "triumph of rhetoric" whenever issues large or small are

Ours is an unavoidably Postmodern culture, and we have become a Postmodern church.

decided by the person with the most compelling "personal story" or by the person with the loudest argument. We experience the epistemological "dead end" (i.e., *"ultimate truth is unknowable"*) of Postmodernism when personal opinions concerning spiritual/doctrinal issues become self-validating (it's true because I believe it). We experience the nihilistic effects of Postmodernism in calls by religious teachers and leaders to "question everything." We experience the self-centered individualism of Postmodernism when therapy replaces theology (*"It's true because it makes me feel better about myself"*). Ours is an unavoidably Postmodern culture, and we have become a Postmodern church. And that requires a brief explanation.

Jean-François Lyotard (10 August 1924 – 21 April 1998) was a French philosopher, sociologist, and literary theorist. He is well known for his articulation of postmodernism in the late 1970s. In his writings Lyotard highlights what he sees as the increasing skepticism of our Postmodern culture toward "meta-narratives" and their reliance upon some form of "transcendent and universal truth":

"Simplifying to the extreme, I define postmodern as incredulity toward metanarratives . . . . The narrative function is losing its functors, its great hero, its great dangers, its great voyages, its great goal. It is being dispersed in clouds of narrative language . . . . Where, after the metanarratives, can legitimacy reside?"[9]

In the vocabulary of Postmodernism a "meta-narrative" is ANY big, transcendent or universal story which claims 1) to explain reality in all its particulars, and 2) to be universally binding upon all people everywhere, demanding that they respond to the story in either acceptance or rejection, in either faith or unbelief. No one can escape either the demands or the consequences of such a meta-narrative. Lyotard's observation is quite profound when we understand the question he is asking, *"If truth cannot be found in 'meta-narratives', where CAN it be found?"*[10]

There are other aspects of Postmodernism which impact the Church, such as its skepticism toward institutions (i.e., institutional churches), but its skepticism toward meta-narratives (and particularly toward religious meta-narraitves) is one of Postmodernism's greatest challenges to evangelical, biblical Christianity. Why?

And They Dreamt Of A Kingdom

Because the Scriptures clearly present *"the Gospel of the Kingdom"* as an all-encompassing, universally binding meta-narrative which calls everyone everywhere to repent and believe. In other words, the story of the Kingdom is a meta-narrative of the very kind that Postmodernism rejects. Indeed, it is impossible to understand the Biblical story, either in whole or in part, apart from God's all encompassing plan and intention to establish His Kingdom *"on earth as it is in heaven."* Personal discipleship, life in the community of the Church and our place in the world around us can only be understood in terms of the "big story" meta-narrative of the Kingdom of God and our role in it. For these reasons alone, it is imperative that we, as biblical disciples in a Postmodern context, understand the "big story" of the Kingdom of God and that we be able to explain and articulate it to those around us who might be seeking to understand the call of *"the Gospel of the Kingdom."*

The Story Of The Kingdom In Four Bite-Sized Stages

Big ideas are often best understood when presented in smaller pieces. This principle applies as we seek to better grasp and understand the story of the Kingdom of God. For purposes of simplicity, we can better understand the "big story" of the Kingdom of God by examining it in four smaller pieces which we will call "stages":

Stage 1 - The Inauguration of The Kingdom - Think of this as the Kingdom of God from eternity past up to the time of Jesus' first Advent.

Stage 2 - The Incarnation of The Kingdom - This second stage embraces the earthly ministry of Jesus from His birth through His Ascension and return to the Father.

Stage 3 - The Continuation of The Kingdom - This third phase encompasses the on-going work of the Church to proclaim and manifest the Kingdom from the time of Jesus' Ascension into heaven until his bodily, visible return to earth at the end of the present Age (commonly referred to as Jesus' "second coming"). This is the stage we find ourselves in today.

Stage 4 - The Consummation of The Kingdom - This final stage begins with the bodily visible return of Jesus at the end of this present Age to establish the Age to Come, and continues through the Millennium and into the "Eternal State."

Stage 1 - The Inauguration of The Kingdom

"All Thy works shall give thanks to Thee, O LORD, And Thy godly ones shall bless Thee. They shall speak of the glory of Thy Kingdom, and talk of Thy power; to make known to the sons of men Thy mighty acts, and the glory of the majesty of Thy Kingdom. Thy Kingdom is an everlasting kingdom, And Thy dominion endures throughout all generations." (Psalms 145:10-13)

To speak of the "inauguration" of God's Kingdom is, in fact, a misnomer. By common definition, to "inaugurate" something is *"to bring about the beginning of that thing."* But the Old Testament Psalmist and other Scriptures make it clear that the Kingdom of God has no beginning, *"Thy Kingdom is an everlasting kingdom."* To be "everlasting" (Hebrew: *'olam*) is to be eternal, and to be eternal is to have no beginning . . . and no end. [11]

There are few passages anywhere in Scripture which speak more eloquently about the Kingdom of God than the above passage by the Old Testament Psalmist. In language both poetically beautiful and theologically profound - penned nearly a thousand years before Jesus - the Psalmist demonstrates that the people of God have always known and understood something about the Kingdom of God. In the process the Psalmist defines the Kingdom of God as Jehovah's kingly rule, what the Psalmist refers to as His "dominion." Both the Psalmist and the people of God understood that the Kingdom of God means that Jehovah reigns as King and that His reign knows no boundaries of space, time or geography. His rule - His "dominion" - is everlasting. It is eternal and unending whether we look backward through eternity past, or whether we look forward into eternity future. God's Kingdom - His Kingly rule and dominion - is both majestic and everlasting, whether seen from the Old Testament or from the New Testament.

> *. . . the Kingdom of God means that Jehovah reigns as King and that His reign knows no boundaries of space, time or geography.*

What Nebuchadnezzar Learned About The Kingdom. Nowhere in the Old Testament is this principle of the Kingdom of God as God's Kingly rule and dominion better taught and illustrated than in the Book of Daniel. Reading the fourth chapter of the book of Daniel we might come away with the impression that King Nebuchadnezzar of Babylon (604-562 B.C.) was not exactly the brightest spiritual bulb in the box. There is no question that he was a great and powerful King who ruled over the greatest empire of his day. But God saw things differently. In spite of specific warnings from God delivered through Daniel, Nebuchadnezzar refused to humble himself. God was forced to cut him down to size and to take Nebuchadnezzar on a little personal journey of discovery. In the process, Nebuchadnezzar discovered something about himself as well as about the Kingdom of God. He discovered that although he was "a great king," only God is King. He discovered that, while the "kings" of this world may have their dominions over geographic areas and may rule over them for a season, only God has everlasting dominion over all. Only the Kingdom of God *"endures from generation to generation."* Men and kings may briefly rule over nations, but only Jehovah is King over all. Even "kings" must submit to the rule and dominion of the King.

"At the end of the days I, Nebuchadnezzar, lifted my eyes to heaven, and my reason returned to me, and I blessed the Most High, and praised and honored him who lives forever, for his dominion is an everlasting dominion, and his kingdom endures from generation to generation." (Daniel 4:34; see also Daniel 6:26)

Here is the critical point. It is so profound that even a spiritually dim bulb like Nebuchadnezzar eventually saw the light. In *"this present age,"* the Kingdom of God is **NOT** primarily a place, a territory, a physical realm or a piece of geography. Nebuchadnezzar wasn't acknowledging God's dominion over a piece of property, a particular country or even a particular people. Nebuchadnezzar was acknowledging God's rule, reign and dominion over EVERYTHING. The Kingdom of God is a person, not a piece of geography. It is a rule rather than a realm. The Kingdom of God exists in the person of Jehovah, the King. On five different occasions the Scriptures sum up Jehovah's Kingly rule and dominion by simply declaring, *"The Lord reigns!"* (See 1 Chronicles 16:31; Psalm 93:1; Psalm 96:10; Psalm 97:1; Psalm 99:1). The Kingdom of God represents the summation of

> *The Kingdom of God is a person, not a piece of geography. It is a rule rather than a realm.*

And They Dreamt Of A Kingdom

this simple reality: Jehovah-God reigns as Lord and King. Multiple biblical writers, speaking with one voice, all declare, *"How great are his signs, how mighty his wonders! His kingdom is an everlasting kingdom, and his dominion endures from generation to generation."* (Daniel 4:3) God is King and He rules as King. Everywhere. Over everything. And, over everyone.

Rebels Against The Rebellion. We've established that the Scriptures clearly present Jehovah-God reigning as Lord and King. But there is more to the story. The Scriptures are equally clear that He is also King over a world in rebellion. The story of that rebellion unfolds in the third chapter of Genesis. In His kingly rule and dominion - which was His by right of creation - God appointed man to tend His creation, starting with the Garden (Genesis 2:15). Man, the creature fashioned in God's own image by God's own hand, was given great freedom and responsibility over the rest of creation. In his creaturely dominion as regent over God's creation, man was given authority to exercise dominion over God's world, limited by only one prohibition: that he not eat from the tree of the knowledge of good and evil (Genesis 2:16-17). We are not told how much time transpired between the warning and the rebellion, but in the end it didn't matter. Adam and Eve acted presumptively and foolishly. They rebelled against God's kingly rule, disobeyed His specific instructions and ate of the tree. Let's be clear. Mankind's rebellion, which began in the Garden of Eden and continues even today, wasn't against a place, a political jurisdiction or a country. It was a rebellion against the King Himself and His rule over them. This was personal.

The results of our rebellion-in-Adam were nothing short of catastrophic. In the fifth Chapter of Romans the Apostle Paul describes the extent of the moral and spiritual catastrophe which befell mankind and all of creation as a consequence of that initial rebellion. He writes that through Adam and Eve's rebellion, *"sin came into the world through one man, and death through sin, and so death spread to all men because all sinned"* (Romans 5:12). According to Paul, through this one catastrophic act of rebellion, the curse of sin and rebellion "went viral," infecting every man, woman and child who descended from that first couple. Because one had sinned, ALL had sinned and experienced the corruption that flowed from that one mad act of rebellion against Jehovah-God's kingly rule. Through mankind's rebellion, God's Kingdom reign and rule over His creation and His creature was rejected. God still reigned as King, but now his rule and His Kingship were no longer recognized by His rebellious subjects.

Ed Stetzer tells the true story of Tennessee's secession from the Union during the American Civil War. The residents of eastern Tennessee disagreed with the action taken by their State in seceding from the Union. Following Tennessee's secession from the Union, East Tennessee seceded from the rest of Tennessee. As a result, the residents of East Tennessee were *"in rebellion against the rebellion."* Stetzer then compares this situation with that of believers and the Kingdom of God:

"In many ways we as believers in Christ - followers of another Ruler, citizens of another kingdom - are much like the people of East Tennessee in Civil War America. We live among a world system that, even though ultimately under the reign of a sovereign God, temporarily exerts a competing authority that seeks to enforce an unjust, unrighteous order on those it claims to rule. The Supreme Court, for example would later find that the secession of the southern states was an illegal and illegitimate act. Their confederacy had no legal authority. Thus, the United States was always

legally sovereign over those states. They just didn't know it. And so it is with us. The world's illegal rebellion is illegitimate. It certainly feels real, of course - IS real - but it doesn't change the reality that God is still Ruler of everything. Though people may think they have rebelled, they have not - and cannot - ultimately escape the fact that King Jesus still is sovereign."[12]

The entire sweep of biblical history, from Genesis to Revelation, can be summed up as the story of God's unfolding plan to quell this rebellion and to redeem and restore His rebellious creatures to fellowship with Himself and to full citizenship in His Kingdom. Jehovah-God would begin by choosing a person (Abraham, Genesis 12) and a people (Abraham's descendants) with which to build a nation (Israel). That nation would become his unique possession from among all the peoples of the earth. They would enter into a covenant with the King to live in submission to His Kingly rule and dominion.

"Now therefore, if you will indeed obey my voice and keep my covenant, you shall be my treasured possession among all peoples, for all the earth is mine; and you shall be to me a kingdom of priests and a holy nation." (Exodus 19:5-6)

Their kingdom would be an earthly reflection of His Kingdom. He would teach them the requirements for being a holy people living in obedience to a holy God. He would impart His laws and words to them, and they would teach and impart those words to others. By their corporate life together as a people and as a nation they would serve as witnesses to God and His Kingdom.

"You are my witnesses," declares the LORD, "and my servant whom I have chosen, that you may know and believe me and understand that I am he. Before me no god was formed, nor shall there be any after me. I, I am the LORD, and besides me there is no savior." (Isaiah 43:10-11)

But the role of this unique people of Israel would go beyond serving as a reflection of and a witness to the Kingdom of God. From the earliest days when He called them into a covenant relationship with Himself, the Lord God promised that through their national lineage He would raise up someone Who would be a shepherd, a deliverer and a King.

"I see him, but not now; I behold him, but not near: a star shall come out of Jacob, and a scepter shall rise out of Israel; it shall crush the forehead of Moab and break down all the sons of Sheth." (Numbers 24:17)

"For to us a child is born, to us a son is given; and the government shall be upon his shoulder, and his name shall be called Wonderful Counselor, Mighty God, Everlasting Father, Prince of Peace. Of the increase of his government and of peace there will be no end, on the throne of David and over his kingdom, to establish it and to uphold it with justice and with righteousness from this time forth and forevermore. The zeal of the LORD of hosts will do this." (Isaiah 9:6-7)

"But you, O Bethlehem Ephrathah, who are too little to be among the clans of Judah, from you shall come forth for me one who is to be ruler in Israel, whose coming forth is from of old, from ancient days . . . . And he shall stand and shepherd his flock in the strength of the LORD, in the majesty of the name of the LORD his God. And they shall dwell secure, for now he shall be great to the ends of the earth. And he shall be their peace." (Micah 5:2-5)

The promises were many and clear. One day Jehovah-God would raise up from among His chosen people a unique and "anointed" person who would be a shepherd, a servant, a Savior and a King. And His arrival would mark the incarnation of the Kingdom.[13]

And They Dreamt Of A Kingdom

Stage 2 - The Incarnation of The Kingdom

"And in the days of those kings the God of heaven will set up a kingdom that shall never be destroyed, nor shall the kingdom be left to another people. It shall break in pieces all these kingdoms and bring them to an end, and it shall stand forever." (Daniel 2:44)

From that time Jesus began to preach and say, "Repent, for the kingdom of heaven is at hand." (Matthew 4:17; see also Luke 4:43)

The above passage from the Old Testament Prophet Daniel expresses the consistent message and promise of the Old Testament. One day Jehovah-God would establish His Kingdom - His kingly rule - on earth. The competing rebellious kingdoms of God's enemies would be crushed. Injustice, hunger, disease and even death itself would be destroyed. And all men would come under the Kingly rule of God in the person of His promised Messiah or "anointed one." These as-yet-unfulfilled promises of a coming Messianic Kingdom led by a Messiah-King hung in the air when Jesus came to Israel proclaiming, *"Repent, for the kingdom of heaven is at hand."* The Kingdom of God was indeed "at hand." It arrived in the person of the Messiah-King Himself, Jesus, God's "anointed one." The incarnation of the Kingdom meant that Jehovah-God, the King of all creation, had taken on human flesh in order to dwell among His rebellious subjects and to accomplish their redemption and restoration (John 1:14; Matthew 20:28).

But there was a problem. The Jewish community of Jesus' day was expecting something different. They were looking for a political and military leader who would defeat their Roman oppressors and establish a literal, visible Kingdom in Jerusalem just as Jehovah had promised through His prophets, *"Behold, the days are coming, declares the LORD, when I will raise up for David a righteous Branch, and he shall reign as king and deal wisely, and shall execute justice and righteousness in the land"* (Jeremiah 23:5). The Jews of Jesus' day wanted a conquering King who would crush their enemies and rule and reign *"on the throne of David and over his kingdom, to establish it and to uphold it with justice and with righteousness from this time forth and forevermore."* (Isaiah 9:7)

But contrary to popular expectations, built upon popular misunderstandings of various Messianic Scriptures, Jesus had not come to lead a conquering army, to save them from their Roman enemies and to establish an earthly Kingdom. He had come to save them from the root cause of all their problems. He had come to deliver them from their underlying sin and rebellion, *"But as he considered these things, behold, an angel of the Lord appeared to him in a dream, saying, 'Joseph, son of David, do not fear to take Mary as your wife, for that which is conceived in her is from the Holy Spirit. She will bear a son, and you shall call his name Jesus, for he will save his people from their sins.'"* (Matthew 1:20-21)

Redemption from sin, rather than deliverance from Rome, was God's plan for this stage of His Kingdom.

Redemption from sin, rather than deliverance from Rome, was God's plan for this stage of His Kingdom. In the process of accomplishing that planned redemption Jesus manifested the reality and the power of God's Kingly Rule. He demonstrated His Kingly rule over disease by healing the sick, the lame and the blind. He demonstrated His Kingly rule over the demonic spiritual realm by casting out demons and delivering those bound by demonic oppression. He demonstrated His Kingly rule over creation itself by changing water into wine and stilling storms with a word. He demonstrated His power to eliminate hunger in the Kingdom of God by multiplying fish and bread to feed the multitudes. And He demonstrated His power over sin and death by raising people from the dead, and by rising from the grave Himself. The Gospel writer, chronicling Jesus' ministry, summed it up this way: *"And he went throughout all Galilee, teaching in their synagogues and proclaiming the gospel of the kingdom and healing every disease and every affliction among the people."* (Matthew 4:23; see also 9:35). Jesus taught the Kingdom, proclaimed the Kingdom and manifested the Kingdom. But there was more. Not only did Jesus proclaim the Kingdom of God, He commanded His disciples to make the Kingdom of God the heart of their message, too. When He commissioned His disciples in Matthew Chapter 10 He gave them clear instructions: *"And as you go, preach, saying, 'The **kingdom of heaven** is at hand.'"* (Matthew 10:7; see also Luke 9:2). His message became their message.

"Lord, Is It Now?." The issue of an earthly Messianic Kingdom lingered in people's minds throughout Jesus' earthly ministry. It surfaced again in Jesus' trial before Pilate, the Roman Governor. In order to gain an offense punishable by death the Jewish religious leaders accused Jesus of claiming to be a "king" in opposition to Caesar (John 19:12). Pilate asked Jesus about this charge: *"Jesus answered, 'My kingdom is not of this world. If my kingdom were of this world, my servants would have been fighting, that I might not be delivered over to the Jews. But my kingdom is not from the world.'"* (John 18:36) Jesus' response was clear and unambiguous. He was, indeed, a "king," but not of any earthly kingdom. *"My kingdom is not of this world."* Not yet. This is the *"now . . . but not yet"* reality of the Kingdom.

But this issue of an earthly Kingdom would arise one last time during Jesus' post-resurrection appearances to His disciples in the forty days between His resurrection and ascension, *"So when they had come together, they asked him, 'Lord, will you at this time restore the kingdom to Israel?' He said to them, 'It is not for you to know times or seasons that the Father has fixed by his own authority. But you will receive power when the Holy Spirit has come upon you, and you will be my witnesses in Jerusalem and in all Judea and Samaria, and to the end of the earth.'"* (Acts 1:6-8)

Even at this late hour in their relationship with Jesus, the disciples still nurtured the idea that Jesus had come to establish and rule over a physical earthly Kingdom. Jesus didn't deny either the possibility or the reality of a future earthly Kingdom. He simply said (paraphrasing), *"That's not your concern right now. Leave that to the Father."* Jesus turned the focus of the discussion away from the possibility of an earthly Kingdom and toward that spiritual power which His disciples would need in order to be His witnesses. Jesus wanted them to grasp the immediate reality that the power to preach, teach and manifest the reality of the Kingdom of God must be their priority. And those were Jesus' last words on the subject before ascending into heaven.

> *Jesus taught the Kingdom, proclaimed the Kingdom and manifested the Kingdom. He also made twelve disciples of the Kingdom.*

Stage 3 - The Continuation Of The Kingdom

The Gospels make it clear that the Kingdom of God constituted the heart of

And They Dreamt Of A Kingdom

Jesus' message and ministry. The Kingdom of God is so prominent in the Gospel of Matthew that it is frequently referred to by New Testament scholars as the "Gospel of the Kingdom." Jesus taught the Kingdom, proclaimed the Kingdom and manifested the Kingdom. He also made twelve disciples of the Kingdom. In His post-resurrection appearances following His death and resurrection, Jesus again emphasized the Kingdom of God in His conversations with His disciples. When Luke, the Physician, wants to summarize Jesus' post-resurrection ministry in the 40 days between His resurrection and ascension, he describes it in terms of the Kingdom of God, "He (Jesus) presented himself alive to them after his suffering by many proofs, appearing to them during forty days and speaking about the Kingdom of God." (Acts 1:3) Let this sink in for a moment. Jesus regarded the message of the Kingdom as so important that He spent His last 40 days on earth with His disciples talking about the Kingdom. What do you and I talk about when time is short?

The end of Jesus' earthly ministry was not the end of the message of the Kingdom of God. Quite the contrary. The life, message and ministry of Jesus had been all about the Kingdom. Because those early disciples had spent three years learning about the Kingdom from the King Himself, the good news of the Kingdom of God continued on and became the message of the early New Testament Church. When we read the New Testament, particularly the Book of Acts, we see the disciples themselves preaching the

> . . . the good news of the Kingdom of God continued on and became the message of the early New Testament Church.

Kingdom of God where ever they went. "But when they believed Philip preaching the good news about the Kingdom of God and the name of Jesus Christ, they were being baptized, men and women alike." (Acts 8:12) Philip, "the Evangelist," one of Jesus "disciples of the Kingdom," did what Jesus had taught him to do. He preached the good news about the Kingdom of God. Jesus' disciples - and the churches they established - taught, proclaimed and manifested the message of the Kingdom of God.

The Apostle Paul, the great "Apostle to the Gentiles," proclaimed the Kingdom of God wherever he went (See Acts 14:21-22; 19:8; 20:25; 28:23), all the way to Rome: "And he stayed two full years in his own rented quarters, and was welcoming all who came to him, preaching the kingdom of God, and teaching concerning the Lord Jesus Christ with all openness." (Acts 28:30-31) Paul wasn't talking about or advocating an earthly Kingdom which would compete with Rome for power and position, but a spiritual Kingdom in which Jesus, the Messiah-King, would rule the hearts and minds of men through faith. This is the Kingdom which Paul proclaimed.

But Paul not only proclaimed the good news of the Kingdom of God (just as Jesus and His disciples had done), he also taught the believers and churches under his care about the Kingdom of God. Writing to young believers in the city of Colossae (in western Asia Minor, modern day Turkey), Paul explained their Christian experience with these words: "He (God the Father) has delivered us from the domain of darkness and transferred us to the kingdom of his beloved Son, in whom we have redemption, the forgiveness of sins." (Colossians 1:13-14) Paul's message was simple. Through their response of faith to the good news of the Kingdom of God, these formerly blind and rebellious subjects of the "domain of darkness" had been redeemed, their sins had been forgiven, and they had been transferred to "the Kingdom of His beloved Son."

According to Ed Stetzer, *"That word 'transferred' refers to the removal of people from one place of residence to another, repositioned for the purpose of forming a new colony. Paul's use of that word in describing salvation implies that we have not only been transferred into Christ's kingdom but also commissioned to be a part of outposts of that Kingdom wherever God leads us to go . . ."*[14]

Similarly, Paul tells the believers in the Roman colony of Philippi that, as believers and disciples of the Kingdom, their loyalties and their citizenship have undergone a radical change, *"But our citizenship is in heaven, and from it we await a Savior, the Lord Jesus Christ . . ."* (Philippians 3:20). This was a profound declaration to make to believers in a Roman colony where Roman citizenship was highly prized. The implication is clear. To be a citizen of the Kingdom of God is to be loyal to King Jesus above all else.

> *To be a citizen of the Kingdom of God is to be loyal to King Jesus above all else.*

The earthly ministry of Jesus was defined by the call for all men to repent and to believe the good news of the Kingdom. That call and that message continue on in the preaching and teaching of the Church. When we look at the life of the early Church we quickly discover that they didn't *"do evangelism"* as you and I understand it today. To our knowledge they never led anyone in "the sinner's prayer" and never challenged anyone to "ask Jesus into their hearts." And they never encouraged anyone to "join the church." Rather, the early Church proclaimed the Kingdom, taught the Kingdom and lived the Kingdom. And unbelievers - both Jews and Gentiles - responded in faith to the message of the Kingdom of God which they heard and saw manifested in the lives of these Kingdom-oriented believers. This is *"The Continuation of the Kingdom,"* the on-going ministry of God's people, which has continued for nearly 2,000 years. And it will continue until Jesus returns (literally, personally, bodily, visibly) to bring about *"The Consummation of The Kingdom."*

Stage 4 - The Consummation of The Kingdom

"On this mountain the LORD of hosts will make for all peoples a feast of rich food, a feast of well-aged wine, of rich food full of marrow, of aged wine well refined. And he will swallow up on this mountain the covering that is cast over all peoples, the veil that is spread over all nations. He will swallow up death forever; and the Lord GOD will wipe away tears from all faces, and the reproach of his people he will take away from all the earth, for the LORD has spoken. It will be said on that day, 'Behold, this is our God; we have waited for him, that he might save us. This is the LORD; we have waited for him; let us be glad and rejoice in his salvation.'" (Isaiah 25:6-9)

Just as the Old Testament Scriptures had promised a coming Messiah-King, those same Scriptures promised a future day when the Kingdom of God and the reign of the King would become a reality upon the Earth. The above passage from the Prophet Isaiah is just one of many such passages describing the blessings of that coming future earthly Kingdom - the Kingdom of God (for another, see Isaiah 9:1-11).

Throughout His earthly ministry Jesus made it clear, to anyone who would listen, that the Kingdom of God would not come in its fulness until He returned at *"the end of the age"* to personally bring *"this present age"* to an end. Writing to disciples in the Asian province of Galatia, the Apostle Paul explains that the present age is

And They Dreamt Of A Kingdom

spiritually and morally at enmity with the Kingdom of God. Paul refers to it as *"the present evil age"* (Galatians 1:4). The Greek word translated "evil" (*poneros*) refers to that which is inherently, morally evil (from which we get our English word "pornography"). In his second letter to the believers in the Greek city of Corinth the Apostle Paul further defines the evil nature of *"this present age"* by describing Satan as *"the god of this age"* who is able to blind the minds of unbelievers against the gospel (2 Corinthians 4:4).

Writing to disciples in the Asian City of Ephesus, Paul warns believers that they are engaged in spiritual warfare against this spiritual evil, *"For we do not wrestle against flesh and blood, but against the rulers, against the authorities, against the cosmic powers over this present darkness, against the spiritual forces of evil in the heavenly places. Therefore take up the whole armor of God, that you may be able to withstand in the evil day, and having done all, to stand firm"* (Ephesians 6:12-13). The moral and spiritual evil of this present age will not end

> *The moral and spiritual evil of this present age will not end and the Kingdom rule of Jesus be established, until Jesus returns at the end of the age.*

and the Kingdom rule of Jesus be established, until Jesus returns at the end of the age. Until that day the arrival of the Kingdom in all its fulness - *"on earth as it is in heaven"* (Matthew 6:10) - remains a promise for a future day when the risen and ascended Jesus returns at the end of this present evil age, separates the "sheep" from the "goats," judges all men for what they have done with the message of the Kingdom, and establishes His Kingdom on earth with Jesus as Messiah-King over all.

"Then the seventh angel blew his trumpet, and there were loud voices in heaven, saying, 'The kingdom of the world has become the kingdom of our Lord and of his Christ, and he shall reign forever and ever.' And the twenty-four elders who sit on their thrones before God fell on their faces and worshiped God, saying, 'We give thanks to you, Lord God Almighty, who is and who was, for you have taken your great power and begun to reign.'" (Revelation 11:15-17)

The *"Consummation of the Kingdom"* is coming, but not today. Not yet. The day is coming when King Jesus will return. He will make an end of the kingdoms of men. Their kingdoms will become His Kingdom. He will establish His Kingdom *"on earth as it is in heaven"* and will reign and rule with His saints for a thousand years (Revelation 20). Every Old Testament promise of a King and a Kingdom will be fulfilled. And once His promises have been fulfilled and all enemies have been defeated, He will create a new heavens and a new earth in which the Kingdom of God will become an eternal reality which shall have no end (Revelation 21).

The fulness of the Kingdom of God remains a promise for a coming day. Like an exquisitely wrapped Christmas present, it lies beneath the tree awaiting the "Christmas morning" of Jesus Second Advent. Our name is clearly on the gift tag, a pledge designating it for us. But not yet. Today we have the thrill and anticipation of knowing something of what's in the exquisitely wrapped box. We have all the emotions of being both teased and blessed at the promise of the incredible gift which awaits us. But its fulness remains a mystery, awaiting the day when it will be ours to open and enjoy. It is here and it is ours, but not quite yet. And like the disciples quizzing Jesus concerning His time table for this Kingdom, we must await the times and seasons appointed and known only by the Father (Acts 1:6-8).

Questions For Reflection

Reflecting on this Lesson, what did you discover about the Kingdom of God that you did not know before?

Read: Psalm 145:1-21. This Psalm has much to say about the Kingdom. Spend some time reflecting on the attributes (i.e., defining characteristics) of God and his Kingdom. Consider the following:

1. Attributes of the King (145:1-9). As you read this section, see if you can identify ten (10) attributes of God as King.

2. Attributes of God's Kingdom (145:10-13). As you read this section, see if you can identify five (5) attributes of God's Kingdom.

3. Attributes of God's rule over His Kingdom (145:14-20). As you read this section, see if you can identify ten (10) attributes of God's rule over His Kingdom.

4. A Personal Commitment To the King (145:21). Describe the Psalmist's personal commitment to the King.

As disciples of the Kingdom and Ambassadors of the King, we live as "rebels against the rebellion." How does this truth help explain some of the conflicts we as disciples experience in the world?

In His life and ministry, Jesus fulfilled over 300 Old Testament messianic prophecies written no less than 400 years before He was born. What does this truth tell you about God's Kingly reign and rule over the seemingly random events of history? How does this truth encourage you to trust God for His Kingdom plan and purposes for your life as a disciple of the Kingdom?

Key Thought

The Kingdom of God is God's Kingly rule, reign and dominion over His creation, beginning in the hearts of individuals whom He acts to redeem and to call as disciples of the Kingdom.

And They Dreamt Of A Kingdom

5 - The Kingdom And The Church

Just as the story of the Kingdom was the story of the people of God in ancient Israel, the story of the Kingdom is also the story of the Church. Now it's time for us to turn our attention to the role of the Church in that story. We have spent the past four Lessons focusing upon the reality and the nature of the Kingdom of God. In the process we discovered that the Kingdom of God has always existed in the person of the Lord God and that the Kingdom has always been God's plan, beginning in eternity past and continuing throughout "this present age." We discovered that Jesus, the Messiah-King, proclaimed the Kingdom, taught the Kingdom, manifested the Kingdom, made disciples of the Kingdom, and expected His disciples to do the same after He returned to the Father.

But by this point in the discussion someone has begun nervously fidgeting and asking the question, *"What about the Church? Where does the Church fit into God's plan for the Kingdom?"* That's the question we want to answer in this Lesson as we examine the relationship between "the Kingdom" and "the Church." We'll begin our examination of this relationship with a subtle but important observation. Here it is. Jesus NEVER preached a message on "the Church." In

> *A true Jesus-shaped spirituality will be a Kingdom-shaped spirituality.*

three years of ministry as recorded in four Gospels, Jesus only mentioned "the Church" twice (Matthew 16:18; 18:17). But Jesus either referred to or taught about the Kingdom of God over 100 times!

There is a point to be grasped here. Jesus was all about the Kingdom. Jesus taught the Kingdom, proclaimed the Kingdom and manifested the Kingdom. He also made twelve disciples of the Kingdom. In turn, Jesus expected His disciples to be Kingdom-oriented believers with a Kingdom-oriented message. As disciples of Jesus, we don't proclaim "church," "our church" or "the Church." We proclaim a Kingdom, a Savior, and a Messiah-King. A true Jesus-shaped spirituality will be a Kingdom-shaped spirituality. We teach the Kingdom, we proclaim the Kingdom, we manifest the Kingdom and we make disciples of the Kingdom. And when disciples of the Kingdom gather together for worship, teaching, mutual ministry and fellowship they call themselves "the Church," the _ekklesia_ or *"the assembly of those who have been called out."*[15] And this brings us to our first of several important principles concerning the relationship between the Kingdom and the Church.

The Kingdom Creates the Church. Several years ago a friend of mine rattled my paradigm with a simple but profound statement. *"Jesus never told anyone to plant churches,"* he said over a cup of coffee, *"Jesus told us to make disciples."* If that statement doesn't set you back on your heels for a few moments and make you think, then you need to stop and let the full impact sink in. For His part, Jesus declared that

> *The Kingdom of God creates the Church, not the other way around.*

He would build His Church (Matthew 16:18). For our part, He commanded us to make disciples. This truth confronts us with an uncomfortable question: Why do we attempt to build (or "plant") churches while asking God to make disciples, rather than the other way around?

The bottom line is this. The Kingdom of God creates the Church, not the other

And They Dreamt Of A Kingdom

way around. As we proclaim the Kingdom, teach the Kingdom and make disciples of the Kingdom, the eventual result will be the planting of churches - *"assemblies of those who have been called out"* - as those Kingdom disciples gather together to worship the King. The Church is the product of the Kingdom. Let's state it this way: Make disciples of the Kingdom and the result will be the planting of churches. Plant "churches" and the result may or may not be the making of disciples of the Kingdom. And this spiritual reality confronts us with a question concerning our priorities. Is it our priority to make disciples, or to plant churches?

The Kingdom is God's plan. Discipleship is His method. And the Church is the by-product. The Kingdom produces the Church as a by-product of discipleship. If we make disciples, the result will be a Church. If we try to begin by "planting a church," the probabilities are high that the result will be an organization of religious consumers, not disciples. When we lose sight of this truth we can quickly become distracted by "the masses." Unfortunately, it is impossible to disciple the masses. Jesus couldn't do it, and didn't try. Why do we?

The Kingdom of God Is the "Big Story" of Which the Church Is the "Smaller Story." The reality that the Kingdom produces or creates the Church leads to another important principle concerning the relationship between the Kingdom and the Church. The Kingdom of God is the "big story" of which the Church, including your particular church fellowship, is the "smaller story." If you aren't a part of the Kingdom, a disciple of the Kingdom, then you are not part of the Church, even though you might be part of an organized "church." No one enters the Kingdom by joining a church. As we will discover moving forward, you and I must first be "born again" into the Kingdom of God before we can assemble together with other born again believers and disciples of the Kingdom as a genuine part of the Church.

> *No one enters the Kingdom by joining a church.*

The Church is created when individuals respond in faith and obedience to the message of the Kingdom. By faith we acknowledge, confess and repent of our sins, including our personal sin of rebellion against His Kingly rule, asking God's forgiveness based upon the sacrificial death of Jesus for our sins. We exercise faith in Jesus the Messiah-King as our savior and deliverer from rebellion, sin and death. In humility and faith we submit to His Kingly rule in our lives and become life-long disciples of the Kingdom, committed to living personal lives of radical faith and radical obedience. When we gather together with other disciples of the Kingdom we constitute the Church, a manifestation of the Kingdom of God in a still-fallen and lost world, a smaller part of a much larger whole.

Disciples Of The Kingdom Are The Building Blocks Of The Church. Disciples of the Kingdom are the living stones which God Himself is using to build His spiritual temple, *"you yourselves like living stones are being built up as a spiritual house, to be a holy priesthood, to offer spiritual sacrifices acceptable to God through Jesus Christ."* (1 Peter 2:5) And when those living stones gather together, whether in the homes of those disciples or in special buildings set aside for that purpose, we refer to those gatherings as "church." Without the message of the Kingdom there are no disciples. Without disciples there are no living stones. And without living stones there is no Church.

In the 1st Century world of Jesus and the early Church, Jews gathered in assemblies known as Synagogues which had originated during the Babylonian captivity some 400 years earlier. The term "Synagogue" (from the Greek verb *sunago*, meaning *"to gather together"*) referred primarily to the official gathering of 10 adult male Jews. Only secondarily did it come to refer to the place where they gathered.

> *Disciples of the Kingdom are the living stones which God Himself is using to build His spiritual temple.*

Following the day of Pentecost the early believers, who were mostly Jews, continued to attend synagogue and to worship in the Temple in Jerusalem. But they also added an aspect that had been missing among pious Jews. They began to meet in one another's homes (i.e. they met "house to house." See Acts 2:46).

Jewish converts to Christianity were soon banned from synagogues and open persecution soon made attendance at Temple services difficult (As Paul discovered in Acts 21). As the Church spread into predominantly Gentile (i.e., non-Jewish) areas, neither Synagogue nor Temple attendance were important to Gentile converts. But the Church, consisting of Jewish and Gentile disciples of the Kingdom, continued to meet house-to-house. The Church, gathering in homes, began to replace the Synagogue as the focus of Christian activity. And like the original meaning of "synagogue," the designation "church" referred to any assembly of Christians gathering together for worship, irrespective of the place. It designated the gathering of those who had been called out of the domain of darkness and had been transferred into the Kingdom of God's Son (Colossians 1:13). The Church was a gathering of disciples of the Kingdom.

The Church Is A Witness To The Kingdom. The Church is not the Kingdom, and this truth needs some explanation. From our perspective as believers and disciples of the Kingdom, our understanding of Church must be based upon a better understanding of the Kingdom. Our calling as the Church is to teach the Kingdom, preach the Kingdom, manifest the Kingdom and make disciples of the Kingdom. We can only do that by better understanding the Kingdom. It is NOT the calling of the Church to teach itself, proclaim itself, to exalt itself, or even to urge others to "join the church" (a concept entirely foreign to the New Testament). Rather, as disciples of the Kingdom our calling is to bear personal witness to the reality of the Kingdom of God, *"And this gospel of the kingdom shall be preached in the whole world for a witness to all the nations, and then the end shall come"* (Matthew 24:14).

But from the perspective of the curious unbeliever, the situation is somewhat different. While the believer studies the Kingdom, the unbeliever studies the Church. Whether knowingly or unknowingly, whether for good or for ill, the unbeliever counts upon the Church to provide a true and genuine witness to the Kingdom. Everything the unbelieving world knows about the Kingdom of God it learns through the witness of disciples of the Kingdom (collectively known as "the Church") as we teach, preach and manifest the Kingdom of God individually and as a corporate body. The Church - composed of

> *. . . as disciples of the Kingdom our calling is to bear personal witness to the reality of the Kingdom of God.*

disciples of the Kingdom - is God's witness concerning His Kingdom to an unbelieving world. What are you bearing witness to? Your "church" or the Kingdom of God?

And They Dreamt Of A Kingdom

The Church Is The Instrument Of The Kingdom. The fulness of the Kingdom of God remains a future promise, to be fulfilled when Jesus returns at the End of the Age. Until then, Jesus acts through His Church, utilizing it as His instrument to continue His mission of teaching, proclaiming and manifesting the Kingdom of God. This is true in at least four ways. ***First,*** the Church is God's instrument for *proclaiming the message of the Kingdom*, a message which has not changed since Jesus proclaimed it: *"Repent, for the kingdom of heaven is at hand."* ***Second,*** the Church is God's instrument for *manifesting the power of the Kingdom*, what Scripture refers to as *"the powers of the Age to Come"* (Hebrews 6:5). The power of the Kingdom of God is seen and experienced as the Church prays for people to be set free from the power of sin (salvation), from sickness and disease (healing), from demonic oppression (deliverance) and even from death itself (eternal life). ***Third,*** the Church is God's instrument for *revealing the mysteries of the Kingdom* as it teaches the truths of Scripture to those who respond in faith and become disciples of the Kingdom (Matthew 13:11). ***Fourth,*** the Church is the instrument for *manifesting the love, mercy and kindness of the Kingdom* through good deeds done in the name of Jesus, the King (Matthew 5:13-16; 25:31-46).

The Organized Church As It Exists Today Has Lost The Kingdom of God. Given what we have learned up to this point about the Kingdom creating the Church, how can the church lose the Kingdom? How can that happen? It happens because we fail to preach the Kingdom, teach the Kingdom and manifest the Kingdom. We come to believe that we are too spiritually sophisticated for such a basic message as *"The Kingdom of God is at hand. Repent, and believe the good news."* As a result, we simply ignore it and go on to more interesting topics. It happens when we confuse our priorities and attempt to reverse engineer the message and the process. We begin by proclaiming "church" and inviting people to "come and see." It proceeds by taking surveys to learn what people want to hear. It culminates with a sermon series entitled "Yea, God" complete with a giant loaf of *"Wonder Bread"* suspended from the ceiling to illustrate (wait for it . . .) how "wonderful" God is. True story. I was there. *Sigh.*

Did the crowds who came and saw this "spiritual loaf" ever hear the message of the Kingdom proclaimed, taught or manifested? Not while I was there. Sorry. Are the masses who respond to this reverse engineered and highly-processed "spiritual white bread" believers and disciples of the Kingdom? Or has the radical message of the Kingdom (*"repent of your sin, deny yourself, take up your cross and follow me"*) been replaced with something else: a stage prop, a building, a bistro, a concert, a snappy 40-day purpose driven program, or something else only tangentially related to the Kingdom, if at all. The topic of the Kingdom may have occasionally come up in a conversation or it may have received honorable mention in a sermon series, but not because anyone actually took it seriously.

The late Michael Spencer once observed that Christians today have created a spirituality that wants Jesus on the cover, but not in the book. The same could be said of the Kingdom of God. While the Kingdom may still occasionally appear on the cover of our books, the message, the power, the wonder and the mystery of the Kingdom of God have disappeared from the life of the very Church which owes its existence to Jesus' proclamation of the Kingdom.

If the "bad news" is that the church of our day has lost the Kingdom of God, then the good news is that God is restoring it. The even better news is that He wants to restore the Kingdom of God to your house and to the church which meets there. The greatest, most profound manifestation of the Kingdom of God that your friends and neighbors will ever see will be what they see take place in your organic house church. It is through the on-going witness of disciples of the Kingdom, gathering as the *ekklesia* (Church), that your friends, neighbors and others who are seeking spiritual truth will encounter the reality of the Kingdom

If the "bad news" is that the church of our day has lost the Kingdom of God, then the good news is that God is restoring it.

and experience the reality of God's Presence in a community of believers. Through the instrumentality of that witness they will experience the reality of forgiveness, the reality of answered prayer, the reality of healing from sickness and disease, the reality of deliverance from demonic bondages and more. In short, it is through the instrumentality and witness of the Church that meets in your house that they will touch, taste and experience the reality of the Kingdom of God, and be forever changed by it.

Questions For Reflection

Reflecting on this Lesson, what did you learn about the relationship between the Kingdom of God and the Church that you did not know before?

How does the Kingdom of God create the Church? How would you explain this to a new believer?

How does your own discipleship bear witness to the Kingdom of God as opposed to a "church" or other religious organization.

Describe how the Church is an instrument of the Kingdom? How do you see yourself as an instrument of the Kingdom?

How is this statement true (or not true) in your own life: *"It is through the instrumentality and witness of the Church that meets in your house where (unbelievers) will touch, taste and experience the reality of the Kingdom of God, and be forever changed by it."*

Key Thought

The Kingdom of God creates the Church by making disciples of the Kingdom who gather together as the Church.

And They Dreamt Of A Kingdom

6 - Disciples Of The Kingdom

"Therefore every scribe who has become a disciple of the Kingdom of Heaven is like a master of a house, who brings out of his treasure what is new and what is old." (Matthew 13:52)

"The cross where Jesus died became also the cross where His apostle died. The loss, the rejection, the shame, belong both to Christ and to all who in very truth are His. The cross that saves them also slays them, and anything short of this is a pseudo-faith and not true faith at all." - A.W. Tozer, *The Divine Conquest*

"Jesus never called us to lead. He calls us to follow. Leaders wear crosses. Followers bear them." - Neil Cole

In 2012 LifeWay Research (the research arm of the Southern Baptists) conducted a survey of more than 4,000 people concerning their spiritual lives and level of maturity. After crunching and analyzing the responses the researchers at LifeWay identified what they considered to be eight biblical factors which, according to them, consistently figure in the life of a maturing believer. These "attributes of discipleship" which LifeWay identified are: Bible engagement, obeying God and denying self, serving God and others, sharing Christ, exercising faith, seeking God, building relationships, and unashamed transparency.

Part of a long-term LifeWay project called the Transformational Initiative, the Transformational Discipleship Assessment survey was quite extensive.[16] The research was conducted in three phases. First, LifeWay researchers interviewed recognized "discipleship experts." Next, LifeWay polled 1,000 Protestant pastors in the United States. Finally, more than 4,000 Protestants church-goers from both the U.S. and Canada were surveyed. According to LifeWay, the purpose of the survey was to help church leaders discover how best to help their members grow.

I want to be clear at this point. I am not necessarily opposed to surveys, as they can often clarify what people are doing, thinking or believing at a particular point in time. Nor am I opposed to the "eight biblical factors" listed above. But I believe the survey (along with its results) raises as many questions as it purports to answer. For example, can being a disciple of the Kingdom really be reduced to eight principles? Is that what Jesus did? And doesn't this come perilously close to reducing biblical "discipleship" to something that will fit on a bumper sticker (O.K., in this case, a BIG bumper sticker!)? Will we soon be deluged with the "latest and greatest" program curriculum announcing *"Eight Steps To Making Disciples In Only 40 Days?"* My guess would be that it's coming.

But what is particularly troubling about the whole matter is what appears to be an underlying assumption that the way to understand biblical discipleship is to interview professing Christians about their discipleship habits. Really? Granted, there are many godly and mature individuals whose lives, examples and teachings could (and should) teach us a few things about what it means to follow Jesus. But if we truly want to better understand what it means to be a disciple of the Kingdom, shouldn't we start by asking the King what it means to be His disciple? Shouldn't Kingdom discipleship begin with the King? If we are "ambassadors of Christ," wouldn't it be helpful to hear from the King Himself concerning what He expects of His ambassadors?

And They Dreamt Of A Kingdom

Why This Matters

"Now the eleven disciples went to Galilee, to the mountain to which Jesus had directed them. And when they saw him they worshiped him, but some doubted. And Jesus came and said to them, 'All authority in heaven and on earth has been given to me. Go therefore and make disciples of all nations, baptizing them in the name of the Father and of the Son and of the Holy Spirit, teaching them to observe all that I have commanded you. And behold, I am with you always, to the end of the age.'" (Matthew 28:16-20)

Following His resurrection, Jesus spent 40 days appearing to His disciples and talking with them about the Kingdom of God. Finally, the day came when it was time for Him to leave them and return to the Father. It was a critical moment of farewells and last instructions. So, what last words did Jesus give His disciples and the Church? The heart of Matthew's account is found in verses 19 and 20, *"Go therefore and make disciples of all nations, baptizing them in the name of the Father and of the Son and of the Holy Spirit, teaching them to observe all that I have commanded you. And behold, I am with you always, to the end of the age."* (Matthew 28:19-20)

We need to take a moment to understand the structure of this passage, based upon the Greek text, which is as follows: *"(As you are) going, make disciples (by) baptizing them (and by) teaching them."* I have long thought that students of New Testament Greek would do themselves (and the Church) a favor by studying Classical Greek in addition to the Koine Greek of the New Testament. One of the benefits might be a better understanding of passages like this one from Matthew. Greek is known for its use of participles to set the stage or to describe the circumstances surrounding the action of the finite verb in a sentence. It is not unusual for a sentence in a Greek historical narrative to contain

> *The only imperative in the sentence is "make disciples." It was Jesus' last command to His own disciples; what they were to do "as they were going."*

several "circumstantial participles," all describing the circumstances surrounding the action of the finite verb. In this verse from Matthew, the finite verb (*matheteuo*) is a command, *"make disciples."*[17] The participle *poreuthentes* (from the middle deponent verb *poreuomai*, meaning "to go") sets the circumstances surrounding the command to make disciples, namely, *"as you are going."*

This verse is frequently translated, *"Go, and make disciples."* While it is permissible to translate this participle simply as "go," there are two problems. First, the conjunction "and" is absent in the Greek, which leads to the second problem. It diminishes the imperative force of the finite verb ("make disciples") by suggesting that "go" is also an imperative (i.e., *"Go and make"*). It is not. The only imperative in the sentence is "make disciples." It was Jesus' last command to His own disciples; what they were to do *"as they were going."* A simple, accurate rendering of this passage would be, *"As you are in the process of going (wherever that might be), make disciples."*

We began this section with a question disguised as a tease: *"Why This Matters."* Biblical discipleship, what it means to be a disciple and what it means to make disciples, is at the heart of everything Jesus did and taught. Discipleship was so important to Jesus that His last instructions to those who would lead His Church forward constituted a command to be obeyed, not a suggestion to take into consideration: "Make Disciples." That's why it matters. Because it matters to Jesus.

There is much more we could say about this passage, but I want to briefly focus on the last two participles in this verse, "baptizing" and "teaching." In Greek grammar these two participles are known as "instrumental participles" or "participles of means." In relation to the finite verb of the sentence ("make disciples"), they serve to answer the question, *"How do we make disciples?"* The answer is simple. We make disciples by baptizing those who respond to the message of the Kingdom (water baptism constitutes the act of public identification with Jesus and with the believing community), and by teaching them the same things Jesus taught His disciples (which is what the rest of this book is all about).

So, What Is A Disciple?

"A disciple is not above his teacher, nor a servant above his master. It is enough for the disciple to be like his teacher, and the servant like his master." (Matthew 10:24-25)

The command to "make disciples," and the prominent role of teaching as a primary instrument in the process of disciple-making, forces us to examine what it means to be a "disciple." At its heart, biblical discipleship as practiced by Jesus consisted of a relationship between a teacher and a student. The word "disciple" itself (Greek: *mathetes*) means "a learner" or "a student." Without this relationship between a teacher and a student, there is no discipleship.

Let's reflect for a moment. Jesus' challenge and task on earth was profoundly simple. In a span of three years He must impart to a handful of individuals sufficient eternal truth to transform their lives and carry both the message of the Kingdom and a growing Church forward until His return at the end of the Age. The method He chose to accomplish this task was elegantly simple. He would pick twelve unlikely individuals and spend the next three years pouring Himself into them. They would be His "disciples," his "padawan learners," if you will. In their company He would preach, teach and model everything they would need to know about the Kingdom of God in order to carry His Church forward after He was gone. Discipleship was Jesus' plan and method for the Kingdom from now until His return.

> *Discipleship was Jesus' plan and method for the Kingdom from now until His return.*

The concept of discipleship was common in the ancient world. Notable teachers, philosophers and rabbis had their schools of disciples. The Greek philosopher, Plato, was a disciple of Socrates in Athens. Up until the time of his conversion the Apostle Paul had been a disciple of the great Jewish Rabbi, Gamaliel (Acts 22:3). But while the concept of discipleship was common, the discipleship of Jesus was different. He called the unlikely, not the most promising or the most popular. Uneducated fishermen, a despised tax collector, a political zealot, and others of no reputation at all (do we even know anything about Thomas, other than He doubted Jesus' resurrection without proof?).

The discipleship of Jesus was different in another way. It required faith, not in a body of teaching, but in Jesus Himself. Faith in His teaching was important, but believing in Jesus Himself was indispensable. Their belief in Him might start small,

And They Dreamt Of A Kingdom

with a faith based upon the testimony of others, but it must grow to a point where believing in the King and His Kingdom rises above everything else and declares, *"Lord, to whom shall we go? You have the words of eternal life, and we have believed, and have come to know, that you are the Holy One of God."* No rabbi had ever made such demands of his disciples. This was different.

> *Faith in His teaching was important, but believing in Jesus Himself was indispensable.*

The discipleship of Jesus was different in another way. Jesus required absolute commitment. This absolute commitment might begin with a simple invitation to "come and see" (John 1:39), but it would soon grow to a call: *"Follow me"* (Matthew 4:19). This simple phrase, "follow me," occurs 21 times in three gospels, all but one of them being found on the lips of Jesus. And when Jesus told people to "follow me" His words didn't represent an invitation so much as a command. But accepting the invitation - obeying the command - came at a price: absolute commitment to Jesus above everyone and everything else (See Mark 10:28).

Total commitment meant selling one's possessions and giving everything to the poor when possessions were the obstacle standing in the way of obedience (Luke 18:22). Total commitment meant leaving a lucrative tax business to follow Jesus (Matthew 9:9), or being unavailable either to bury one's own father (Luke 9:51), or even to say "good bye" to one's family (Luke 9:61). In short, the total commitment required to be a disciple of Jesus meant a profound death to self and to the normal human commitments one would expect or could look forward to. Friends. Family. Business. Possessions. And to make this point unmistakably clear, Jesus stated this discipleship principle in no uncertain terms . . . twice.

". . . whoever does not take his cross and follow me is not worthy of me. Whoever finds his life will lose it, and whoever loses his life for my sake will find it." (Matthew 10:38-39)

"If anyone would come after me, let him deny himself and take up his cross and follow me. For whoever would save his life will lose it, but whoever loses his life for my sake will find it." (Matthew 16:24-25)

In an age like ours, when crosses have been reduced to costume jewelry worn by people with little or no biblical commitment, Jesus' declaration here doesn't carry the emotional impact that it did in the 1st Century. Jesus' listeners would have been shocked to hear Him equate discipleship with crucifixion. A cross was a cruel, deliberately painful, despised and feared Roman instrument of execution. The Romans hadn't invented crucifixion. It had been practiced by the ancient Persians, Carthaginians and Macedonians. The Romans simply perfected it as an instrument of punishment and terror. In the year 71 B.C. Roman Legions under Marcus Licinius Crassus put down a slave rebellion led by a Thracian slave named Spartacus (known as the Third Servile War, 73–71 BC). Having defeated the slave army in battle, Crassus ordered his legions to crucify six thousand captured survivors along a 125 mile stretch of the Apian Way between Capua and Rome. A warning to any other would-be rebels. The Jewish historian Flavius Josephus records how, during the Maccabean period in Palestine prior to Christ, the Maccabean King Alexander Jannaeus (103-76 B.C.) crucified 800 Pharisees who opposed his rule.[18] That is what a "cross" meant to the people of Jesus' day. It meant death, and not a pleasant one.

Someone once observed that there was one thing you knew with certainty about a man carrying a cross out of the city. You knew he wasn't coming back. For those whom Jesus called to be His disciples His call required a response of total commitment of radical faith and radical obedience to Himself as their Master, Lord and Teacher. No coming back. That's what it means to be a disciple of the Kingdom. You must go "all in," or go home. It was that commitment which set the disciples apart from the crowds of "believers" who followed Jesus' ministry but were never heard from again, except to cry "Hosanna" on Palm Sunday and "crucify Him" only a week later. And it is this distinction between "believers" and "disciples" which we need to consider next.

That's what it means to be a disciple of the Kingdom. You must go "all in," or go home.

Questions For Reflection

Reflecting on this Lesson, what did you discover about what it means to be a disciple that you did not know before?

Explain what it is about your own life which sets you apart as a disciple of the Kingdom, as opposed to simply being another "follower" or "believer" in Jesus.

Key Thought

A disciple of the Kingdom is someone who has made an absolute commitment of faith and obedience to Jesus as his Master, Lord and Teacher.

49

And They Dreamt Of A Kingdom

7 - Believers Versus Disciples

"Now when he was in Jerusalem at the Passover Feast, many believed in his name when they saw the signs that he was doing. But Jesus on his part did not entrust himself to them, because he knew all people and needed no one to bear witness about man, for he himself knew what was in man." (John 2:23-25)

"Christianity without discipleship is always Christianity without Christ. It remains an abstract idea, a myth which has a place for the Fatherhood of God, but omits Christ as the living Son . . . . There is trust in God, but no following of Christ." - Dietrich Bonhoeffer, **The Cost of Discipleship**

And now for the elephant in the room, or more specifically, the spiritual elephant in the church: *"What is the relationship between 'believers' and 'disciples'"*? Let's begin our consideration of the question with the above passage from the Gospel of John. We are told in John 2:13 that Jesus went up to Jerusalem for the Feast of the Passover. While there Jesus cleansed the temple of the money changers (John 2:14-17) and prophesied His own death and resurrection (John 2:18-22). Then John gives us the passage which we quote above. While only two verses long, this passage is a "block buster." It offers us insight into how Jesus regarded the crowds who followed Him and who "believed" in Him. The Greek text of this passage contains a play on words based upon the Greek verb *pisteuo* (*"to believe"*). An accurate paraphrase of this verse might be something like this, *"many believed in his name . . . . But as for Jesus, He didn't believe in them."*

Let's admit the truth up front. This is a disturbing passage. It confronts us with a reality we would rather ignore, namely, that Jesus didn't entrust Himself to everyone who came along claiming to believe in Him. The average church would have led these people in a "group sinner's prayer," made them members, elders and deacons and invited them to teach a class or serve on a committee. Jesus, for His part, ignored them (ouch!). Jesus didn't take such people too seriously (Ouch, again!). As Morris notes, *." . . we should probably not regard them as having a profound faith. They believed because they saw the 'signs.' While such a faith is better than none, it is not the deepest faith. It is no more than a beginning."*[19]

Modern Christianity devotes its attention to the crowds. Biblical Christianity devotes its attention to the disciples. Jesus wasn't looking to accumulate a crowd of "believers." His ministry was to call out and raise up disciples of the Kingdom who would carry His message of the Kingdom to the uttermost corners of the earth, regardless of the cost. And to accomplish this discipleship task He was willing to experience every church's worst nightmare - negative church growth! Jesus understood that the "believing" crowds would come and go, depending upon their whims and His popularity. But Jesus wasn't seeking popularity. He was seeking to establish His Kingdom in the hearts, minds and lives of men who would carry His message of the Kingdom to the ends of the earth. And for that He needed disciples, not followers or even "believers."

> *Modern Christianity devotes its attention to the crowds. Biblical Christianity devotes its attention to the disciples.*

And They Dreamt Of A Kingdom

"Believers" Who Stone Jesus

The above passage from John 2 helps to explain another curious incident later in Jesus' ministry recorded in John Chapter 8. In the first half of the Chapter (verses 1-29) Jesus interacts with Jewish religious leaders (Scribes and Pharisees), beginning with a woman caught in the act of adultery (8:1-11). Jesus proceeds to declare, *"I am the light of the world"* and to warn the Jewish religious leaders that *"unless you believe that I am (he, i.e., "God") you will die in your sins."* (John 8:24). Then, in verses 30-32 we have an interesting development: *"As he was saying these things, many believed in him. So Jesus said to the Jews who had believed in him, 'If you abide in my word, you are truly my disciples, and you will know the truth, and the truth will set you free.'"* (John 8:30-32)

It appears that some portion of "the Jews" (John's catch-all term for Jewish religious leaders) "believed" in Jesus (verse 30). Jesus responds to these new believers by instructing them on what it means to be His disciples (verse 31-32). What occurs next is stunning. For the next 26 verses, through the end of the Chapter, these new believers argue with Jesus over their relationship to Abraham. At one point, Jesus tells these new believers (same context), *"You are of your father the devil"* (John 8:44). They respond by calling Jesus a demon-possessed Samaritan (John 8:48). Finally, the entire episode ends with these new believers rejecting Jesus' claim to divinity (*"Before Abraham was, I Am"*) and attempting to stone Him (John 8:58-59). Not the way most of us want our "new believers" class to end. As Morris observes, *"This section of discourse is addressed to those who believe, and yet do not believe. Clearly they were inclined to think that what Jesus said was true. But they were not prepared to yield Him the far-reaching allegiance that real trust in Him implies."* [20]

> *Biblically speaking, a profession of belief is only as valid as the discipleship which flows from it.*

There's a reason why Jesus didn't trust the crowds who "believed" in Him, besides the reality that they were fickle and superficial. He wasn't looking for "believers." He was looking for "disciples." Biblically speaking, a profession of belief is only as valid as the discipleship which flows from it. When it comes to the issue of professing believers versus disciples this is a spiritual principle we need to fully grasp. While only God knows the true condition of the heart, a profession of belief which never manifests itself in discipleship is questionable . . . at best. As we will soon discover, such "belief" is like sown seed which sprouts quickly, but soon dies for lack of root or due to the cares of this life. It never bears fruit. And fruitfulness - not profession - is the sign of genuine faith and discipleship (more about this in Lesson 39).

Receiving and Believing

This issue of "believers" versus "disciples" nearly always leads quickly to the following passage from the John's Gospel: *"He came to his own, and his own people did not receive him. But to all who did receive him, who believed in his name, he gave the right to become children of God, who were born, not of blood nor of the will of the flesh nor of the will of man, but of God."* (John 1:11-13)

Based upon all we have learned thus far about Jesus and His message, there is really only one plausible interpretation of this passage. Jesus' life, message and ministry were all about the Kingdom of God, *"Jesus came into Galilee, proclaiming the gospel of God, and saying, 'The time is fulfilled, and the kingdom of God is at hand; repent and believe in the gospel'"* (Mark 1:14-15). What Jesus' own people did not receive was His message concerning the Kingdom of God. Whatever else the

What Jesus' own people did not receive was His message concerning the Kingdom of God.

crowds around Jesus may or may not have believed, those who received and believed Jesus' message of the Kingdom were (and are) the ones to whom He gave *"the right to become children of God."*

It is always surprising, even eye opening, to see who actually receives the message of the Kingdom and who doesn't. The religious leaders of Jesus day, for the most part, never received it. But guess who did? The thief dying on the cross next to Jesus. He understood that Jesus was all about the Kingdom. Set aside what you think you know, and listen with fresh ears to this conversation:

"One of the criminals who were hanged railed at him, saying, 'Are you not the Christ? Save yourself and us!' But the other rebuked him, saying, 'Do you not fear God, since you are under the same sentence of condemnation? And we indeed justly, for we are receiving the due reward of our deeds; but this man has done nothing wrong.' And he said, 'Jesus, remember me when you come into your kingdom.' And he said to him, 'Truly, I say to you, today you will be with me in Paradise.'" (Luke 23:39-43)

Do you understand what just transpired? The thief, dying on the cross next to Jesus, received the message of the Kingdom, believed the message of the Kingdom and spent the remaining moments of his life as a disciple of the Kingdom. But as you probably noticed, there was a second thief dying on another cross on the other side of Jesus. His attitude was quite different.

He was willing to "believe" that Jesus was the Christ, but only if Jesus would deliver him on his terms, *"Save yourself and us!"* There is an irony in the responses of these two men to their situations. The first thief was, in fact, fulfilling one of Jesus' primary requirements for a disciple; death to self, even if it meant death on a cross. He didn't ask to be delivered. He asked to be remembered in the Kingdom. That is the faith of a disciple of the

In the Presence of the King, one man died a disciple, while the other died a thief. Which are you? And which am I?

Kingdom. It is the faith of one who understands that *"there are far, far better things ahead than any we leave behind."* But the second thief had no interest in dying on a cross for his faith. He didn't want to be remembered. He wanted to be delivered. In the end, he experienced neither. The second thief had a "belief" that only extended as far as his own needs. In the Presence of the King, one man died a disciple, while the other died a thief. Which are you? And which am I?

Let's be clear. In the Kingdom of God, salvation, redemption from sin and deliverance from the domain of darkness, is by faith. As Paul told the Ephesian believers, *"For by grace you have been saved through faith. And this is not your own doing; it is the gift of God, not a result of works, so that no one may boast"* (Ephesians 2:8-9). Salvation is by faith, not by discipleship. Salvation and the Kingdom are a gift, not a reward. And according to Paul, even the faith to believe is a gift. We have nothing to boast about with respect to either our faith or our salvation.

But if "faith" is the *sine qua non* of biblical Christianity, then discipleship is the Q.E.D. or *quod erat demonstrandum* of genuine faith.[21] Simply put, faith is the necessary essence of our relationship with Jesus. And our discipleship represents our life-long demonstration of what we profess to believe. What does your life demonstrate about what you claim to believe?

Raising The Bar of Discipleship

"True religion," wrote A. W. Tozer, *"confronts earth with heaven and brings eternity to bear upon time."* The same can be said of true discipleship. True discipleship confronts each of us with the reality of the Kingdom of God, and brings the demands of that Kingdom to bear upon our daily lives. Jesus set a high bar for those who would answer His call to discipleship in the Kingdom. And He refused to lower that bar to accommodate those unwilling to measure their lives by it. Instead, he was constantly raising it.

> *With Jesus, discipleship continually became more challenging, not less. The lessons got harder, not easier.*

With Jesus, discipleship continually became more challenging, not less. The lessons got harder, not easier. To overturn the tables of the Temple money changers once was a statement of principle which took everyone by surprise (John 2:13ff) and got the attention of 1st Century Judaism. But to do so again, at the end of His ministry, was to raise the bar of obedience and to throw down the gauntlet before people who already wanted to kill Him . . . and would soon do so! Jesus was in the business of raising the bar for those who would follow Him. Not lowering it. And that alone deserves our thoughtful reflection.

Commenting upon the state of the Church in his generation, A.W.Tozer observed, *"The Church has surrendered her once lofty concept of God and has substituted for it one so low, so ignoble, as to be utterly unworthy of thinking, worshiping men. This she has done not deliberately, but little by little and without her knowledge, and her very unawareness only makes her situation all the more tragic."*[22]

Tozer's observation is equally true today concerning our concept of discipleship. The church of the 21st Century has lowered the bar of discipleship to the point of all but eliminating it altogether. Contrary to New Testament teaching, all believers are now disciples. To qualify as a disciple all anyone needs to do is show up, take a class, complete a workbook and curriculum, and get involved in a church activity or program. And the money changers now take debit cards, which you can use to pay for your class materials. Tozer continues:

"This loss of the concept of majesty has come just when the forces of religion are making dramatic gains and the churches are more prosperous than at any time within the past several hundred years. But the alarming thing is that our gains are mostly external and our losses wholly internal; and since it is the quality of our religion that is affected by internal conditions, it may be that our supposed gains are but losses spread over a wider field."[23]

Simply substitute the word "discipleship" for the word "majesty" in the above quote, and our generation is linked with Tozer's and our point is driven home with fresh power and urgency. For the contemporary church to measure its "supposed gains" by its outward success (the size of the campus, or the budget or attendance) while ignoring the absence of committed disciples able to bear fruit and reproduce themselves in the lives of others, is to experience *"losses spread over a wider field,"* masquerading as success.

It is time for the Church to re-set the bar of discipleship in the Kingdom as established and set by Jesus Himself. But to do so may well challenge our religion-shaped spirituality to its breaking point and force us to re-examine our structures and the things that shape us. And that is where we need to go next.

Questions For Reflection

Reflecting on this Lesson, what did you learn about what it means to be a disciple that you did not know before?

In your own words, how would you describe the difference between a "believer" and a "disciple"? How does your description apply to you?

Read: 2 Timothy 2:1-2. What does this passage from Paul's second letter to Timothy tell us about the importance he and the early church placed upon the concept of discipleship?

What are you doing in your own life, ministry or church to reproduce the discipleship process which Paul described to Timothy and which Jesus practiced with His disciples?

Key Thought

As disciples of the Kingdom, our discipleship embodies our life-long demonstration of what we profess to believe about Jesus and the Kingdom of God.

And They Dreamt Of A Kingdom

8 - The Things That Shape Us

"We shape our buildings; thereafter they shape us."
- Sir Winston Churchill

In the Battle of Britain during World War 2 the British House of Commons sustained heavy bomb damage. On October 28, 1944, during the rebuilding of the House of Commons, Winston Churchill spoke to Parliament and made the above observation. I would suggest that Churchill's observation was probably more insightful than even he understood. We all begin with values which guide us as we shape our buildings, our "structures." But at some point along the way, our buildings - our structures - begin to shape our values. The same truth applies to our spiritual lives, what I refer to throughout this book as our "spirituality." When it comes to matters involving our "spirituality" - how we understand such things as God, faith, obedience, etc. - we are generally shaped by one of two things: values or structures. This is as true for you and me as it was for Jesus' first disciples.[24]

Our spirituality represents the embodiment and daily expression of everything we believe concerning Scripture, God, worship, truth, sin, redemption, faith, obedience and our life in the Kingdom of God. The people of God had begun their spiritual journey some 20 centuries before Jesus with a faith-driven, Jehovah-shaped spirituality embodied by Abraham. The spiritual values of that Jehovah-shaped spirituality were later codified by God through Moses in "the Law," forged in the fires of faith, holiness, and obedience upon Mount Sinai. But over the intervening centuries the fires of that Jehovah-shaped spirituality had gone cold. The values of the Law had been superceded by a religious structure and a religious legalism, devoid of faith. Personal faith and obedience to God had become lost in a religion-shaped spirituality fashioned around structures rather than values, law rather than grace, sacrifice rather than mercy, outward conformity rather than inward transformation and tradition rather than truth.

> *Our spirituality represents the embodiment and daily expression of everything we believe concerning Scripture, God, worship, truth, sin, redemption, faith, obedience and our life in the Kingdom of God.*

By the time of Jesus, the embodiment of that religion-shaped spirituality could be seen on full display in the religious leadership of 1st Century institutional Judaism. The religion-shaped spirituality they had created and the religious structures they controlled had become more important to them than the faith they had lost or the God they claimed to worship. By the time Jesus came on the scene, the religion-shaped spirituality of 1st Century Judaism was simply unsuited for the Kingdom. It represented the structure of an old wineskin which could not hold the new wine and values of the Kingdom. It must be challenged and eventually laid aside. This is frequently true of wineskins which men create. It is even true today.

Jesus Versus The Disciples

When Jesus first called His disciples, they were men with a deeply ingrained religion-shaped spirituality, bequeathed to them by 1st Century Judaism. Nearly everything they thought they knew about the God of Israel they had learned from the institutional religious structure of 1st Century Judaism. And it showed. They regarded

And They Dreamt Of A Kingdom

all Gentiles (non-Jews) as "unclean" and refused to associate with them (Acts 10:28), because that's what Judaism taught. They despised Samaritans (John Chapter 4), just as they had been taught, and were ready on a moment's notice to call down fire from heaven to consume them (Luke 9:52-54). Their religion-shaped spirituality told them to avoid all Gentiles, most women (outside of family members), lepers and tax-collectors in particular and "sinners" in general. It was a sin to heal anyone on the Sabbath, and a man was probably born blind because either he or his parents had sinned (John 9:2). According to what they had been taught, God was a "legalist," and one could not be truly religious or spiritual without obeying the more than 5,000 religious rules and regulations ("traditions of the elders") which governed 1st Century Judaism.

Then they met Jesus. And for the next three-and-a-half years He would shake and bend their religion-shaped spirituality to the breaking point. As they traveled with Him along the highways and byways of Israel, they watched in stunned disbelief as He ministered to both women AND Samaritans, and allowed a woman of questionable character ("a sinner") to minister to Him (Luke 7:36-39). They watched Him heal lepers with a touch, when a spoken word would have accomplished the same thing. They even joined Him as He dined in their homes (Matthew 26:6) because He wanted to make a point about ministry to "the least of these." They accompanied Him as He dined in the homes of tax-collectors, "hung out" with assorted "sinners" and ministered to a gentile woman and her daughter (Matthew 15:22-28). They watched as He healed on the Sabbath in order to provoke a confrontation with the leaders of institutional Judaism (Matthew 12:10; Mark 3:2; Luke 14:3). There was more. With Jesus, there always is. But you get the point.

For three-and-a-half years Jesus challenged everything His disciples knew about God, faith, religion and spirituality.

For three-and-a-half years Jesus challenged everything His disciples knew about God, faith, religion and spirituality. Jesus challenged their understanding of God until He was their understanding of God. He challenged their understanding of religious authority until He was their understanding of religious authority. He challenged their understanding of obedience to God until they understood that obedience to Him WAS obedience to God. And He challenged their understanding of spirituality and religion until He embodied their understanding of spirituality and religion. He challenged them to rid themselves of all "other things" in their spiritual lives until He and He alone embodied *"the main thing"* in their spiritual lives.

Twelve Changed Men

After spending three-and-a-half years with Jesus, the disciples emerged from the events of the crucifixion and resurrection as profoundly changed men. Gone (for the most part) was the religion-shaped spirituality inherited from 1st Century Judaism. In its place was a Jesus-shaped spirituality fashioned by Jesus and suited for life, ministry and discipleship in the Kingdom of God. Scripture recognizes and points out this profound change early in the Book of Acts. In their first post-resurrection encounter with the disciples, the Jewish religious authorities found themselves at a loss to explain who these people were until they *"began to recognize them as having been with Jesus."* (Acts 4:13) The disciples had been changed beyond recognition. They were no longer the obedient Jewish religionists Jesus had first called along the shores of Galilee. They were now men who had been profoundly transformed by a Jesus-shaped spirituality. They were now disciples of the Kingdom.

Later in the book of Acts we read, *"and the disciples were first called Christians in Antioch"* (Acts 11:26). The Greek word for "Christians" is what we call a "diminutive" - a word formed by adding a suffix to a root word in order to indicate "smallness." The Greek term "Christians" literally means "little Christ-ones." We don't know who first referred to the disciples in Antioch as "Christians."

> *A Christian is a disciple of the Kingdom who manifests a Jesus-shaped spirituality.*

I suspect it was people outside the Church who intended the label as something approaching a slur. If so, they unwittingly paid those early disciples the highest possible compliment. They accused them of looking like Jesus. They accused them of manifesting a Jesus-shaped spirituality.

Today, we are very loose with our terminology. We describe someone as a Christian simply because they attend a church service and make some nominal profession of faith. Our standards for what constitutes a Christian are really quite low. Not so in the early church. "Christian" was the label given by unbelievers who watched the early disciples manifest a Jesus-shaped spirituality in their daily lives, and in the face of mounting persecution. We could restate it this way. Biblically speaking, a Christian is a disciple of the Kingdom who manifests a Jesus-shaped spirituality.

What Shapes You?

At the end of the day you and I embody the things we believe and which have shaped us. We are either the living embodiment of a set of religious rules and beliefs given to us by the religious structures which have shaped us, or we are the embodiment of a daily relationship with the living, risen Jesus. We are either disciples of the Kingdom of God and its values or we are disciples of a religious organization and its values.

> *At the end of the day you and I embody the things we believe and which have shaped us.*

We are either the embodiment of a Jesus-shaped spirituality, fashioned around Jesus and the values of the Kingdom, or we are the embodiment of a religion-shaped spirituality, fashioned around the values and structures of someone or something else.

What is a Jesus-shaped spirituality? It is the life of a disciple who looks like Jesus and who sounds like the Kingdom of God, as opposed to looking and sounding like some religious leader and his (or her) organization. A Jesus-shaped spirituality is one which challenges us to become disciples of the Kingdom by submitting our lives to the Lordship of Jesus, the Messiah-King, and to follow him in daily obedience. Jesus wants to challenge our understanding of God until He IS our understanding of God. He wants to challenge our understanding of religious authority until He IS our understanding of religious authority. He wants to challenge our understanding of obedience to God until we understand that obedience to Him IS obedience to God. And He wants to challenge our understanding of spirituality and religion until He IS our understanding of spirituality and religion. In short, Jesus wants to challenge us to rid ourselves of all "other things" in our spiritual lives until He and He alone embodies *"the main thing"* in our spiritual lives.

The pursuit of a Jesus-shaped spirituality means cutting our ties with the comfortable and safe religious traditions, customs and assumptions we may have known, and embracing the wildness of the Kingdom of God as proclaimed by an itinerant Rabbi and carpenter from Nazareth Who now rules as Messiah and King. The religion-shaped spirituality you may have known in the past is not a reliable guide to who Jesus is, or what He wants you to do today. A Jesus-shaped spirituality must be pursued on Jesus' terms and no others. That was the first lesson Jesus' disciples had to learn, and it is a lesson we need to learn (again) as well.

Values, Structure And Discipleship

"You never change a structure until you change a value. We do not transplant systems and structures. We transplant values and life." - William Beckham

Reflecting on the current state of the church in the early years of the 21st Century, there is a fundamental reality which confronts us regarding our lack of disciple-making in the church today. The nature of discipleship - the relationship between a teacher and a student - presents the contemporary church with a conundrum. Specifically, it presents us with a fundamental conflict between our values on the one hand (i.e., making disciples as Jesus commanded) and our structure on the other (large organized churches led by paid staff). Our structures are designed to attract and entertain the masses. They are not designed to make disciples. According to the National Congregations Study conducted at Duke University, 90% of all church congregations in America have 350 or fewer people.[25] Using this as a benchmark, the pastor of such a church would need to be roughly thirty times more effective than Jesus in order to disciple his (or her) congregation the way Jesus did.[26] Simply stated, our current church structure all but guarantees that the vast majority of the people attending our churches will never be discipled in any biblically meaningful way, so long as they are part of that structure. Our structure guarantees our failure at the primary task we have been given to accomplish, the impartation of Kingdom values to the next generation of believers and disciples.

If discipleship as modeled and commanded by Jesus is one of our core values, and if our current structure of church guarantees our inability to implement that value, then we are confronted with a fundamental crisis which demands a choice on our part. We must choose either to embrace the "value" of discipleship and allow that value to shape and change our structures, or to admit to ourselves that our structures have become our value and that we have, indeed, been conquered by our structures and the religion-shaped spirituality which they inevitably produce.

If our goal is to attract and entertain the masses, and to lead them into some form of nominal profession of "belief," then the "multi-campus/megachurch" model is by far the best methodology. It works, at least for that purpose. But if our goal is to follow the example and the command of Jesus to make disciples who are fruitful and reproduce themselves by making more disciples, then we must do things differently. Jesus lived His life to please an audience of One, to train an audience of twelve and to proclaim the Kingdom of God to an audience of whoever would listen. Jesus focused His time and effort on a handful of disciples, challenging their religion-shaped spirituality - inherited from 1st Century Judaism - to its breaking point. And in its place

He shaped them with a spirituality molded around Himself and the values of the Kingdom.

Jesus didn't raise up and train "worker bees" for a religious program, not even a "missions" program. He ushered in a Kingdom by investing Himself in twelve key people. They were His plan, and the Kingdom of God was His program. Jesus' goal was to establish the Kingdom of God in the hearts, minds and lives of a handful of men. And He chose the methodology best suited to achieving that goal. That's how Jesus made disciples of the Kingdom of God. I believe that is what He would do if He were making Kingdom disciples today. And that is what we must do, too. The remainder of this book is devoted to examining the ministry of Jesus with those twelve men and the values He sought to teach them.

Questions For Reflection

Reflecting on this Lesson, what did you learn about how our values and our structures shape us and what we believe?

Spend some time reflecting on your own discipleship. What are the "values" which have shaped your discipleship? Where did you learn those values, from Jesus and the Kingdom or from someone or something else? How are you imparting those values to others? What is the difference between a "value" and an "activity"?

Key Thought

You and I are the embodiment of what we believe and the values which have shaped us. We are either the living embodiment of a set of religious rules and beliefs given to us by the religious structures which have shaped us, or we are the embodiment of a daily relationship with the living, risen Jesus.

And They Dreamt Of A Kingdom

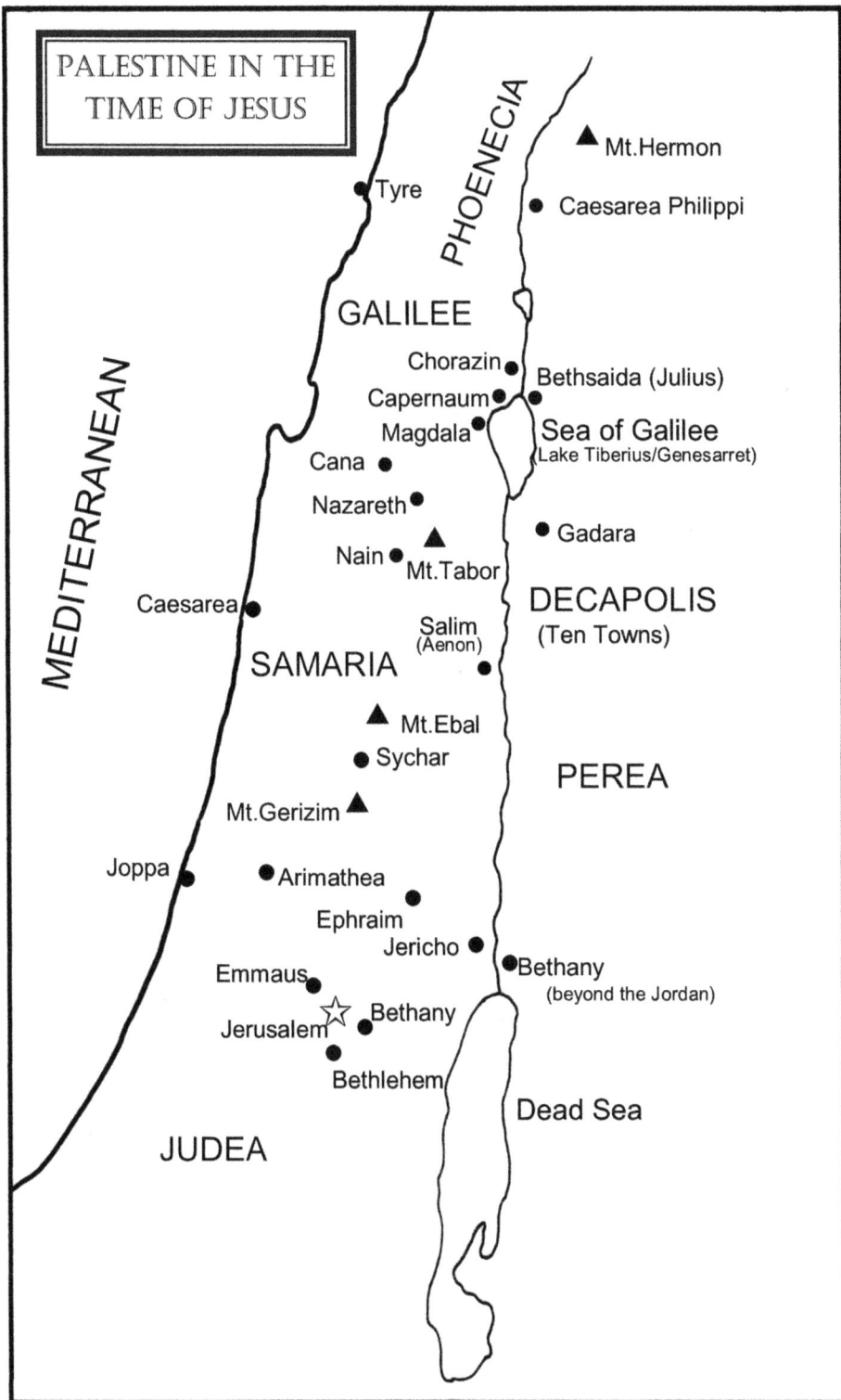

PALESTINE IN THE TIME OF JESUS

MEDITERRANEAN

PHOENECIA

Tyre

Mt. Hermon

Caesarea Philippi

GALILEE

Chorazin

Bethsaida (Julius)

Capernaum

Magdala

Sea of Galilee
(Lake Tiberius/Genesarret)

Cana

Nazareth

Nain

Mt. Tabor

Gadara

DECAPOLIS
(Ten Towns)

Caesarea

Salim
(Aenon)

SAMARIA

Mt. Ebal

Sychar

PEREA

Mt. Gerizim

Joppa

Arimathea

Ephraim

Jericho

Bethany
(beyond the Jordan)

Emmaus

Jerusalem

Bethany

Bethlehem

Dead Sea

JUDEA

And They Dreamt Of A Kingdom

9 - Beginnings

"The next day again John was standing with two of his disciples, and he looked at Jesus as he walked by and said, 'Behold, the Lamb of God!' The two disciples heard him say this, and they followed Jesus. Jesus turned and saw them following and said to them, 'What are you seeking?' And they said to him, 'Rabbi' (which means Teacher), 'where are you staying?' He said to them, 'Come and you will see.'" (John 1:35-39)

Discipleship Reading: *John 1:35-51*   **When:** *Summer, A.D. 26*
Contextual Reading: *John Chapter 1*   **Where:** *Bethany*

In the Kingdom of God, every journey of discipleship has a beginning. And for five young Galilean seekers, each of their personal discipleship journeys would begin inauspiciously along the banks of the Jordan River somewhere in the Summer of A.D. 26. And that's were we want to begin. Writing over 100 years ago, A.B. Bruce summed up this moment in time when he wrote, *"All beginnings are more or less obscure in appearance, but none were ever more obscure than those of Christianity."*[27]

After a profound silence of some 400 years (since the last Old Testament prophet, Malachi), the prophetic voice of God had once again been heard in Israel. John, the promised messenger and Messianic forerunner, appeared in the wilderness of Judea around the Jordan River proclaiming a message of repentance, baptism and the Kingdom of God (Mark 1:4). His arrival embodied the fulfillment of a promise given seven hundred years earlier, *"As it is written in Isaiah the prophet, 'Behold, I send my messenger before your face, who will prepare your way, the voice of one crying in the wilderness: 'Prepare the way of the Lord, make his paths straight'"* (Mark 1:2-3).

The impact of John's message on 1st Century religious Judaism was profound, *"And all the country of Judea and all Jerusalem were going out to him and were being baptized by him in the river Jordan, confessing their sins."* (Mark 1:5) The masses went out to hear the prophetic message of John the Baptizer, and somewhere among the masses of the curious and the interested were two young men from Galilee who embraced John's message and became His disciples. And there, on the banks of the Jordan River, they heard John's testimony concerning a young Rabbi from Galilee named Jesus.

"The next day he saw Jesus coming toward him, and said, 'Behold, the Lamb of God, who takes away the sin of the world! This is he of whom I said, 'After me comes a man who ranks before me, because he was before me' . . . . And I have seen and have borne witness that this is the Son of God." (John 1:29-34)

Events unfolded quickly. The next day, when Jesus appeared on the scene again, John repeated his witness of Jesus as "the Lamb of God." Hearing the testimony of one whom they had come to respect and trust, these two young men came to a conclusion concerning the Rabbi from Nazareth. Andrew, one of the two, explained it to his brother, Simon Peter, this way, *"We have found the Messiah."* Based upon John's testimony, these two young Galileans decided to follow Jesus. When Jesus noticed their interest, He presented them a simple question: *"What are you seeking?"* Their answer suggests that they weren't really sure. Jesus' response, *"Come and see,"* was not so much a call to discipleship as an invitation to hang out with Him for a while and to get to know Him.[28] They accepted Jesus' invitation. Andrew told Peter, and the two of them told Philip, who then told Nathaniel. The next day, when Jesus decided to leave Judea and return to Galilee, He didn't travel alone. Five young Galilean seekers traveled with Him, unaware that, from this day forward, their lives would never be the same. [29]

As we observed earlier, in the Kingdom of God, all discipleship journeys have a beginning. For these five seekers their journeys into discipleship began with a short term mission adventure based upon the testimony of John and the invitation of Jesus. We really don't know what their faith consisted of at this point. Andrew thought they had found the promised Messiah. Nathaniel was momentarily overwhelmed by Jesus' supernatural knowledge of him. What they genuinely believed about Jesus or the Kingdom is unclear. But that would soon change.

A Borrowed Faith

All five men began this journey of discipleship with a "borrowed" faith in Jesus, a belief borrowed from someone else who believed. And a borrowed faith can only take us so far. It is one thing to believe that Jesus is the Messiah because John the Baptizer said so. It is quite another to discover it for oneself because of time spent with Jesus. A borrowed faith would be enough for five would-be disciples to begin their journey, but it would not be sufficient for very long. Before these men could enter into the discipleship which Jesus desired for them, their borrowed faith must become a faith of their own possession.

Every journey of discipleship into the Kingdom of God is a journey of faith which each of us must take for ourselves. Others can help, encouraging us with their words and their example. But we must believe for ourselves. No one can believe for us. Like children growing up in the shadow of a parents' faith, the day eventually comes when the faith of the parent is no longer sufficient to carry the child forward. The child must believe for himself (or herself). The faith of the parent must become the faith of the child's own possession, or the day will come when they will discard it along with other borrowed things in their life.

Jesus understood another truth we would do well to embrace. We should never be afraid to say to someone who is seeking, *"Come and see."* It is a simple invitation to walk with us, to spend time together, to build a relationship and to explore life in the Kingdom. All too often we don't encourage interested non-believers to "come and see" simply because we have nothing to show them but a "sinner's prayer" followed by a series of religious meetings. Our reluctance to invite others to "come and see" reflects a lack of depth and confidence in our own walk of faith and discipleship. While "come and see" may not have the ring of finality of a "sinner's prayer," it may be much more honest and genuine for everyone involved. It is how a borrowed faith, or even a curious faith, grows into a genuine faith. It is how many journeys of discipleship begin, including the journeys of five young Galileans. It is how many journeys of discipleship have come to a personal declaration of *Veni Vidi Crédidi* - *"I came, I saw, I believed."*[30]

Questions For Reflection

Spend some time reflecting on your own spiritual journey. How much of what you believe has been borrowed from other people (parents, teachers, pastors, friends). Why are you a disciple of Jesus (or not)? Is it because you personally believe, or is it because others said you should believe and you have simply "borrowed" their faith? How have you turned the "borrowed" aspects of your spiritual journey into a faith of your own possession?

Who are the people in your life you have invited to simply "come and see" and to explore a relationship with Jesus? How would you do that without taking them to a religious meeting?

Key Thought

Every journey of discipleship into the Kingdom of God is a personal journey of faith which each of us must take for ourselves.

And They Dreamt Of A Kingdom

10 - A Wedding In Cana

"This, the first of his signs, Jesus did at Cana in Galilee, and manifested his glory. And his disciples believed in him." (John 2:11)

Discipleship Reading: *John 2:1-12*
Contextual Reading: *John Chapter 2*

When: *Summer, A.D. 26*
Where: *Cana, in Galilee*

Background

"On the third day there was a wedding at Cana in Galilee, and the mother of Jesus was there. Jesus also was invited to the wedding with his disciples." (2:1-2)

From where John was baptizing by the Jordan River, east of Jerusalem,[31] Jesus and his five would-be disciples undertook the three-day walk to Galilee in northern Israel which they all called home. The village of Cana was located roughly nine miles north of Nazareth (in what is now known as Khirbet Qana). Jesus would visit Cana twice during His recorded ministry (John 2:1 and 4:46), and Nathaniel was from there (John 21:5).

The wedding to which Jesus and His five would-be disciples were invited appears to have been a wedding among family friends. Weddings in the ancient Near East of Jesus' day were an important social event, involving what can be best described as a "legal reciprocity." This meant that there were mutual expectations. The bridal party was expected to provide for the guests who attended, while the guests were expected to bring suitable gifts. It was not a matter to be taken lightly. Potentially, there could be legal penalties for the party which failed to live up to expectations.

In a Jewish wedding there was a betrothal period which was much more serious than today's "engagement." It represented a solemn pledge by both participants and required a divorce to break. Mary and Joseph were in the betrothal period when she conceived Jesus. Jewish weddings took place on a Wednesday if the bride was a virgin and on a Thursday if she was a widow. On the day of the wedding, the Bridegroom and his friends would make an evening procession to the bride's house to receive the Bride. The Bridegroom and the bridal party would then return to the Bridegroom's house where a celebration and a wedding banquet was held. This feast was often a prolonged affair and could last for several days.

The Crisis

"When the wine ran out, the mother of Jesus said to him, 'They have no wine.' And Jesus said to her, 'Woman, what does this have to do with me? My hour has not yet come.' His mother said to the servants, 'Do whatever he tells you.'" (2:3-5)

Somewhere early in the course of the celebration, the supply of wine for the banquet ran out. Over the years commentators have suggested that perhaps the young couple was too poor to supply a large number of guests with an unlimited supply of wine. Whatever the reason behind the shortage, it represented a crisis on several levels. It was socially embarrassing and could bring the entire celebration and the banquet to a halt. But there was more. It presented the possibility of a devastating legal liability because the guests could claim that the bridal party had breached their

obligation to adequately provide for the guests. In short, it was a crisis.

It was at this critical juncture that Mary, Jesus' mother, approached Jesus concerning the situation. As we observed earlier, the wedding party and family appear to have been family friends, which would help explain both Mary's concern over the situation and her attempt to solicit Jesus' involvement. On first glance, Jesus' response to His mother seems somewhat brusk and insensitive. But there is a deeper reality at work. Jesus had not yet begun His public ministry. That day still lay several weeks in the future. At this moment in time Jesus must be clear concerning the boundaries of His ministry, and that includes letting His mother know that she cannot dictate the terms or the timing of that ministry. For her part, Mary understood her son well enough to know that He would act, in spite of the fact that she never asked or suggested a specific course of action. How do we know this? Because the gospel writer tells us, *"His mother said to the servants, 'Whatever He says to you, do it.'"*

Jesus' Unexpected Response

"Now there were six stone water jars there for the Jewish rites of purification, each holding twenty or thirty gallons. Jesus said to the servants, 'Fill the jars with water.' And they filled them up to the brim. And he said to them, 'Now draw some out and take it to the master of the feast.' So they took it." (2:6-8)

My suspicion is that Jesus' response to the situation took those involved by surprise. It was "outside the box" and involved six stone water jars or cisterns. The Jews of Jesus' day practiced frequent ritual religious washings, including prior to meals. As we will discover later, this ritual practice would create a controversy later in Jesus' ministry. Water was stored in these stone jars or cisterns until it was needed for these ceremonial washings. Each jar would have held between 25 and 30 gallons of water (for a total of around 150 to 180 gallons). Jesus instructed the servants to fill the jars with water, and then to take some of the water to the head waiter ("master of the feast"). It was then that things got, well, interesting.

The Miracle And The Gift

"When the master of the feast tasted the water now become wine, and did not know where it came from (though the servants who had drawn the water knew), the master of the feast called the bridegroom and said to him, 'Everyone serves the good wine first, and when people have drunk freely, then the poor wine. But you have kept the good wine until now.'" (2:9-10)

Like watching a pebble dropped into calm water, we can only watch and imagine the chatter of conversation rippling through the wedding banquet as word of what had just happened began to spread. It wouldn't be long before the servants told others what they knew, what they had seen, and what Jesus had done. In a matter of a few minutes, or as long as it took the servants to fill the cisterns with water, Jesus had transformed 150-to-180 gallons of water into high-quality celebration wine, enough to sustain the wedding feast and celebration for several days if necessary. In addition, he had transformed a potential social embarrassment (if not an out-right disaster) into a blessing, while fulfilling the responsibility of a good wedding guest to give an appropriate gift. And He had done it all with five seekers and would-be disciples quietly observing and absorbing every unfolding moment.

And His Disciples Believed

"This, the first of his signs, Jesus did at Cana in Galilee, and manifested his glory. And his disciples believed in him." (2:11)

Someone once observed that God is always at work doing many things at once. You and I tend to be one dimensional in our perspective, one of the frustrating limitations of being human. Far too often, all we can see is what God is doing (or not doing) in our lives at this particular moment in time, generating questions such as, *"Why has God allowed this disaster to happen to me? Doesn't He care?"* God, on the other hand, sees not only the needs of our unique situation, but how our situation is tied to the situations of those around us. He understands how the ripple effects of His dealings in our lives will affect many people. Yes, God, in the person of Jesus, cared. But He cared about everyone involved and how all of their lives would be profoundly touched and transformed by how He responded to the needs of this young couple. Mary saw only the potential disaster that could unfold. Jesus saw an opportunity to transform disaster into blessing while generating ripple effects which would touch the entire wedding party. The headwaiter saw only good wine which had been (supposedly) held back. The servants saw the miracle which created the wine. And five young would-be disciples witnessed the Messiah of Israel unexpectedly manifesting His glory at a wedding celebration. And, as a result, they believed in Him.

> *Someone once observed that God is always at work doing many things at once.*

Welcome to the Kingdom of God, and to what it means to be a disciple of that Kingdom. Over the next three years these men would witness Jesus perform many miraculous signs (John 20:30-31).[32] But few, if any, would have the profound impact that this one undoubtedly had on them. This one caused them to believe in Jesus for themselves, transforming their borrowed faith into the gift of faith which they would own for themselves for the rest of their lives. Their faith would be challenged and would undoubtedly grow in the years ahead. But in a very real sense, their faith began on this day at a wedding in Cana as they watched the Messiah of Israel manifest His glory, transforming disaster into blessing and water into wine.

Our journey of discipleship into the Kingdom of God is not measured by how many miraculous signs we have seen or experienced. It is measured by that one sign which illumines our heart, ignites faith to believe and transforms our borrowed faith into a faith which we possess for our own. This was that sign and that moment for these five would-be disciples. They now believed in Jesus, not because of the testimony of John the Baptizer or anyone else. They now believed in Jesus because they had witnessed the manifestation of His glory for themselves. And that is the beginning of genuine discipleship in the Kingdom of God.

And They Dreamt Of A Kingdom

Questions For Reflection

Reflecting on this Lesson, what did you learn about Jesus ability to transform disaster into blessing?

What have been the significant moments in your own spiritual journey into the Kingdom which have ignited faith in your own life, challenging you to believe God for greater things?

This is the first of the seven miraculous signs of the Gospel of John. Each sign reveals the supernatural transforming power of the Kingdom of God and challenges the reader to believe. What did you discover from this event that would encourage you to believe that Jesus can transform the disasters of your life into blessing?

Key Thought

Our journey of discipleship into the Kingdom of God is not measured by how many miraculous signs we have seen or experienced, but by that one sign which illumines our heart, ignites faith to believe and transforms our borrowed faith into a faith of our own possession.

---

11 - Zeal For Thy House

"The Passover of the Jews was at hand, and Jesus went up to Jerusalem. In the temple he found those who were selling oxen and sheep and pigeons, and the money-changers sitting there. And making a whip of cords, he drove them all out of the temple, with the sheep and oxen. And he poured out the coins of the money-changers and overturned their tables. And he told those who sold the pigeons, 'Take these things away; do not make my Father's house a house of trade.' His disciples remembered that it was written, 'Zeal for your house will consume me.'" (John 2:13-17)

Discipleship Reading: John 2:13-25   **When:** Spring, A.D. 27
Contextual Reading: John 2   **Where:** Jerusalem

Jesus Begins His Public Ministry

The Spring of A.D. 27 had arrived, and with it the Feast of Passover. Jesus and His five would-be disciples had spent the previous Summer/Fall of A.D. 26 and the Winter of A.D. 27 in their home region of Galilee. Beyond that, we know very little about those silent months. But all that was about to change. With His five new believers and would-be disciples in tow, Jesus made the trip south to Jerusalem where they would celebrate the Feast of Passover together and where Jesus would launch His public ministry.

Jesus would begin His public ministry in the Temple in Jerusalem. Rebuilt by Zerrubabel in 516 B.C., after its destruction by the Babylonians 70 years earlier, and dramatically expanded by Herod the Great, the Jerusalem Temple represented the heart and soul of 1st Century Judaism. And at no time was this more true than during the feast of Passover. During Passover the population of Jerusalem swelled as Jewish worshipers from around the Mediterranean world descended upon Jerusalem and the Temple to celebrate Passover, offering the prescribed sacrifices and obtaining the required Passover lamb. For these purposes, foreign coins needed to be exchanged for the Temple coins required to make the necessary purchases.[33] And all of these services were conveniently provided for a fee by the religious/political sect known as the Sadducees, who oversaw and administered all Temple functions. In short, Passover had become a big business, all conducted within the courts surrounding the Temple itself. This was the stage onto which Jesus stepped to begin His public ministry.

A Prophetic Act

Jesus began His ministry with an act which would prove prophetic of His entire ministry. This "cleansing of the Temple" (as it has come to be known), represented a prophetic challenge to the religion-shaped spirituality of 1st Century Judaism which had reduced the Kingdom God to an ethnic/political heritage, an inflexible body of religious traditions, and a business of carefully constructed and controlled religious activities. For the sake of the Kingdom of God and world

Jesus knew that the old wineskin of 1st Century religious Judaism must be challenged to its breaking point so that a new wineskin could emerge and the new wine of the Kingdom could be poured out.

redemption, Jesus knew that the old wineskin of 1st Century religious Judaism must be challenged to its breaking point so that a new wineskin could emerge and the new wine of the Kingdom could be poured out. That challenge would begin on this day.

But Jesus' cleansing of the Temple was prophetic in another way. It foreshadowed the "zeal" with which He would undertake and pursue His mission. Watching all of this unfold, Jesus' would-be disciples remembered the words of Psalm 69:9, *"For zeal for your house has consumed me."* Jesus was consumed by Godly "zeal," and that needs to be explored. The root meaning of the Hebrew word rendered "zeal" in Psalm 69:9 (*qin'ah*) conveys the idea of "jealousy" (literally, "jealous zeal"). The same three-consonant root appears in one of the very Names of God, *"for you shall worship no other god, for the LORD, whose name is Jealous, is a jealous God"* (Exodus 34:14). "Jealousy" is not an attitude God manifests, but an attribute which defines and describes who God is in His essential nature. In His cleansing of the Temple Jesus manifested the "jealous zeal" of God in at least four ways.

First, *Jesus manifested the "jealous zeal" of God for His holiness.* In His "Jealousy," the God of Scripture is a consuming fire, *"For the LORD your God is a consuming fire, a jealous God."* (Deuteronomy 4:24) This speaks of His holiness, that quality of God's essential nature whereby He is totally and completely separated from sin and is singularly devoted to His own glory. Jesus understood that, in the midst of the materialism, the commercialism and the religious activity which now filled the courts of the Temple, 1st Century religious Judaism had lost the holiness and the glory of God. As God's Messiah, Jesus was "jealous" to see the holiness and the glory of God restored to His people.

Second, *Jesus manifested the "jealous zeal" of God for our pure and unadulterated worship.* The clear message of all Old Testament warnings against idolatry underscores a basic spiritual truth: God is jealous for our worship, *"for you shall worship no other god, for the LORD, whose name is Jealous, is a jealous God."* (Exodus 34:14) He will not share our worship with anyone or anything, including religious traditions. Jesus saw that the religion-shaped spirituality of 1st Century Judaism was preventing the true worship of God, worship which was being lost daily amidst all of the commercial/religious activity now filling the Temple.

Third, *Jesus manifested God's "jealous zeal" to save His people.* In His "jealous zeal" the Lord God will clothe Himself in armor and fight for His people and for their salvation just as the prophet Isaiah declared, *"He put on righteousness as a breastplate, and a helmet of salvation on his head; he put on garments of vengeance for clothing, and wrapped himself in zeal as a cloak."* (Isaiah 59:17; see also Isaiah 42:13) On this particular day, the fight for the salvation of God's people took the form of a young Rabbi from Nazareth cleansing the Temple of animals and money changers. Later in His ministry, this "jealous zeal" would impel Jesus to condemn the Pharisees as hypocrites whose religious traditions were preventing the salvation of God's people, *"But woe to you, scribes and Pharisees, hypocrites! For you shut the kingdom of heaven in people's faces. For you neither enter yourselves nor allow those who would enter to go in."* (Matthew 23:13) But on this day in the Temple, the "jealous zeal" of God's Messiah saw the religion-shaped spirituality of the Sadducees and the Temple coming between the people of God and their salvation. And He would have none of it.

Fourth, and finally, *Jesus manifested God's "jealous zeal" to see His Kingdom* *manifested.* This zeal for the Kingdom had been prophesied 700 years earlier by the Prophet Isaiah, *"Of the increase of his government and of peace there will be no end, on the throne of David and over his kingdom, to establish it and to uphold it with justice and with righteousness from this time forth and forevermore. The **zeal** of the LORD of hosts will do this."* (Isaiah 9:7) We need to be clear at this point. The "jealous zeal" of Jesus was not for a building, and certainly not for a Temple building which He knew would be reduced to a pile of rubble not many years later. As He drove the money changers and the animals from the Temple precinct, the "jealous zeal"

The "jealous zeal" of Jesus was not for a building, and certainly not for a Temple building which He knew would be reduced to a pile of rubble not many years later.

of Jesus expressed the consuming fire of God's holiness, God's unrelenting jealousy for our true worship, His undimmed jealousy to redeem His people, and His eternal desire to see His Kingdom manifested. And that divine "jealous zeal" is what five young believers and would-be disciples witnessed on this day in the Temple. It was an object lesson they would not forget.

The Consequences of Our Zeal

But such "jealous zeal" has its consequences, and we see them unfold in this passage. The first consequence is prophetically described in the last half of Psalm 69:9, *"and the reproaches of those who reproach you have fallen on me."* To walk in a divine zeal which challenges the existing religious traditions and religion-shaped spirituality of the day is to draw the reproach of those who have a vested interest in perpetuating those traditions. And Jesus now attracted the reproach of the Sadducees who ruled the Temple. They now demanded that Jesus perform a miraculous "sign" to validate His authority to do these things. Jesus would, in fact, perform many miraculous signs over the next three years of public ministry, all of which would be rejected by the Sadducees and the other religious leaders of Judaism. But on this day, Jesus offered them the greatest "sign" of all: His own resurrection. The Sadducees would eventually reject that sign, too. But His disciples would remember the prophecy after it happened, and would believe.

"Jealous zeal" has another consequence. It tends to excite the masses, and so it did here. *"Now when he was in Jerusalem at the Passover Feast, many believed in his name when they saw the signs that he was doing."* (John 2:23) There are always masses[34] of people ready to respond to what they see as revolutionary zeal, and they will respond with a "belief" that is both quick and shallow. But Jesus was no starry-eyed, idealistic revolutionary out to quickly gather a large following for a cause by overturning the existing order. He was the Son of God on a mission to redeem fallen humanity. He understood the fickleness and deceitfulness of the human heart far better than we do. And this was a lesson which five young would-be disciples needed to learn early in their own discipleship.

"There are two levels of believing in Jesus' name - that spoken of in John 1:12, which carries with it the authority to become God's children, and that spoken of here. The former level involves unreserved personal commitment, the practical acknowledgment of Jesus as Lord, but it will not be attained as long as 'we see the signs but see not him.'" [35]

75

And They Dreamt Of A Kingdom

What The Disciples Saw That Day

On this day in the Temple, five young would-be disciples of the Kingdom witnessed the zeal of Jesus, and discovered at least two important lessons(in addition to the "unspoken" lesson of, *"Wow, hanging out with Jesus is never boring!"*). They discovered the "jealous zeal" of Jesus for the things of God and the Kingdom of God. This is an important lesson for every disciple of the Kingdom. Our zeal will become our focus, and the things which excite our zeal will become the things which consume our focus.

This was no idle lesson for these men. In 1st Century Judaism there was a sect of Jews known as "the Zealots." According to the Jewish Historian, Flavius Josephus, the Zealots were Jews who *"agree in all other things with the Pharisaic notions; but they have an inviolable attachment to liberty, and say that God is to be their only Ruler and Lord."* (*Jewish Antiquities*, 18.1.6) Their radical commitment to Jewish independence from Rome would lead to the Great Jewish Revolt (A.D. 66–73) and the eventual destruction of Jerusalem and the Temple. Misplaced zeal can have disastrous consequences, both for us and for those we disciple. As disciples of the Kingdom, the focus of our zeal is to be God and His Kingdom.

But they discovered something else on this day in the Temple. They discovered that "jealous zeal" for the things of God and the Kingdom of God has consequences. If they were to truly be His disciples, and disciples of His Kingdom, they must be prepared to experience those consequences. They must be prepared for rejection and persecution by religious leaders whose religious structures are challenged by the spiritual truths of the Kingdom. And they must be prepared to resist the call of the "masses" who are easily led, but whose commitment is shallow and untrustworthy. It was a lot for five Galilean fishermen and would-be disciples to absorb. And their journey into discipleship and the Kingdom of God was just getting started.

Questions For Reflection

Reflecting on this Lesson, what did you learn about Jesus and His "zeal" that you did not know before?

Take a few moments and reflect on your own "zeal." If someone were to examine your life, what things would they conclude are the focus of your "zeal?" How many of those things are directly related to your life as a disciple of the Kingdom?

Read Revelation 3:14-22 (Jesus letter to the Church at Laodicea). What role did "zeal" (or a lack of zeal) play in Jesus' rebuke of the believers in that church? How do Jesus' words to those early Christians apply to your own spiritual journey. What did the risen Christ command them to do in response (see 3:19)?

Key Thought

As disciples of the Kingdom, the focus of our zeal is to be God and His Kingdom. Our zeal becomes our focus, and the things which excite our zeal become the things which consume our focus.

And They Dreamt Of A Kingdom

12 - The New Birth

"Now there was a man of the Pharisees named Nicodemus, a ruler of the Jews. This man came to Jesus by night and said to him, 'Rabbi, we know that you are a teacher come from God, for no one can do these signs that you do unless God is with him.' Jesus answered him, 'Truly, truly, I say to you, unless one is born again he cannot see the kingdom of God.'" (John 3:1-3)

Discipleship Reading: *John 3:1-21*　　　　**When:** *Spring, A.D. 27*
Contextual Reading: *John Chapter 3*　　　　**Where:** *Jerusalem*

A Man Named Nicodemus

A popular book on the topic of biblical discipleship declares that *"disciples are made, not born."* On reflection, it proves to be one of those subtle-yet-profound statements which is both true and false. And that deserves an explanation. The statement is true in the sense that genuine discipleship takes work, both on the part of the teacher as well as on the part of the student. Genuine discipleship doesn't take place in the absence of intentionality and commitment. In that sense, disciples ARE made. But in a strictly biblical sense the above statement is false. Disciples must, in fact, be born. Or more correctly speaking, they must be "born again." And this is one of the first lessons every would-be disciple of the Kingdom must grasp, including five would-be disciples from Galilee, and another would-be disciple by the name of Nicodemus.

Genuine discipleship doesn't take place in the absence of intentionality and commitment.

We need to get to know Nicodemus just a little. Nicodemus was a Pharisee. Within the Judaism of Jesus' day there were three primary religious "sects": the Pharisees, the Sadducees and the Essenes (although Josephus refers to the Zealots as a "fourth sect"). The Pharisees were devoted students of the Old Testament Law and were legendary for their strict observance of the Law and its related "traditions of the elders" (see Mark 7:3-5). They were non-Levites, which meant they were not part of the hereditary priesthood of the Temple in Jerusalem. They were the religious teachers of Israel and exercised strong influence over the Synagogues and the daily religious life of the average Jew. People held them in high regard. In his capacity as a Pharisee and teacher, Nicodemus was no spiritual novice. He was among the best and the brightest that 1st Century Judaism had to offer. The Sadducees represented a hereditary priestly aristocracy (being Levites) who accepted only the first five books of the O.T. (the Pentateuch) as authoritative. These were the political leaders of Israel. They were known for their willingness to make accommodations with Rome and dominated both the Temple in Jerusalem and the Jewish national ruling council of 71 elders called the Sanhedrin. As *"a ruler of the Jews"* Nicodemus was both a Pharisee and a member of the ruling Sanhedrin.

As a ruler and teacher of Israel, Nicodemus had taken notice of Jesus' initial ministry. Jesus appears to have made quite an impression, not only upon Nicodemus but upon others as well, *"Rabbi, **we** know that you are a teacher come from God, for no one can do these signs that you do unless God is with him."* Nicodemus never explains who the "we" are, but he obviously isn't speaking just for himself.

For His part, Jesus ignores the compliment that Nicodemus tries to pay Him

And They Dreamt Of A Kingdom

(declaring Him to be *"a teacher come from God"*). As the wise master-teacher that He is, Jesus cut through the religious pleasantries of Judaism in order to get to the heart of what was really troubling this "teacher of Israel." Nicodemus has unspoken questions about the core message of Jesus' ministry, the Kingdom of God. Jesus knows something that Nicodemus has yet to learn. Jesus understands that Nicodemus cannot reach the Kingdom of God by means of the religious Judaism

Jesus understands that Nicodemus cannot reach the Kingdom of God by means of the religious Judaism so familiar to Nicodemus.

so familiar to Nicodemus. So, as a wise master-teacher, Jesus begins the conversation by offering Nicodemus a piece of spiritual truth designed to shake his religious paradigm to its very core: *"Jesus answered him, 'Truly, truly, I say to you, unless one is born again he cannot see the kingdom of God.'"*

Like so many of Jesus' teachings, the truth He offers Nicodemus is designed both to reveal and to conceal, forcing the listener to wrestle with its meaning. Jesus employs a Greek word (*anothen*) which can be properly understood two different ways. On the one hand, it could be rendered as "again" or "anew" or "from the beginning," which is how Nicodemus understood it (*"You must be born all over again"*). On the other hand, it could be correctly understood as meaning "from above" or "from heaven," which is how Jesus meant it (*"You must experience a heavenly birth"*). Either way, Jesus' declaration forced Nicodemus to re-think everything he thought he knew about the Kingdom of God.[36]

For Nicodemus, this piece of spiritual truth struck like a thunderbolt from a clear sky, *"in one sentence (Jesus) sweeps away all that Nicodemus stood for, and demands that he be re-made by the power of God."* [37] It was nothing short of devastating for any good religiously observant Jew. But it was especially devastating for religious teachers and leaders like Nicodemus, who believed that the Kingdom of God was the unique possession and national birthright of Judaism. To be Jewish was to be in the Kingdom. But the truth Jesus shared so simply contained implications which now challenged Nicodemus with three stunning realities. If what Jesus was saying was true, then the Kingdom of God was NOT the unique possession of religious Judaism. Next, if what Jesus was saying was true,

With one simple declaration of truth Jesus swept away everything Nicodemus believed in and which had given his religious life meaning.

not even religiously observant Jews were "in the Kingdom." Finally, and most devastating of all, this simple truth meant that entrance to the Kingdom of God was impossible by any means known to religious Judaism, including Nicodemus.

With one simple declaration of truth Jesus swept away everything Nicodemus believed in and which had given his religious life meaning. The profound nature of the moment was not lost on this teacher and ruler of Israel. He who had undoubtedly taught others about the Kingdom of God and Israel's role in it now found himself standing outside of that very Kingdom and unable to gain entrance by any means he understood. As New Testament scholar, F.F. Bruce, observed concerning Nicodemus,

"He himself had probably taught others the conditions required for admittance to the kingdom of God, for enjoying the life of the age to come, but he had never heard these conditions expressed in the terms which Jesus now used. Keeping the commandments of God, doing his will day by day, were terms which he would have understood; but what was meant by this strange language about being 'born of the Spirit'?" [38]

Nicodemus' response to Jesus told the story, *"How can these things be?"* The full impact of Jesus' statement weighed heavily as Nicodemus wrestled with the reality that his own entrance into the Kingdom now looked as impossible as re-entering his own mother's womb and being born a second time.

At this point in the conversation you and I might think that Jesus would try to comfort Nicodemus, perhaps even offer to lead him in a "sinner's prayer" to be born again. That's what you and I would do. But that isn't what happened. Jesus, for His part, was unrelenting with this would-be disciple of the Kingdom. There was more truth that Nicodemus needed to hear and embrace, so Jesus pressed in. *"Do not marvel that I said to you, 'You must be born again. The wind blows where it wishes, and you hear its sound, but you do not know where it comes from or where it goes. So it is with everyone who is born of the Spirit."* Not only is entrance to the Kingdom of God impossible without a heavenly birth, but even that very birth is outside of Nicodemus' control. It is the Spirit of God - unpredictable and uncontrollable in His comings and goings - Who brings about this new birth, with the result that we are *"born of the Spirit."* Simply stated, the heavenly birth, which Nicodemus needs and by which the individual enters the Kingdom of God, is a sovereign act of God by His Holy Spirit, beyond the control of the religion-shaped spirituality of Judaism that Nicodemus knew so well.

As if all that has transpired thus far is not enough, Jesus is not yet finished shaking the religious worldview of this would-be disciple. Gently but firmly Jesus chides Nicodemus for his lack of knowledge concerning these spiritual truths. *"Jesus answered him, 'Are you the teacher of Israel and yet you do not understand these things? Truly, truly, I say to you, we speak of what we know, and bear witness to what we have seen, but you do not receive our testimony. If I have told you earthly things and you do not believe, how can you believe if I tell you heavenly things?'"* (John 3:10-12).

But Jesus had yet to reveal the greatest truth of this encounter. As a wise master-teacher, Jesus had waited for just the right moment. And that moment had now arrived.

"And as Moses lifted up the serpent in the wilderness, so must the Son of Man be lifted up, that whoever believes in him may have eternal life. For God so loved the world, that he gave his only Son, that whoever believes in him should not perish but have eternal life." (John 3:14-16)

All biblical teaching, from the Old Testament to the New, concerning salvation, the Kingdom of God and eternal life now found its summation in the words of Jesus to Nicodemus. It is difficult to adequately describe the significance of this moment in the life of this would-be disciple. He had begun His encounter with Jesus thinking that this itinerant rabbi might be *"a teacher come from God,"* someone who might be able to enlighten him concerning the Kingdom of God. Now, in the midst of their conversation, Nicodemus discovers that he is, in fact, in the Presence of the very Son of the Most High. Jesus now reveals to Nicodemus that salvation, entry into the Kingdom of God by means of the new birth and even eternal life itself are all one and the same. And to experience all of these things, Nicodemus needs only one thing: faith - "belief" - in God's only Son, Jesus. To believe in Jesus is to avoid perishing under God's condemnation of the world. To believe in Jesus is to experience a new and heavenly birth. To believe in Jesus is to enter the Kingdom of God and to have "eternal life."

Resolution Versus Reflection

John's record of this encounter between Jesus and Nicodemus concludes without any "resolution." In twenty-one short verses it is over, and we are left to wonder. Did Nicodemus "believe" in Jesus? Was he "born again"? Did he ever become a disciple of Jesus? We don't know and are never told. Nicodemus appears two more times in the Gospel of John, once speaking out on Jesus' behalf before the Sanhedrin (John 7:50-51) and again at the tomb of Jesus, bringing spices to prepare His body for burial (John 19:39). After that, Nicodemus disappears from

. . . throughout His ministry Jesus purposely intended that His teaching generate questions and force personal reflection.

the biblical record, leaving us to wonder and reflect. And that's the point. You and I want resolution. We want an answer to the question, *"Whatever happened to Nicodemus."* But throughout His ministry Jesus purposely intended that His teaching generate questions and force personal reflection. He expressed no desire to give formulaic answers, or to impart instant faith in four points and a prayer. In the Kingdom of God, discipleship means asking questions of ourselves and of Jesus. Genuine discipleship requires a personal willingness to allow His truth to reshape our spiritual lives around the answers we discover. We must wrestle, reflect . . . and believe.

Resolution asks, *"Did Nicodemus ever experience the new, heavenly birth?"*
Reflection asks, *"Have I ever experienced the new birth?"*

Resolution asks, *"Will we see Nicodemus in the Kingdom of God?"*
Reflection asks, *"Will I be in the Kingdom of God?"*

Resolution asks, *"Did Nicodemus ever believe in Jesus and experience eternal life?"*
Reflection asks, *"Have I believed in Jesus for eternal life?"*

You and I must stand along-side Nicodemus and learn the same paradigm-shaking reality that he had to learn. The Kingdom of God is not the birthright or possession of any religious group, nor can entrance to the Kingdom be gained by any religious observance which men can devise. There are no exceptions. Entrance to the Kingdom of God can only be gained - by one and by all - through belief in Jesus and the personal experience of a new and heavenly birth by the Spirit of God. This is the necessary starting point for all would-be disciples of the Kingdom. This is where genuine discipleship in the Kingdom of God begins. But it is not where it ends.

Questions For Reflection

Reflecting on this Lesson, what did you learn about being "born again" and the Kingdom of God that you did not know before?

Read: 1 Peter 1:3 and 1 Peter 1:22-25. Writing some thirty years after the events of John 3, which Peter probably witnessed first hand, Peter is addressing gatherings of disciples throughout Asia Minor (modern day Turkey). What description from John 3 does Peter use to describe these disciples? What does Peter's description tell us about the impact which the incident with Nicodemus must have had upon him and the early church?

Spend some time reflecting on your own born again experience. How did it change you? How would you describe your born again experience to someone who does not share your faith? If you find yourself struggling with this issue, then I would encourage you to stop now and read Lesson 43 - "The Good News of The Kingdom."

Key Thought

A Disciple of the Kingdom is someone who has responded to the good news of the Kingdom, has believed in Jesus and has experienced a new birth by the Spirit of God.

And They Dreamt Of A Kingdom

13 - He Must Increase

"John answered, 'A person cannot receive even one thing unless it is given him from heaven. You yourselves bear me witness, that I said, 'I am not the Christ, but I have been sent before him.' The one who has the bride is the bridegroom. The friend of the bridegroom, who stands and hears him, rejoices greatly at the bridegroom's voice. Therefore this joy of mine is now complete. He must increase, but I must decrease.'" (John 3:27-30)

Discipleship Reading: *John 3:22-36*   **When:** *Spring/Summer, A.D.27*
Contextual Reading: *John 3*   **Where:** *Aenon, near Salim*

John the Baptizer was unique in many ways. His birth, name, Naziritic lifestyle, calling and prophetic message had all been miraculously announced to John's father, Zechariah, by the angel Gabriel (Luke 1:11-20). He would be a forerunner, *"in the spirit and power of Elijah, to turn the hearts of the fathers to the children, and the disobedient to the wisdom of the just, to make ready for the Lord a people prepared."* (Luke 1:17)

When John emerged from the Judean wilderness and stepped onto the stage of public ministry *"in the fifteenth year of the reign of Tiberius Caesar,"* his appearance and his message rattled the leadership and galvanized the people of 1st Century Jerusalem. He looked like an Old Testament Nazirite and sounded like an Old Testament prophet. He was both. It seemed as though Elijah himself had returned, just as Malachi, the last Old Testament prophet, had foretold.[39] His message resonated among his hearers with prophetic authority as he proclaimed, *"Repent, for the kingdom of heaven is at hand."* (Matthew 3:2) The impact of John's ministry was profound. *"Then Jerusalem and all Judea and all the region about the Jordan were going out to him, and they were baptized by him in the river Jordan, confessing their sins."* (Matthew 3:5-6).

Masses of people from Jerusalem and the surrounding area turned out to hear John's message, to repent of their sins and to be baptized by him. But religious leaders also came, demanding to know who he considered himself to be, and by what authority he did these things. John and his message represented a threat to their carefully constructed religious structure. Such a threat could not go unchallenged:

"And this is the testimony of John, when the Jews sent priests and Levites from Jerusalem to ask him, 'Who are you?' He confessed, and did not deny, but confessed, 'I am not the Christ.' And they asked him, 'What then? Are you Elijah?' He said, 'I am not.' 'Are you the Prophet?' And he answered, 'No.' So they said to him, 'Who are you? We need to give an answer to those who sent us. What do you say about yourself?' He said, 'I am the voice of one crying out in the wilderness, 'Make straight the way of the Lord,' as the prophet Isaiah said.'" (John 1:19-23)

John's response was eloquent but simple. His calling and his message were his authority. John saw himself as nothing more than a forerunner and a messenger for someone greater than himself (John 1:26-34). In the cultural context of the 1st Century, a forerunner was an official whose sole responsibility consisted of preparing a city and a region for an upcoming royal visit. The King is coming, and everything must be made ready for his arrival, right down to straightening and paving the roads the royal procession would travel on. Once the King arrived, the task of the forerunner was complete. His was a calling to planned obsolescence.

And They Dreamt Of A Kingdom

And that is where John found himself on this day in the late Spring or early Summer of A.D. 27. at a place called *"Aenon, near Salim."* The actual location is debated. Aenon is the Greek version a Semitic term meaning "spring." In the water-poor Middle East, places owning a spring tend to be named after the water source. Writing at the end of the 3rd Century, A.D., Eusebius, places Aenon *"near Salem, where John used to baptize, as is written in the Gospel according to John, and the site is shown until this very day, at the eighth milestone from Scythopolis towards the south, near Salim and the Jordan."* It was probably near the upper source of the Wady Far'ah, an open valley extending from Mount Ebal to the Jordan, a location full of "springs" on the West side of the Jordan.

There, on this day, several of John's disciples approached him with questions about his ministry. The King had arrived in the person of Jesus, the Rabbi from Nazareth. John had personally baptized Him and publicly testified that Jesus was *"the Lamb of God Who takes away the sin of the world."* (John 1:29) Now, Jesus had begun His public ministry, and John's work as His forerunner was winding down. His public ministry had been as brief as it was profound, spanning less than a year, by most estimates. The crowds which had once followed John in impressive numbers now turned their attention to Jesus. *"All are going to him,"* was the description given by one of John's remaining disciples. It would get worse. In a matter of only a few weeks, John would be arrested and imprisoned by Herod Antipas. After languishing in prison for another year, John would be executed on a drunken whim by a King whom John had chastised for adultery (Matthew 14:1-12).

It is at this critical turning point in his life and ministry that we discover the depth of John's self-awareness concerning himself, his ministry and his calling. John is unconcerned about someone else's success at his expense, *"A person cannot receive even one thing unless it is given him from heaven."* He continues by reminding his remaining disciples that they themselves heard him openly declare that he is not the Christ. He is not "the bridegroom." Jesus is. He is the friend of "the bridegroom," who now *"rejoices greatly at the bridegroom's voice."* John then sums up His understanding of His own place and ministry in a simple but profound observation: *"He must increase, but I must decrease."* In God's sovereign plan for John's life and ministry, his destination was oblivion, not notoriety.

> *John would never see the great tree which would grow from the seed he sowed during his brief ministry.*

John the Baptizer would not live to see his five young followers become committed disciples of Jesus, or Apostles who would carry the good news of the Kingdom to the ends of the earth. John would never see the great tree which would grow from the seed he sowed during his brief ministry. But the more John's ministry decreased in importance in the eyes of the masses, who left him to follow Jesus, the more significant John's ministry became as the forerunner of all which followed.

Welcome to one of the most important lessons you and I will ever learn about our walk as disciples of the Kingdom. Our calling and our task is to decrease so that Jesus can increase. Jesus will grow in importance, while we will recede into the background of what God is doing. As disciples of the Kingdom, the organic growth of the Kingdom means that what God plants through us will grow to far exceed us. In the process, Jesus will be glorified and we will scarcely be remembered, if at all. The destination of every successful disciple of the Kingdom is oblivion, not notoriety. In the Kingdom of God, our significance is inversely proportional to our importance.

Questions For Reflection

Reflecting on this Lesson, what did you discover about discipleship in the Kingdom of God that you did not know before? How can you take what you discovered and apply it to your own discipleship?

Take some time to reflect on this statement: *"In the Kingdom of God, our significance is inversely proportional to our importance."* What do you see as the difference between being "important" and being "significant"? Which are you?

How will the seed of the Kingdom which God is sowing through you grow into something that will outlast and far exceed you?

Key Thought

As disciples of the Kingdom, the organic growth of the Kingdom means that what God plants through us will grow to far exceed us.

And They Dreamt Of A Kingdom

14 - With Jesus In Samaria

"Now when Jesus learned that the Pharisees had heard that Jesus was making and baptizing more disciples than John (although Jesus himself did not baptize, but only his disciples), he left Judea and departed again for Galilee. And he had to pass through Samaria." (John 4:1-4)

Discipleship Reading: John Chapter 4:1-42   **When:** Summer, A.D. 27
Contextual Reading: John Chapter 4   **Where:** Samaria, Sychar

Journeys Of Necessity

It is now the Summer of A.D. 27. We do not know exactly how much time Jesus spent in the Jerusalem area following the Passover. But it is now time for Jesus and His band of five would-be disciples to leave Judea and head north, back to Galilee and home.

Between Judea and Galilee lay the land of Samaria. The Jews of 1st Century Judaism regarded Samaritans as "half-breeds," products of interbreeding between a Jewish remnant and Assyrians, Babylonians and other non-Jewish locals over the centuries (starting with the Assyrian conquest of the northern Kingdom of Israel in 721 B.C.). They practiced their own form of Judaism and the rivalry between the Samaritans and the Jews was intense. A good Jew would not speak to a Samaritan and would go out of his way to avoid one. When it came to making the trip from Judea to Galilee, a strict religiously observant Jew would make the effort to avoid Samaria by first heading east and crossing the Jordan River into the Transjordan before heading north. Jesus, however, took the more direct route, passing directly through Samaria. This choice all but guaranteed contact with Samaritans along the way.

The Greek text of verse four says, *"It was necessary for Him to pass through Samaria."* The Greek verb <u>deo</u> *("to be necessary")* suggests something more than the demands of geography. It suggests a *"necessity born from duty."* For Jesus, this journey through Samaria wasn't about geography. It was about doing what was absolutely necessary for the message of the Kingdom, *"The expression points to a compelling divine necessity. Jesus had come as 'the light of the world.' It was imperative that this light shine to others than Jews."* [40]

Throughout His ministry, everything Jesus did He did with a greater purpose in mind. This was particularly true when it came to His relationship with those who would become His disciples. And it was true with respect to this "journey of necessity" through Samaria. Jesus understood that the good news of the Kingdom of God could not be limited by the religion-shaped spirituality of 1st Century Judaism which marginalized and excluded nearly all non-Jews, including Samaritans. If the good news of the Kingdom was to reach beyond Judaism to the

> *Throughout His ministry, everything Jesus did He did with a greater purpose in mind.*

greater Gentile world, then the religion-shaped spirituality of Judaism must be challenged and replaced with one fashioned around Jesus Himself. These five would-be disciples were about to receive a "baptism-by-fire" lesson in what it means to be disciples of the Kingdom.

A journey through Samaria all but guaranteed extended contact with

And They Dreamt Of A Kingdom

Samaritans. That contact began in earnest when six weary travelers stopped to rest by the village well in the small town of Sychar near Shechem. While His five disciples went in search of food, Jesus engaged in a conversation with a Samaritan woman who had come to draw water from the well. Most Sunday School versions of this encounter focus on Jesus' interaction with the woman. While Jesus' interaction with this woman is certainly important, we want to focus our attention on how Jesus used this journey and this incident to teach His disciples the meaning of discipleship. So, I'm going to skip over the traditional Sunday School version of this story and examine the discipleship lessons at work here. And from a discipleship perspective, Jesus undertook this "journey of necessity" for at least three critical reasons.

First, Jesus took this "journey of necessity" through Samaria in order to challenge the religion-shaped spirituality of exclusion which so dominated 1st Century Judaism. Through His encounter with this Samaritan woman Jesus challenged this "spirituality of exclusion" on at least three levels.

Jesus challenged this "spirituality of exclusion" on a personal level. He did this by having a private conversation with a woman who was not a family member. From within the perspective of 1st Century Judaism, this act alone was profound. As Morris observes, *"Whatever might be thought of the propriety of asking for a drink, no Rabbi would have carried on a conversation with a woman."* [41] We know this from the reaction of Jesus' disciples when they returned from their scavenger hunt, *"And at this point His disciples came, and they marveled that He had been speaking with a woman; yet no one said, 'What do You seek?' or, 'Why do You speak with her?'"* (John 4:27) These five would-be disciples understood what was occurring on a personal level, and they were

> For His part, Jesus knew that one day God would pour out His Spirit on both male and female disciples without distinction.

stunned by it. The Greek word translated "marveled" (*thaumadzo*) communicates the idea of "incredulous surprise."Jesus was breaking well-entrenched Jewish social convention in order to have a private conversation with a woman concerning the Kingdom of God. For His part, Jesus knew that one day God would pour out His Spirit on both male and female disciples without distinction, just as the prophet Joel had promised (Joel 2:28-29; and Acts 2:18). And one day the Apostle Paul would declare to believers in Galatia that *". . . there is no male and female, for you are all one in Christ Jesus"* (Galatians 3:28). But Jesus also knew that those days would never come without this day and this lesson. And so a religion-shaped spirituality, which regarded women as inferior, must be confronted and challenged to its breaking point.

Jesus also challenged this "spirituality of exclusion" on an ethnic level. Not only was she a woman, but she was a Samaritan (see our earlier discussion above on the relationship between Jews and Samaritans). John makes it clear that this was a problem by inserting a parenthetical comment into his record of the conversation, *"The Samaritan woman therefore said to Him, 'How is it that You, being a Jew, ask me for a drink since I am a Samaritan woman?' [For Jews have no dealings with Samaritans]."* (John 4:9) Writing some 50 or more years after the event, the Apostle John understood how profound this moment had been, both for Jesus and for His Church. Reaching out to those who had been marginalized by a religion-shaped spirituality was at the heart of Jesus' mission. The day would come when Jesus would send His Church out to be His witnesses and to proclaim the good news of the Kingdom *"in Jerusalem and in all Judea and Samaria, and to the end of the earth."* (Acts 1:8) But Jesus knew that day would never come if this day did not come first, if His disciples were not set free from a religion-shaped spirituality which marginalized and excluded all non-Jews from the Kingdom of God. And that process of being set free would begin here in Samaria.

Finally, Jesus challenged this "spirituality of exclusion" on a moral level. In addition to being a woman and a Samaritan, she was a woman of questionable morals, *"He said to her, 'Go, call your husband, and come here.' The woman answered and said, 'I have no husband.' Jesus said to her, 'You have well said, 'I have no husband'; for you have had five husbands, and the one whom you now have is not your husband; this you have said truly'."* (John 4:16-18) We need to be clear at this point. Jesus neither ignored nor condoned this woman's immorality. He pointed out her adulterous lifestyle, making it clear that He was well aware of what sort of person she was. But beyond that, Jesus did not condemn her. Jesus' mission (both then and now) was not to condemn, but to redeem (John 3:17). And such a mission of redemption demanded that He spend considerable time with "sinners," even to the point of being criticized by those religious leaders who clung so tightly to their religion-shaped spirituality (Matthew 9:10-11). Jesus' response to such criticisms was always the same, *"I have not come to call the righteous but sinners to repentance."* (Luke 5:32) Jesus was unwilling to allow the good news of the Kingdom to be restricted or denied by a religion-shaped spirituality of exclusion, regardless of the reason.

> *Jesus was unwilling to allow the good news of the Kingdom to be restricted or denied by a religion-shaped spirituality of exclusion, regardless of the reason.*

Second, Jesus took this "journey of necessity" through Samaria in order to challenge His disciples with a vision for the spiritual need and harvest beyond the limited confines of Judaism. After the disciples returned from their search for food, the woman returned to town with a mission of her own, *"So the woman left her water jar and went away into town and said to the people, 'Come, see a man who told me all that I ever did. Can this be the Christ?'"* (John 4:28-29) What she left behind was one Messiah and five somewhat confused would-be disciples who were trying to process what had just happened. But Jesus was not yet done with this lesson. When the disciples urged him to eat, Jesus' response caught them off guard, *"I have food to eat that you do not know about."* What was He talking about? Had someone else brought Him something to eat? Like a skilled master teacher Jesus pressed home the *"ah ha!"* moment of this lesson, *"Jesus said to them, 'My food is to do the will of him who sent me and to accomplish his work.'"*

> *To be a disciple of the Kingdom is to have a hunger - even a zeal - for doing the will of God that supercedes our hunger or desire for anything else. Even food.*

I have often wished that I could have been there to see the expression on the faces of these would-be disciples as Jesus turned lunch into a master lesson on what it means to be a disciple of the Kingdom. To be a disciple of the Kingdom is to have a hunger - even a zeal - for doing the will of God that supercedes our hunger or desire for anything else. Even food. Men (and women) hunger for many things in this present evil age: food, sex, money, power, love, fame, adulation and more. As disciples of the Kingdom, our hunger for doing the will of God must supercede all of these. And in the process, it must supercede any religion-shaped spirituality that would prevent us from doing His will.

But the lesson was not quite over (actually, it would last for another two days, but more about that in a moment). Jesus continued,

"Do you not say, 'There are yet four months, then comes the harvest'? Look, I tell you, lift up your eyes, and see that the fields are white for harvest. Already the one who reaps is receiving wages and gathering fruit for eternal life, so that sower and reaper may rejoice together. For here the saying holds true, 'One sows and another reaps.' I sent you to reap that for which you did not labor. Others have labored, and you have entered into their labor.'" (John 4:35-38)

In the agricultural life of ancient Israel there was a period of four months between the end of sowing and the beginning of the harvest. Jesus and His would-be disciples sat by Jacob's well and watched people from the village, dressed in their white robes, coming out to greet them at the urging of the woman. Jesus saw a harvest which was immediately ready and required no waiting before bringing in.[42] And that was the problem. It was simple, but profound. When these five would-be disciples looked around themselves at the surrounding territory and its people, they saw only "Samaritans"; people they had been taught all of their lives to despise as "half-breeds." When Jesus looked around at the same territory and its people, He saw people who needed the good news of the Kingdom; a spiritual harvest in need of laborers.

For the sake of world redemption and the Kingdom of God, Jesus knew that these five would-be disciples, like all disciples who would eventually follow Him, must sacrifice their limited vision of the world and embrace His much larger vision of the world. They must come to see the lost and the marginalized through Jesus' eyes. And for this they must allow their religion-shaped spirituality to be broken, transformed and re-molded into one shaped around Jesus Himself. That was why Jesus had taken them on this "journey of necessity"

Some discipleship lessons simply cannot be taught. They must be caught.

through Samaria. Some discipleship lessons simply cannot be taught. They must be caught. It was time for these five would-be disciples to "catch" the vision.

As if to punctuate the lesson with an exclamation point, something happened next which I am certain these young would-be disciples never saw coming. People from the local village asked Jesus to stay with them for an additional couple of days, *"Many Samaritans from that town believed in him because of the woman's testimony, 'He told me all that I ever did.' So when the Samaritans came to him, they asked him to stay with them, and he stayed there two days."* (John 4:39-40) Imagine the moment. Five would-be disciples, who probably didn't want to be in Samaria in the first place, and were probably looking for the fastest way out, were now invited to stay longer! I suspect that Jesus didn't put the issue up for a vote. They stayed an additional two days.

We are left to imagine what took place during those two days. Perhaps the disciples heard the woman recount her conversation with Jesus (more than once, would be my guess, which would explain how we came to have a record of the conversation in the Gospel of John). One thing is certain. It was a fruitful two days for the Kingdom of God, *"And many more believed because of his word. They said to the woman, 'It is no longer because of what you said that we believe, for we have heard for ourselves, and we know that this is indeed the Savior of the world.'"* (John 4:41-42). The faith which many Samaritans had "borrowed" from the testimony of a woman they all knew well now became a genuine faith of their own possession, *"for we have heard for ourselves, and we know that this is indeed the Savior of the world."* Faith grows where the Kingdom is sown. Even in Samaria. And that leads to our third and final discipleship point in this episode.

> *Faith grows where the Kingdom is sown. Even in Samaria.*

Third, Jesus took this "journey of necessity" through Samaria in order to demonstrate and practice a spiritual principle He would later teach. If you sow the seed of the Kingdom, you will reap the fruit of the Kingdom. We can only wonder how much of the ministry of the Apostles in Samaria in Acts 8 involved reaping what had been sown by Jesus in John 4. But one thing quickly becomes clear. By the time the disciples heard Jesus teach the parable of the sower (which we will examine later), they had watched Him practice the principle of "Kingdom seed sowing" in His own ministry for at least a full year. Some lessons must be demonstrated before they can be taught and understood. Sowing seed wasn't simply a "lesson" for Jesus, it was His way of life. It's how He "did ministry." And it is how He expects us to do ministry, too.

> *If you sow the seed of the Kingdom, you will reap the fruit of the Kingdom.*

Discipleship Lessons In Contagious Truth

In the Kingdom of God, many truths cannot be taught. They must be caught. These truths must be personally experienced before they can be fully understood. In the Kingdom of God, spiritual growth and maturity are the result of truth experienced over time. Far too much of what passes for discipleship in our western Evangelical, Bible-believing churches today comes from books and classrooms, rather than from "journeys of necessity" taken with Jesus through the Samarias of our world. Truths have been taught, but they have not been caught. And all too often it is in books and classrooms where religion-shaped spiritualities get formed and people get inoculated against "the Jesus virus." It is in Samaria where disciples of the Kingdom get permanently infected with the values of the Kingdom and where their religion-shaped spirituality gets challenged to its breaking point, and transformed into one which looks, thinks and sounds like Jesus.

> *In the Kingdom of God, spiritual growth and maturity are the result of truth experienced over time.*

This reality confronts us with another reality. In the Kingdom of God, profound ministry most often occurs in places where you and I don't really want to go. For this reason alone, as disciples of the Kingdom, our "journeys of necessity" with Jesus often take us to places we would really rather avoid. But, as author A.W. Tozer once observed, when it comes to fruitful ministry, "miracles follow the plow."[43] If we want to

And They Dreamt Of A Kingdom

see Jesus perform miracles of transformation in our life and ministry then we must be willing to follow Him to people and to places we would rather avoid. We must allow the Lord of the harvest to yoke us to Himself as He plows fallow ground that no one else has been willing to plow. It is the example of Jesus, the history of His Church and the calling of every would-be disciple of the Kingdom. Including you and me.

Questions For Reflection

Reflecting on this Lesson, what did you discover about discipleship in the Kingdom of God that you did not know before?

How has God used a personal journey of necessity into the "Samaria" of your world to emphasize how certain truths must be caught before they can be taught? How has He used such truth and such journeys to challenge your own religion-shaped spirituality?

Key Thought

In the Kingdom of God, many truths cannot be taught; they must be caught during personal journeys of necessity into places where you and I would rather not go.

15 - Repent

"Now after John was arrested, Jesus came into Galilee, proclaiming the gospel of God and saying, 'The time is fulfilled, and the kingdom of God is at hand; repent and believe in the gospel.'" (Mark 1:14-15)

Discipleship Reading: *Mark 1: 14-15*   `**When:** *Summer, A.D. 27*
Contextual Readings: *Mark 1; Matthew 4; Luke 4*   **Where:** *Galilee*

The Summer of A.D. 27 was now underway as Jesus and His five would-be disciples left Samaria and headed home to Galilee. Somewhere along the way Jesus probably received the news that John the Baptizer, His forerunner (and 2nd cousin), had been arrested by Herod (Matthew 4:12; Mark 1:14). John would languish in Herod's prison for another year before being executed. Arriving in Galilee, Jesus soon discovered that the fame of His exploits in the Temple during the feast of Passover had preceded Him home, spread by Galileans who had also attended the feast. In Jerusalem Jesus had announced the beginning of His public ministry with practical and prophetic actions which upset the religious status quo.

Now, as He returned to Galilee to begin what would be some 18 months of extended ministry, Jesus proclaimed a message that would prove equally challenging to the religious status quo, *"The time is fulfilled, and the kingdom of God is at hand; repent and believe in the gospel."* The biblical writers never tell us exactly how and where Jesus proclaimed His message of repentance. Their reason behind this omission was simple. They wanted to communicate an overall impression that repentance was the message which characterized Jesus' entire ministry, not a unique message preached on limited occasions. And that reality invites us to look closer.

> *. . . repentance was the message which characterized Jesus' entire ministry, not a unique message preached on limited occasions.*

Background

When John the Baptizer, the forerunner of Jesus, came preaching a message of repentance, every Jew who heard that message understood what it meant. Repentance - or the lack of repentance - had played a critical role in the national life of God's people. In the New Testament, the concept of repentance is expressed by the Greek word *metanoia*. Like its Old Testament counterparts,[44] the word denotes a profound change of mind or heart which produces a profound change of direction or behavior. Repentance had been at the heart of the messages delivered by the Old Testament prophets. Through them, the God of Israel had continually confronted the sins of His wayward people, warning them of dire consequences and calling them to repent of their sin and rebellion, and to return to Him.

But Israel chose not to listen and not to repent . . . with disastrous consequences. In 721 B.C. the Northern Kingdom of Israel perished at the hands of the Assyrians as punishment for their sins and their refusal to repent. 135 years later, in 586 B.C., the Southern Kingdom of Judah fell to the Babylonians and was taken into Captivity for their refusal to respond to the prophetic call of God to repent, delivered through the prophet Jeremiah. The people of God in the Old Testament understood what repentance meant. They had simply chosen to NOT obey, and had paid a high price for their disobedience. Such was the background when John exploded on the religious landscape, proclaiming a public call for God's people to repent.

But John was only the forerunner, sent to prepare the way for someone greater. Jesus was the fulfillment. And when Jesus followed John, proclaiming, *"The time is fulfilled, and the kingdom of God is at hand; repent and believe in the gospel,"* every religiously-observant Jew who had heard John's message now understood what it meant (Mark 1:15; see also Matthew 4:17). God was once again calling His people to repent. But this time it was different. This time it was personal. The long-promised Kingdom of God had arrived in the person of the Messiah-King, Who now called upon all men - beginning with God's covenant people - to repent of their sin and rebellion and to embrace His Kingly rule and authority. And that was profound.

Jesus On Repentance

It is critical that you and I understand the role repentance played throughout Jesus' ministry. Indeed, Jesus Himself defined His own ministry in terms of repentance, telling the Pharisees (and His disciples), *"I have not come to call the righteous but sinners to repentance"* (Luke 5:32). In the Kingdom of God, the journey of biblical faith and discipleship begins with a call to personal repentance from our sin and rebellion. Whatever blessings of abundant life might one day flow to those who believe (John 10:10), they are all contingent upon the willingness of

In The Kingdom of God, the journey of biblical faith and discipleship begins with a call to personal repentance from our sin and rebellion.

the individual to repent of their sins and to embrace God's Messiah-King. We must not take the message of repentance lightly. Jesus didn't. The call to repentance lay at the heart of His proclamation of the Kingdom. Failure to repent represented nothing less than a rejection of the Kingdom, leading Jesus to denounce those cities where He had performed many miracles but where the people failed to repent,

"Then he began to denounce the cities where most of his mighty works had been done, because they did not repent. 'Woe to you, Chorazin! Woe to you, Bethsaida! For if the mighty works done in you had been done in Tyre and Sidon, they would have repented long ago in sackcloth and ashes.'" (Matthew 11:20-21)

Here the biblical writer "lifts the veil" to reveal Jesus' purpose behind the miraculous signs and wonders He performed. His purpose was NOT to amaze and entertain the masses. Rather, His purpose was to confront people with the supernatural reality of the Kingdom of God, calling them to repent of their sin and rebellion, and to believe. Conversely, Jesus did not hesitate to confront His listeners with the consequences which lay ahead for all those who refused to repent,

"There were some present at that very time who told him about the Galileans whose blood Pilate had mingled with their sacrifices. And he answered them, 'Do you think that these Galileans were worse sinners than all the other Galileans, because they suffered in this way? No, I tell you; but unless you repent, you will all likewise perish. Or those eighteen on whom the tower in Siloam fell and killed them: do you think that they were worse offenders than all the others who lived in Jerusalem? No, I tell you; but unless you repent, you will all likewise perish.'" (Luke 13:1-5)

With stunning bluntness Jesus contrasts the tragedies of this world (horrible accidents and political massacres) with the greater tragedy of eternal consequences for all who fail to repent and embrace the good news of the Kingdom. The Greek word for "perish" in this passage (*apollumi*) is a primary New Testament word for describing eternal punishment. Jesus wants His listeners to understand that their refusal to repent of their sins and to embrace the message of the Kingdom has eternal consequences.

Jesus placed repentance from sin at the heart of His proclamation of the Kingdom, and He taught His disciples to do the same. We see this first in Mark's account of the commissioning and sending out of the disciples, *"So they went out and proclaimed that people should repent"* (Mark 6:12). But we see it more intentionally expressed by Jesus in one of His last post-resurrection conversations with His disciples. There He specifically emphasizes the role repentance is to play in their future proclamation of the gospel:

> *Jesus placed repentance from sin at the heart of His proclamation of the Kingdom, and He taught His disciples to do the same.*

"Then he opened their minds to understand the Scriptures, and said to them, 'Thus it is written, that the Christ should suffer and on the third day rise from the dead, and that repentance and forgiveness of sins should be proclaimed in his name to all nations, beginning from Jerusalem. You are witnesses of these things.'" (Luke 24:46-48)

Repentance In The Early Church

"The times of ignorance God overlooked, but now he commands all people everywhere to repent" (Acts 17:30)

Speaking to Greek intellectuals on Mars Hill in Athens, the Apostle Paul summarizes the early Church's understanding concerning the importance of repentance in the message of the Kingdom. God now commands ALL people EVERYWHERE to repent. Where did the early Church get its understanding and message concerning repentance? From Jesus and His disciples. Simply stated, the early Church continued what Jesus began.

Like the above passage from Paul's sermon on Mars Hill, the best way to see how the early Church continued what Jesus began is to look at their post-resurrection, post-ascension sermons as they took the message of the Kingdom to the world. The first three chapters of the book of Acts record two public sermons by the Apostle Peter (one of the five early disciples of Jesus). A brief look at these two sermons quickly reveals how the early church continued Jesus' message of repentance.

Peter's sermon on the day of Pentecost - *"'Let all the house of Israel therefore know for certain that God has made him both Lord and Christ, this Jesus whom you crucified.' Now when they heard this they were cut to the heart, and said to Peter and the rest of the apostles, 'Brothers, what shall we do?' And Peter said to them, '**Repent** and be baptized every one of you in the name of Jesus Christ for the forgiveness of your sins, and you will receive the gift of the Holy Spirit.'"* (Acts 2:36-38)

Peter's sermon to the crowd at the Gate Beautiful - *"And now, brothers, I know that you acted in ignorance, as did also your rulers. But what God foretold by the mouth of all the prophets, that his Christ would suffer, he thus fulfilled. **Repent**

therefore, and turn again, that your sins may be blotted out, that times of refreshing may come from the presence of the Lord, and that he may send the Christ appointed for you, Jesus, whom heaven must receive until the time for restoring all the things about which God spoke by the mouth of his holy prophets long ago." (Acts 3:17-21)

These two sermons make it clear that Jesus' call to repentance shaped both the message of the disciples and the message of the early Church. The Church of the New Testament placed the call to repentance at the heart of their proclamation of the Kingdom, just as Jesus had taught them to do. This was also true of the Apostle Paul, who encountered the resurrected Christ on the road to Damascus in Acts 9. Years later, in his defense of the gospel and his ministry before King Agrippa, Paul declared, *"Therefore, O King Agrippa, I was not disobedient to the heavenly vision, but declared first to those in Damascus, then in Jerusalem and throughout all the region of Judea, and also to the Gentiles, that they should **repent** and turn to God, performing deeds in keeping with their repentance."* (Acts 26:19-20)

> *Jesus' call to repentance shaped both the message of the disciples and the message of the early Church.*

The Lost Heart Of Discipleship And The Church

It should be clear by now that the call to repentance and faith was at the heart of Jesus' proclamation of the Kingdom of God. Jesus' disciples heard that message, embraced that message, proclaimed that message and incorporated that message into the DNA of the early church. If we take seriously the message of Jesus concerning repentance and the Kingdom of God, we are led to an unavoidable conclusion. Repentance is a foundational truth for both the Kingdom and the Church. Remove it, and the very nature of the Kingdom and existence of the Church are threatened.

One of the realities concerning Jesus' message of repentance which should unsettle us is that He directed it at the believers of His day - Jews - the very people whom the Old Testament Scriptures named as God's chosen people. If God's chosen people in Jesus' day were in need of repentance, what makes us think that His people today - the Church - are somehow exempt from that same message? Unfortunately, in the contemporary Evangelical churches of the early 21st Century, one seldom hears messages on the need for personal or corporate repentance from sin. And yet, after the command to "listen," the command to "repent" is the most frequent instruction given by the risen Christ to the seven churches of Asia in Revelation Chapters 2 - 3. Biblically speaking, repentance is a matter close to God's heart, beginning in the Church. Repentance in the life of a disciple, or in the corporate life of the Church, is about living out an authentic life of genuine humility and obedience before a watching world, which has yet to see a genuine role model of repentance, forgiveness and obedience. Perhaps

> *. . . after the command to "listen," the command to "repent" is the most frequent instruction given by the risen Christ to the seven Churches of Asia in Revelation Chapters 2 - 3.*

the world will consider the claims of Christ more seriously when it sees disciples of the Kingdom, and the churches they plant, living out a life of repentance, humility, forgiveness and holiness more fully.

Questions For Reflections

Reflecting on this Lesson, what did you learn about the role repentance played in Jesus' message of the Kingdom that you did not know before?

When was the last time you challenged someone with their need to repent of their sin and rebellion in order to enter the Kingdom of God?

Read 1 John 1:5-10. Reflecting on this passage (written to Christians), what role should repentance play in the life of the believer?

Read Revelation Chapters 2-3 (Letters of the Risen Christ to the seven Churches of Asia). What are some of the things the Risen Christ challenges the believers in those Churches to repent over? How do those issues relate to you as a disciple of the Kingdom today?

Key Thought

As disciples of the Kingdom, the call to repentance from sin is at the heart of the good news of the Kingdom we have been commanded to embrace and proclaim.

And They Dreamt Of A Kingdom

16 - Healing A Nobleman's Son

"And at Capernaum there was an official whose son was ill. When this man heard that Jesus had come from Judea to Galilee, he went to him and asked him to come down and heal his son, for he was at the point of death."

Discipleship Reading: John 4:43-54
Contextual Reading: John 4

When: Summer, A.D. 27
Where: Galilee, Cana

The Return To Galilee

After the excursus on repentance in the previous Lesson, it's time to rejoin Jesus and his five would-be disciples on their journey back to Galilee. Having extended their stay in Samaria for an extra couple of days, Jesus and the five headed north. At Sychar the road through Samaria diverged in two directions. One road led toward Nazareth, and beyond Nazareth to Cana. The other road led to Capernaum. Jesus chose the road to Nazareth, and eventually to Cana, where He performed His first miraculous sign the previous year. The ripple effects of that first sign now combine with Jesus new-found fame over recent events to attract a "royal official" in search of a miracle to heal his son who is at the point of death.

We're never told much about this "royal official." [45] He was probably an official in the court of King Herod, who ruled Galilee for the Romans. But we can learn several things about him from his pursuit of Jesus. To begin with, his pursuit reveals his desperation, the desperation of a father whose son is dying. That desperation motivates him to make the sixteen mile trip from Capernaum, where he lives with his son, to Cana where Jesus is. His request, that Jesus *"come down and heal his son,"* reveals a belief that Jesus is limited by time and space and must be physically present in order to help or heal. The stage is now set for Jesus to act, for His disciples to learn and grow, and for this unnamed official to believe.

Miracles, Signs and Wonders

"So Jesus said to him, 'Unless you see signs and wonders you will not believe.'" (John 4:48)

At this point in the story, Jesus takes an unexpected detour into the issue of miraculous signs and wonders. And we have no choice but to follow Him. The phenomenon of miraculous "signs" is an important theme in John's gospel. New Testament scholars generally agree that the writer of John's Gospel organizes his Gospel around seven miraculous "signs."[46] The New Testament uses three primary words to describe the miraculous. A "miracle" (Greek: *dunamis*) describes a work of God's power and emphasizes the powerful nature of the event (John never uses this word to refer to Jesus' miracles). A "wonder" (Greek: *terata*) is a "miracle" which emphasizes the awe-inspiring appearance of the event. This is the

> *Miracles are Signs which cause men to Wonder and which point to God at work, and are intended to result in Repentance and Faith.*

And They Dreamt Of A Kingdom

"wow" factor. Finally, a "sign" (Greek: *semeion*) is a "miracle" which points to something greater than itself and emphasizes the divine purpose of the event, namely, to communicate spiritual truth. We could sum it up this way: *Miracles* are *Signs* which cause men to *Wonder* and which point to God at work, and are intended to result in *Repentance* and *Faith.*

The leaders of 1st Century Judaism frequently asked Jesus for "a sign" to validate His ministry(Matthew 12:38-41; 16:1). And the truth is that Jesus gave them many signs (seven in the Gospel of John alone), all of which they rejected. But Jesus always gave signs on His terms, not theirs; in His timing, not theirs. As we saw in the previous Lesson on repentance, Jesus made it clear that the purpose behind the miraculous signs and wonders He performed was to bring about repentance and faith, *"Woe to you, Chorazin! Woe to you, Bethsaida! For if the miracles had occurred in Tyre and Sidon which occurred in you, they would have repented long ago in sackcloth and ashes"* (Matthew 11:21). In spite of the fact that Jesus performed many signs, people still didn't believe. According to John, their unbelief was rooted in two basic causes: 1) they were spiritually blind, and 2) they loved the glory that comes from man more than the glory that comes from God.

> *Jesus made it clear that the purpose behind the miraculous signs and wonders He performed was to bring about repentance and faith.*

"Though he had done so many signs before them, they still did not believe in him, so that the word spoken by the prophet Isaiah might be fulfilled: 'Lord, who has believed what he heard from us, and to whom has the arm of the Lord been revealed?' Therefore they could not believe. For again Isaiah said, 'He has blinded their eyes and hardened their heart, lest they see with their eyes, and understand with their heart, and turn, and I would heal them.' Isaiah said these things because he saw his glory and spoke of him. Nevertheless, many even of the authorities believed in him, but for fear of the Pharisees they did not confess it, so that they would not be put out of the synagogue; for they loved the glory that comes from man more than the glory that comes from God." (John 12:37-43)

In John 20:30-31the author of the Gospel explains his purpose for writing his account of Jesus life the way he did: *"Many other signs therefore Jesus also performed in the presence of the disciples, which are not written in this book; but these have been written that you may believe that Jesus is the Christ, the Son of God; and that believing you may have life in His name."* According to John, Jesus did *"many other signs,"* but John chose to record these seven particular signs to achieve a specific purpose, namely, *"that you may believe."*

Simply put, the author used the miraculous signs of Jesus to challenge his readers with Jesus' power to transform life's apparent disasters into blessings, and in the process to prick their consciences and call people to repentance and faith. In the Gospel of John, the Kingdom of God is a place where the power of God transforms people, causing them to be born again, and transforming their lives from curse to blessing, from blindness to sight, from darkness to light and from unbelief to faith. Reflecting on Jesus' use of "signs and wonders" and people's responses to them, Leon Morris observes,

"The word [wonder] denotes a portent, something beyond explanation, at

which men can but marvel. Jesus is affirming that people such as the man who had come to Him were lacking in that deep trustful attachment which is of the essence of faith. They looked for the spectacular, and were linked to Him only by a love for the sensational." [47]

As disciples of the Kingdom of God, it is important for us to understand that miraculous signs do not represent a "miracle cure" for people's spiritual blindness or spiritual pride. If people, both then and now, can look at Jesus and not see God, then they can just as easily witness a miraculous sign which He performs and not believe or grasp its meaning. Miraculous signs are intended to challenge our unbelief and confront us with the spiritual reality of an unseen Kingdom. But at best they represent a starting point, a beginning for our faith, not an end.

> *Miraculous signs are intended to challenge our unbelief and confront us with the spiritual reality of an unseen Kingdom.*

A Desperate Faith

"The official said to him, 'Sir, come down before my child dies.' Jesus said to him, 'Go; your son will live.' The man believed the word that Jesus spoke to him and went on his way." (4:49-50)

We cannot avoid the sense of genuine desperation felt by this father. His "little boy" was dying. The Greek word used by the father is not the formal word for son, but the affectionate diminutive for child, which is best translated "little boy."[48] This is a father who is desperate to save his "little boy." And if he was to be saved from death there was no time to waste. Capernaum was at least half-a-day's journey away. They must leave now. Or so he thought.

Jesus' response probably took this desperate father by surprise. He probably expected Jesus to accompany him back to Capernaum. After all, didn't the healer need to be present in order to perform a miracle of healing? But Jesus saw things differently. Jesus saw a "little boy" in need of healing. But He also saw a father who needed to grow in his faith and in his understanding of Who Jesus really was and how God can work - even with a word and even at a distance. And Jesus also saw five would-be disciples who were watching all of this unfold (the word "sponges" pops to mind here). They needed to grow in their faith and understanding of Jesus as the Messiah and King. They needed to see His power to transform sickness into health with nothing more than a spoken word, just as they had witnessed Him transform water into wine with a word.

And so Jesus sent the man away with a simple promise which required him to believe the impossible: his son would live, without a personal visit from Jesus. *"Jesus' words impose a stiff test,"* writes Leon Morris. *"He gives the man no sign. The officer has nothing but Jesus' bare word. But this is enough. He rises to the implied demand for faith. He believes what Jesus says and goes his way."* [49] The man believed Jesus' word, and headed home to Capernaum.

A Growing Faith

"As he was going down, his servants met him and told him that his son was recovering. So he asked them the hour when he began to get better, and they said to him, 'Yesterday at the seventh hour the fever left him.' The father knew that was the hour when Jesus had said to him, 'Your son will live.' And he himself believed, and all

his household. This was now the second sign that Jesus did when he had come from Judea to Galilee." (John 4:51-54)

In the Kingdom of God, faith is never static. As disciples of the Kingdom we are always being challenged to grow in our faith, in our understanding of God's dealings and in our willingness to believe God for greater things. Like five young would-be

In the Kingdom of God, faith is never static.

disciples who began their journeys with Jesus with a borrowed faith, this royal official originally came to Jesus with a borrowed faith which relied upon the testimony of those who had heard or seen Jesus do great - even miraculous - things. Such a borrowed faith, when mixed with desperation, may be sufficient to motivate an individual to seek Jesus out, but it sees Him as little more than a magician, a purveyor of wonders. *In the Kingdom of God, a "magical faith" is no more sufficient than a borrowed one.* It must give way to something more. It must be transformed into a faith which genuinely "believes." For this royal official and desperate father, that moment of transformation first occurs in verse 50, *"The man believed the word that Jesus spoke to him and went on his way."* The Kingdom of God is first manifested in this man's life in a genuine faith which takes Jesus at His word, believes that word, and obeys.

At some point along the journey back to Capernaum the man is met by his servants who bring the news that the man's son is no longer dying but is recovering. Simply put, his "little boy" has been healed. When the man asks for more details, particularly the timing of the change in his son's condition, he realizes that it happened at the very moment when Jesus spoke the word back in Cana. It was a transformational moment, as we read, *"And he himself believed, and all his household."*

But if the man "believed" back in verse 50 when Jesus first told him that his son would live, what does it mean to say that *"he himself believed, and all his household?"* It means that in the Kingdom of God, faith is never static. It grows and matures with every test or trial as we trust God for His promised answer, and as we see His answers unfold before us. The faith of this unnamed official has grown, from a borrowed faith in Jesus as a miracle worker, to a genuine belief in Jesus' spoken word, and finally to a greater and more mature faith with ripple effects of its own sufficient to touch his entire household. [50]

Questions For Reflection

This is the second of the seven miraculous signs of the Gospel of John. Each sign reveals the supernatural transforming power of Jesus and the Kingdom of God, and challenges the reader to believe. How did Jesus transform disaster into blessing in this situation? What did you discover from this "sign" that would strengthen your faith and encourage you to believe that Jesus can transform the disasters of your life into blessing?

As disciples of the Kingdom our faith can never remain static. How is this true in your life? What is God doing in your life today to challenge your faith to grow beyond anything you have experienced up until now?

Key Thought

As disciples of the Kingdom our faith can never remain static, as we are continually challenged to grow in our faith, in our understanding of God's dealings and in our willingness to believe God for greater things.

And They Dreamt Of A Kingdom

17 - Follow Me

"While walking by the Sea of Galilee, he saw two brothers, Simon (who is called Peter) and Andrew his brother, casting a net into the sea, for they were fishermen. And he said to them, 'Follow me, and I will make you fishers of men.' Immediately they left their nets and followed him. And going on from there he saw two other brothers, James the son of Zebedee and John his brother, in the boat with Zebedee their father, mending their nets, and he called them. Immediately they left the boat and their father and followed him." (Matthew 4:18-22)

Discipleship Reading: *Matthew 4:13-22*   **When**: *Spring, A.D. 28*
Contextual Reading: *Matthew 4; Mark 1; Luke 4*   **Where:** *Galilee*

A Time To Reflect

At this point in the New Testament narrative it is obvious that something has happened. Significant time has passed and we need to fill in the gaps.[51] The last time we saw Jesus and His five would-be disciples together was in Cana. The biblical record is not as detailed as we would like for it to be at this point. Apparently, when Jesus left Cana He traveled alone to Nazareth where He preached in the synagogue and was soundly rejected by His home-town crowd (Luke 4:16-31). The lack of any reference to the disciples during that episode suggests the possibility that they did not travel with Him to Nazareth. We can't say with certainty. What we do know is that when our current passage opens, the situation has changed. Several months have passed. It is now the early Spring of A.D. 28. Jesus has moved and relocated His home base from Nazareth to Capernaum. And five would-be disciples have returned to their previous lives and businesses.[52]

Up until this point I have referred to these five men as "would-be disciples." Now, it is time to explain why. By this point in time these five men had spent roughly eighteen months in Jesus' company. Their journey into faith and discipleship had begun with a proclamation and a faith, borrowed from John the Baptizer, that Jesus was, in fact, the promised Messiah. Based on the testimony of John, and the invitation of Jesus to "come and see," they undertook a journey to discover if what they initially believed about Jesus was true.

Much happened in the year that followed. Witnessing Jesus' first miracle at the wedding in Cana, they believed in Jesus for themselves, transforming their borrowed faith into the gift of faith which they would own for themselves for the rest of their lives. Watching Jesus cleanse the Temple in Jerusalem, they discovered the "jealous zeal" of Jesus for the things of God and the Kingdom of God. But they also discovered that such "jealous zeal" has consequences. If they were to truly be Jesus' disciples, and disciples of His Kingdom, then they must be prepared to experience those consequences. Were they prepared to be rejected and persecuted by religious leaders whose religious structures and religion-shaped spiritualities would be challenged by the spiritual truths of the Kingdom which Jesus taught?

Listening to Jesus interact with Nicodemus, these five would-be disciples had their own religion-shaped spirituality challenged to the breaking point as they discovered that entrance to the Kingdom of God was impossible by any means taught to them by 1st Century Judaism. Like Nicodemus, they, too, must be born again by the Spirit of God if they hoped to see the Kingdom of God. Accompanying Jesus through Samaria, these men watched in amazement as Jesus violated religious and social

And They Dreamt Of A Kingdom

conventions of exclusion in order to share the message of the Kingdom. In the process, they found themselves confronted with the reality that, in the Kingdom of God, the most profound ministry often occurs in places and among people you and I would rather avoid. Were they prepared to go to those places and spend time with those people? Listening to Jesus proclaim a message of repentance, these would-be disciples may have remembered how John the Baptizer had preached a similar message. John had been arrested and eventually murdered by Herod for denouncing Herod's marriage to Herodias (the wife of his brother, Philip. See Mark 6:17ff). Would a similar fate befall Jesus . . . and those who followed Him?

It was a lot for five Galilean fishermen to wrap their heads around. They weren't in Synagogue anymore. They had spent nearly a year in the "school of Jesus," and they needed time to process what they had seen and heard. Their religion-shaped spirituality, inherited from 1st Century Judaism, had been challenged to its breaking point. They needed time to decide if this was what they wanted for themselves. The seed of the Kingdom which Jesus had sown into their lives needed time to fully sprout, take root and grow. Jesus, for His part, gave them the time they needed. And, so, the Winter of A.D. 28 found at least four would-be disciples at home in Capernaum by the Sea of Galilee, fishing for a living, mending their nets - just as they had done before they met Jesus - and reflecting on what the next step might be for them and their discipleship with Jesus. They didn't have long to wait.

The seed of the Kingdom which Jesus had sown into their lives needed time to fully sprout, take root and grow.

Follow Me

Every season of reflection and waiting eventually comes to an end. Jesus was back, once again challenging them to take on His yoke. Once again challenging them to "follow me." And that challenge - that "invitation" - deserves a closer look.

In contexts involving discipleship, the phrase "follow me" occurs no less than 11 times in the Gospels (not counting duplicates in parallel passages). You and I are most familiar with those times when Jesus called His eventual disciples to "follow me." But Jesus called other people to "follow me." And for one reason or another they failed to do so, suggesting that there is such a thing as a "failed" call to discipleship. As disciples of the Kingdom it should be as important to us to understand why they failed as it is for us to understand why others succeeded.

"As they were going along the road, someone said to him, 'I will follow you wherever you go.' And Jesus said to him, 'Foxes have holes, and birds of the air have nests, but the Son of Man has nowhere to lay his head.' To another he said, 'Follow me.' But he said, 'Lord, let me first go and bury my father.' And Jesus said to him, 'Leave the dead to bury their own dead. But as for you, go and proclaim the kingdom of God.' Yet another said, 'I will follow you, Lord, but let me first say farewell to those at my home.' Jesus said to him, 'No one who puts his hand to the plow and looks back is fit for the kingdom of God.'" (Luke 9:57-62; Matthew 8:19-22)

Reading this passage and standing alongside the Gospel writer, you and I find ourselves witnesses to three failed calls to discipleship. Two volunteered to be disciples, while one was invited to "follow me." But to our knowledge, all three individuals failed to follow Jesus when given the opportunity. While you and I could try to "parse" the reasons for each failed call, the underlying reason was given earlier by Jesus Himself to His own disciples, *"And he said to all, 'If anyone would come after me, let him deny himself and take up his cross daily and follow me. For whoever would save his life will lose it, but whoever loses his life for my sake will save it"* (Luke 9:23-24). Failed calls to discipleship share a common underlying cause: an unwillingness to take up one's cross and to lay down one's life.

Failed calls to discipleship share a common underlying cause: an unwillingness to take up one's cross and to lay down one's life.

Every call to discipleship is different and unique in its own way, because each person is different and unique. For one person the call to discipleship in the Kingdom comes with a call to "homelessness," to forego the comfort of home and the stability enjoyed by others. For someone else, the call to discipleship means having to forego normal and expected family ties and responsibilities. But regardless of each unique situation (and each person's situation is unique), in the Kingdom of God, genuine discipleship means placing one's hand on the plow of what God is doing and where He is leading, and not looking back. It is difficult - even impossible - to pick up and carry the cross of Jesus while holding on to anything else.

A Time To Choose

On this day by the Sea of Galilee, four would-be disciples were confronted with a choice to answer Jesus' call to "follow me." Up to this point their discipleship had been a curious (but challenging) learning experience in the "school of Jesus." It had begun with an invitation to "come and see" (remember John 1:39). By now these would-be disciples had seen enough to know that, should they answer Jesus' call, their lives would never be the same. They had begun their journey based upon the testimony of others. They must now decide for themselves based upon what they have seen and experienced for themselves. Jesus had given them a few weeks to

Whatever might happen from this point on, their discipleship must be a conscious and intentional choice.

reflect on what they had experienced. Now, the invitation had grown into a semi-command: "Follow me." Whatever might happen from this point on, their discipleship must be a conscious and intentional choice.

There comes a point in time when each of us must choose what we are going to do with Jesus and His call to "follow me." In the Kingdom of God, faith is never static, and neither is our discipleship. Jesus is constantly challenging us to grow and to believe Him for greater things than we have believed Him for in the past. Our discipleship is but a reflection of what we believe.

Jesus' call to discipleship in the Kingdom of God is not something to be taken lightly. The call of the gospel is more than a call to repent from our sin and rebellion and to believe in Jesus as savior and King. It certainly **IS** all of that, but it is so much more. Jesus' call to discipleship embodies a call to embrace a Jesus-shaped spirituality and to live that spirituality out in a life of radical faith and radical obedience as disciples of a radical Kingdom. Our discipleship embodies our lifelong response to Jesus simple command: *"Follow Me."*

And They Dreamt Of A Kingdom

Questions for Reflection

Reflecting on this Lesson, what did you learn about discipleship and Jesus' call to "Follow Me" that you did not know before?

Take some time to reflect on this statement: *"In the Kingdom of God, faith is never static, and neither is our discipleship."* What is God doing today in your own life to challenge your faith and your discipleship to grow?

Take some time to reflect upon your own call to "Follow me." How does your discipleship today reflect your lifelong commitment to a life of radical faith and radical obedience as a disciple of a radical Kingdom?

Key Thought

As disciples of the Kingdom, our daily discipleship embodies our lifelong response to Jesus simple command to "Follow Me."

---

18 - With Jesus On The Sabbath

"And he went down to Capernaum, a city of Galilee. And he was teaching them on the Sabbath, and they were astonished at his teaching, for his word possessed authority." (Luke 4:31-32)

Discipleship Reading: Luke 4:31-44   **When:** Spring, A.D. 28
Contextual Reading: Luke 4; Matthew 8; Mark 1   **Where:** Galilee

It is now the early Spring of A.D. 28, and Jesus' public ministry in Galilee is underway. Having been rejected in His home town of Nazareth, Jesus has moved His base of operation to the busy fishing town of Capernaum on the Sea of Galilee. After a hiatus of several months He has reconnected with the men who traveled with Him on His previous tour of ministry, plus a new one by the name of James, brother of John. Now it is the Sabbath. And with at least four (and probably six) disciples in tow, Jesus headed for the Synagogue in Capernaum to continue the training of His young disciples and to challenge the religion-shaped spirituality of 1st Century Judaism.

At the risk of boring you with technical details, the language of verse 31 deserves our attention. The writer tells us that Jesus *"was teaching them on the Sabbath."* The verbal construction in the Greek is something known as a "periphrastic." It uses the imperfect tense of the verb "to be" with the present participle of "to teach." Simply translated, Jesus *"was continually teaching"* on the Sabbath.[53] Simply put, Jesus is starting a practice which will be a regular part of His ministry: teaching in the Synagogues on the Sabbath. The writer will use the same construction at the end of this passage when he says that Jesus, *"was preaching in the synagogues of Judea"* (Luke 4:44). Teaching in the Synagogues of Galilee on the Sabbath (and later in the Synagogues of Judea) now becomes Jesus' "*modus operandi*" for the next 18 months. He will use His Sabbath teaching to directly challenge the religion-shaped spirituality of 1st Century Judaism, and especially that of the Pharisees who oversaw the daily spiritual life of Israel through the Synagogues.

There is something else about the language of verse 31 which deserves our attention, namely, the response of Jesus' listeners. *"They were astonished at his teaching."* The Greek word "astonished" (*ekplesso*) describes a reaction best summed up as "shock and awe," a feeling which combines fear, consternation and astonishment. On this Sabbath day Jesus' hearers in the Synagogue in Capernaum were "blown away" by what they saw and heard. Welcome to the school of Jesus.

What Word Is This?(Luke 4:33-37)

"And in the synagogue there was a man who had the spirit of an unclean demon, and he cried out with a loud voice, 'Ha! What have you to do with us, Jesus of Nazareth? Have you come to destroy us? I know who you are--the Holy One of God.' But Jesus rebuked him, saying, 'Be silent and come out of him!' And when the demon had thrown him down in their midst, he came out of him, having done him no harm. And they were all amazed and said to one another, 'What is this word? For with authority and power he commands the unclean spirits, and they come out!' And reports about him went out into every place in the surrounding region." (Luke 4:33-37)

I think it would be safe to say that neither Jesus' disciples nor the people attending Synagogue that Sabbath had ever seen or heard anything like this before. What they witnessed that Sabbath Day in the Synagogue was a full-on confrontation between Jesus and a "demonic unclean spirit," a classic conflict between the Kingdom of God and the domain of darkness. As was frequently the case, the very presence of Jesus in the Synagogue was enough to cause this demon to manifest and to cry out.

I've always found it interesting that the demonic realm recognized who Jesus really was (i.e., *"the Holy One of God"*), while the religious leadership of 1st Century Judaism was clueless. It's a dark day in the Church (or Synagogue) when the demons are more discerning than the religious leaders.[54] Over the years commentators have wondered why Jesus told demons to be silent when He cast them out. On reflection, I don't think Jesus had anything to say to the demonic, other than to pronounce their judgment. And that's a short conversation. But there's more. I believe Jesus knew that one day soon the religious leaders would use His acts of deliverance to accuse Him of working in concert with Beelzebub (we'll deal with this later). Extended conversations with these unclean spirits would only reinforce those arguments.[55]

> *It's a dark day in the Church (or Synagogue) when the demons are more discerning than the religious leaders.*

This was a teachable moment in the training of Jesus' disciples, as well as in the spiritual experience of everyone else present in the Synagogue that day. The biblical writer never tells us what Jesus "taught" in the Synagogue that Sabbath day. Why? Probably because the whole experience was the lesson. And it was a lesson which Jesus delivered with "authority" and modeled with "power."

The Greek word for authority (*exousias*) has to do with position and permission. It refers to the right of an individual to exercise power (*dunamis*) due to the position which they hold.[56] Because of His "position" as the second member of the God-head, and as the Son of God acting in perfect submission to the will of His Father, Jesus possessed "authority" - both the right and the permission - to exercise spiritual power. We need to explore this just a little further.

All spiritual power derives from God. In the words of author John White, *"There is one source of supernatural power, and one only. Satan's power is power once entrusted to him by God. God was the Creator of the power just as, being the Creator of all that is, he created Satan himself. The power was meant for use in God's service. It is what we might call embezzled power."* [57]

When Lucifer fell, along with a third of the angelic host, he and his fallen angelic rebels retained that spiritual power which God had bestowed upon them in His service. Lucifer and his followers have "spiritual power," but it is embezzled power. They exercise it apart from God's authority (*exousia*), using it to oppose God's purposes. Such spiritual power, embezzled, misused and devoid of God's authority, now becomes magical power. Is there magic in this world? Yes, there is. But it is demonic.

> *Is there "magic" in this world? Yes, there is. But it is demonic.*

"Whenever anyone, Christian or non-Christian, angel or demon, uses (God's) power for selfish ends . . . the power can be called magical power. It is the same power with the same characteristics put to a wrong use and subtly changed by that

use. Christians who use God's power in this way have begun to act like sorcerers. Angels so using it fall." [58]

Contrary to Lucifer (or Beelzebul), Jesus modeled the exercise of spiritual power in perfect submission to God's authority. The day would soon come when Jesus would commission His disciples with both authority and power to heal the sick, raise the dead, cleanse lepers and cast out demons (See Matthew 10:8). But Jesus knew that such a day could not come without the lesson of this day. Today they must watch and learn as Jesus walked in obedience, taught with authority, and cast out demons with power.

What Everyone Saw That Sabbath

Everyone in the Synagogue that Sabbath Day, including the disciples, discovered the difference between the teaching of Jesus, and the teaching of the religious leaders of 1st Century Judaism. Jesus taught with authority and power. The religious leaders of Jesus' day possessed a pseudo-authority given to them by their religious position, but they lacked the supernatural, spiritual power which Jesus now demonstrated. Religious authority without spiritual power creates a religion-shaped spirituality with the power to imprison those who are free, but no power to free those who are prisoners (Matthew 23:13ff).

> *Religious authority without spiritual power creates a religion-shaped spirituality with the power to imprison those who are free, but no power to free those who are prisoners.*

Before leaving this passage, we should note two things. *First,* all of these events took place on the Sabbath in the local Synagogue, which would become Jesus' regular practice. *Second,* the Pharisees are noticeably absent. These two realities would become increasingly important as Jesus' ministry grew. The Pharisees were the religious sect of 1st Century Judaism which exercised the greatest influence over the religious life of the average Jew. And they did this through their teaching in the Synagogues. On this Sabbath Day in the Synagogue at Capernaum, Jesus had invaded occupied religious territory and had exposed it as spiritually powerless and bankrupt. He had also healed (i.e., deliverance) on the Sabbath. Such direct challenges to their authority, their traditions and their powerlessness would not go unnoticed or unchallenged by the Pharisees. But not on this day. On this day, an amazed (Greek: *thumbos* - literally *"dumbfounded"*) crowd of people left the Synagogue to spread the word concerning Jesus and the events of this exceptional day, *"And reports about him went out into every place in the surrounding region."*

A Sabbath Like No Other (Luke 4:38-41)

"And he arose and left the synagogue and entered Simon's house. Now Simon's mother-in-law was ill with a high fever, and they appealed to him on her behalf. And he stood over her and rebuked the fever, and it left her, and immediately she rose and began to serve them. Now when the sun was setting, all those who had any who were sick with various diseases brought them to him, and he laid his hands on every one of them and healed them. And demons also came out of many, crying, 'You are the Son of God!' But he rebuked them and would not allow them to speak, because they knew that he was the Christ." (Luke 4:38-41)

Jesus spent the remainder of this Sabbath Day doing what He had done earlier in the Synagogue, including giving His watching disciples a "ministry clinic" on what it means to exercise God's authority and power. In the home of Simon Peter, Jesus rebuked a fever the same way He had rebuked the demon earlier, healing Simon's mother-in-law (another Sabbath healing). The Sabbath Day had been instituted by God as a day of rest. On this Sabbath Day, Jesus, the incarnate Son of God and author of the Sabbath Law, spent the Sabbath "resting" and "granting rest" by healing and delivering everyone who came to Him with an affliction.

Time To Move On (Luke 4:42-43)

"And when it was day, he departed and went into a desolate place. And the people sought him and came to him, and would have kept him from leaving them, but he said to them, 'I must preach the good news of the kingdom of God to the other towns as well; for I was sent for this purpose.'" (Luke 4:42-43)

As a life-long student of Greek, I have come to appreciate some of the "nuances" of the language, nuances which frequently get dulled or lost in our English translations. Consider the following more literal rendering of verse 41, *"And the multitude eagerly searched for Him and came to Him and restrained Him, lest He leave them."* This was a grass-roots movement among the masses, who tried to prevent Jesus from leaving. For His part, Jesus could easily have remained and taken advantage of this opportunity to manipulate the masses to whatever end He chose. He chose to leave. The question is, *"Why?"* Why not work with the masses to teach, to heal, to deliver and to build a large grassroots following for the Kingdom of God?

The answer is found by understanding the heart of Jesus' ministry. As we discovered in the episode of cleansing the Temple, Jesus never trusted the masses. He was willing to teach them, to heal them and to minister to them, but He never sought to turn them into a large following. They were not His target audience. He wasn't looking for legions of followers. He was laboring to train disciples.

But there was more. With Jesus, there always is. And it is summed up in this passage, *"It is necessary for me to proclaim the good news of the Kingdom of God to the other cities, also."* The Greek verb translated *"it is necessary"* is the same one we saw earlier in John 4 when Jesus traveled with His disciples through Samaria. Jesus understood His own "journey of necessity." Jesus never allowed His own self-awareness concerning His mission and purpose to be clouded, distracted or determined by the demands of "the multitudes." Jesus lived His life to please an audience of One, to train an audience of twelve, to proclaim the Kingdom of God to an audience of whoever would listen, and to give His life for the sin of the world. His self-awareness would be challenged on a regular basis by the ever-growing crowds which now followed Him, *"and great crowds gathered to hear him and to be healed of their infirmities."* (Luke 5:15) But He would not allow Himself to be distracted by the demands of the multitudes. Later, as His earthly ministry drew to a close, Jesus could declare that He had accomplished His two purposes. He had glorified His Father (John 17:4) and He had kept those whom the Father had given to Him (John 17:6). Can we declare the same at the end of our ministries?

> *Jesus never allowed His own self-awareness concerning His mission and purpose to be clouded, distracted or determined by the demands of "the multitudes."*

Questions for Reflection

Reflecting on this Lesson, what did you discover about the ministry of Jesus that you did not know before?

What is the difference between religious authority and spiritual power?

Describe the difference between Jesus' attitude toward the masses who followed Him, and the attitudes of religious leaders today toward the masses who follow them, their ministry or their church?

How strong is your own sense of self-awareness concerning what God has called you to do? What are the things which distract you from your calling?

Key Thought

As disciples of the Kingdom, we live our lives to please an audience of One, to train an audience of disciples, and to proclaim the Kingdom of God to an audience of whoever will listen.

And They Dreamt Of A Kingdom

19 - Do Not Be Afraid

"But when Simon Peter saw it, he fell down at Jesus' knees, saying, 'Depart from me, for I am a sinful man, O Lord.' For he and all who were with him were astonished at the catch of fish that they had taken, and so also were James and John, sons of Zebedee, who were partners with Simon. And Jesus said to Simon, 'Do not be afraid; from now on you will be catching men.' And when they had brought their boats to land, they left everything and followed him." (Luke 5:8-11)

Discipleship Reading: *Luke 5:1-11*
Contextual Reading: *Luke 5*

When: *Spring, A.D. 28*
Where: *Galilee, Capernaum*

Fishing, Again

The biblical narrative doesn't tell us how much time has passed since that amazing Sabbath Day spent with Jesus. But obviously some time has passed. When the narrative picks up in this passage, the crowds are following Jesus and four disciples have returned to fishing. For His part, Jesus taught the crowd, which was *"pressing in on him to hear the word of God."* But the real focus of His attention was four men who had returned to fishing. There was something these men needed to learn this day. Their return to fishing would provide the opportunity for the lesson.[59]

The reality of their return to fishing is highlighted by Simon Peter's response to Jesus' instructions to let down their nets for a catch, *"Master, we toiled all night and took nothing! But at your word I will let down the nets."* The disciples had returned to fishing because it was what they knew. In times of personal uncertainty we all tend to return to what we know best. Now, they had labored all night at what they knew best. They were professional fishermen, not Jesus. What did He know about fishing or finding a catch? But they had been around Jesus long enough to know better than to ignore His instructions, as "unprofessional" as they might be.

> The disciples had returned to fishing because it was what they knew. In times of personal uncertainty we all tend to return to what we know best.

Then it happened. The sea which had yielded nothing all night in spite of their best professional efforts, now yielded up a harvest of fish so great that their nets began to break. Soon they had filled two boats with fish to the point that the boats were in danger of sinking beneath the load.

It's one thing to witness Jesus' supernatural ministry at arms length, as the disciples had done in the Synagogue on that amazing Sabbath Day. It is quite another thing when the supernatural reality of the Kingdom of God manifests in your fishing boat. The disciples might not understand demonic deliverance, but they understood fishing. This was their "reality." They understood that a night of laboring and fishing with two boats could never produce such an abundant catch. Not in a single night. Not in a week of nights. Peter and his co-laborers were now confronted with the supernatural power of the Kingdom of God on terms they fully understood. They were sitting in a 26-foot fishing sloop, filled to the gunwales with fish to the point of sinking, all because Jesus had spoken the word to lower their nets.

And They Dreamt Of A Kingdom

Two Responses, Two Fears

The Gospel writer records two basic responses by the disciples to this episode. One response was "astonishment." Simon Peter and the rest of the disciples were "astonished" at what happened. This is the same Greek word (*thumbos*) used in Luke 4:36 to describe the response of people in the Synagogue who were "dumbfounded" at the supernatural ministry of Jesus. Now it was the disciples' turn to be "dumbfounded" at the miraculous sign manifesting in their own fishing boats.

As we have already discovered, Jesus' purpose behind the supernatural signs and wonders He performed was NOT to amaze and entertain the masses. It is doubtful that the crowd which Jesus had taught earlier was even aware of what now transpired with the disciples. They were not His intended audience for this lesson. Rather, Jesus' focus was on His disciples. His goal was simple: to confront these men with the supernatural reality of the Kingdom of God and to renew their call to repentance, faith, and discipleship. But, for this to happen, their astonishment must give way to something greater.

His goal was simple: to confront these men with the supernatural reality of the Kingdom of God and to renew their call to repentance faith, and discipleship.

And this leads us to their other response to these events: Fear. Listen to the words of Peter's response to Jesus, *"But when Simon Peter saw it, he fell down at Jesus' knees, saying, 'Depart from me, for I am a sinful man, O Lord.'"* To experience the supernatural power of the Kingdom of God is to experience something of God's holiness. And the response of the human heart to God's holiness is fear, more specifically, *"the fear of the Lord."*

Holiness and the "fear of the Lord" is a shared experience among God's saints throughout the ages. The Prophet Isaiah discovered this reality when He stood in the Temple and experienced a vision of God seated upon His throne, surrounded by angels who continually cried out, *"Holy, holy, holy is the LORD of hosts; the whole earth is full of his glory!"* (Isaiah 6:3) At that moment, Isaiah's response to the holiness of God was remarkably similar to Simon Peter's response to Jesus, *"And I said: 'Woe is me! For I am lost; for I am a man of unclean lips, and I dwell in the midst of a people of unclean lips; for my eyes have seen the King, the LORD of hosts!'"* (Isaiah 6:5)[60] Scripture has much to say about fear, nearly all of which can be summarized into two basic types of fear: *servile* and *sanctified.* [61]

Servile fear is any fear of people, places, things or circumstances apart from God. The human heart is prone to many fears in this fallen world: fear of the unknown, fear of men (and what they can do to us), fear of want and suffering, disaster, sickness and, perhaps the greatest fear of all, the fear of death. The list of things which strike fear into the human heart is as endless and varied as the number of people in the world. But they all have one thing in common. They all have the power to distract us, enslave us, paralyze us and prevent us from obeying God and enjoying the blessing of obedience to His will. All such fears are the collective enemy of the Kingdom of God, and of our discipleship.

Sanctified fear is the type of fear which Scripture encourages, namely, *"the fear of the Lord."* No less than 25 Scriptures teach the blessings of *"the fear of the Lord."* The Scriptures remind us that *"the fear of the Lord is the beginning of wisdom"*

(Psalm 111:10; Proverbs 9:10; 1:7), *"the fear of the Lord is clean"* (Psalm 19:9), *"the fear of the LORD is a fountain of life"* (Proverbs 14:7). The fear of the Lord is to be taught from one generation to the next (Psalms 34:11). The Prophet Isaiah prophesied that the Messiah would be endued with *"the Spirit of wisdom and understanding, the Spirit of counsel and might, the Spirit of knowledge and <u>the fear of the LORD</u>."* (Isaiah 11:2-3). The fear of the Lord is that unique response of the human heart to the holiness of God which produces repentance from sin and faith toward God, and motivates us to obey God in all that He calls us to do. As the Apostle Paul wrote to the believers in the city of Corinth, *"Therefore, knowing the fear of the Lord, we persuade others"* (2 Corinthians 5:11).

This is no academic distinction to be taken lightly and later dismissed. One of the great purposes of God in sending the Messiah, prophesied by Zechariah, father of John the Baptizer, was *"to grant us that we, being delivered from the hand of our enemies, might **serve him without fear,** in holiness and righteousness before him all our days"* (Luke 1:73-75). In the Kingdom of God, the opposite of biblical faith is not doubt or unbelief. It is fear. Servile fear of people, places, things or circumstances apart from God is the mortal enemy of biblical faith, the Kingdom of God and our discipleship. Jesus came to deliver us from the hand of all such "enemies." And He would begin by delivering Simon Peter and his companions from that fear which had returned them to fishing.

> *In The Kingdom of God, the opposite of biblical faith is not doubt or unbelief. It is fear.*

Confronting Our Fears

This was a critical, teachable moment in the life of Simon Peter and his companions. Jesus wasn't merely confronting "fear" in general. Each of us is prone to our unique set of fears. All of them have their spiritual root in a lack of faith on our part in God's ability to meet us at the point of our fear. It is an unswerving principle of discipleship in the Kingdom of God that Jesus will call each of us to trust Him at that point where our obedience to Him intersects our greatest fear. For these four men Jesus was confronting a very specific and personal fear, one which was holding Peter and his companions prisoner and preventing them from fully embracing their call to discipleship.

> *. . . Jesus will call each of us to trust Him at that point where our obedience to Him intersects our greatest fear.*

This episode begs for an answer to an unspoken question: *"Why had they returned to fishing?"* This was the second time that these disciples had left following Jesus in order to return to fishing. But why? The practical reason why such men would leave the discipleship of Jesus and return to their fishing business is a genuine fear concerning how their needs would be met. Fishing was all they knew. It was how they made their living and provided for their families. How would they live if they didn't support themselves by fishing?

Then Jesus showed up, again. In one miraculous moment, He demonstrated that He was more than able to meet their needs. And in that moment of miraculous provision, their servile fear of the future, which threatened to keep them enslaved to fear and bound to their boats, gave way to a genuine - even sanctified - "fear of the

And They Dreamt Of A Kingdom

Lord." From this point on, their lives might not always be overflowing with fish, but their needs would be met. He would provide and it would be enough. It was time for Peter and his companions to let go of their fear of the future, to embrace a healthy and clean fear of God, and to continue on in their discipleship with Jesus, *"Do not be afraid, from now on you will be catching men."* This statement embodied both a command and a declaration. Jesus' word to Peter and His companions was clear, *"Fishing was your old life, but fishing for men is your new life. Do not be afraid to leave the old and embrace the new, because I am more than able to provide for you."*

And They Left Everything

"And when they had brought their boats to land, they left everything and followed him." (Luke 5:1-11)

Welcome to the third call to discipleship for this group of men. Their first "call" took place when Jesus invited five followers of John the Baptizer to "come and see." They did, and in the process they experienced a year of life-changing ministry alongside Jesus. Their second call took place roughly a year later in Capernaum alongside the Sea of Galilee after they had returned to their fishing business. On that occasion the Gospel writer tells us that they, *"Immediately . . . left the boat and their father and followed him."* Now, after what appears to be a matter of only a few days or weeks, they received their third call to follow Jesus. But this time there seems to be a ring of finality in their response, *"they left everything and followed him."*

In their previous calling by the Sea of Galilee, the emphasis was upon the "immediate" nature of their response. But this time was different. An immediate response has given way to a more reflective one. Sometimes enthusiasm makes immediate choices which fear later questions. On this day, in the school of Jesus, these young disciples discovered that the fear of God and our desire to obey Him must replace all other fears and desires. As disciples of the Kingdom, they could not hold on to their fears and their discipleship at the same time. One must give way to the other. But in the end, the disciple who fears God, fears nothing else.

As disciples of the Kingdom, they could not hold on to their fears and their discipleship at the same time.

What The Disciples Learned That Day

You can learn a lot sitting in a fishing boat. The disciples did. They learned that, in spite of all their "professional" expertise, Jesus actually knew more about fishing than they did. If Jesus' plan was to meet their needs through their fishing business, He was certainly able to do so. In abundance! But in the midst of such abundance the disciples were challenged by a deeper lesson. In the midst of abundance they discovered that Jesus wasn't really concerned about their business, but about their obedience. Providing fish - even in great abundance - was the easy part. The God who had spoken creation into existence out of nothing had no problem filling a couple of fishing boats with fish. But transforming the human heart - even the heart of a Kingdom disciple - from slavish, servile fear to genuine faith requires a bit more work. Even for God.

On this day in the Spring of A.D. 28, sitting in a fishing boat on the Sea of Galilee, a group of young disciples learned to confront their fear of the future and of God's provision in their lives. They discovered that the opposite of faith is not doubt, but fear - fear of people, fear of circumstances, fear of how their needs would be met if they followed Jesus the way He was calling them to follow. And they aren't alone.

Fear is a common denominator of the human experience after the fall. The "god" of this present evil age - the "ruler" of this domain of darkness - wants fearful people whose servile fears can be exploited and whose lives can be controlled and manipulated. But in the Kingdom of God, faith conquers and banishes fear. In the Kingdom of God, discipleship is that process by which God raises up a people who fear nothing and no one, save God alone.

On this day, in a fishing boat on the Sea of Galilee, these men learned that discipleship in the Kingdom of God doesn't require us to leave everything we have in order to follow Jesus. Rather, our discipleship in the Kingdom of God requires us to confront our slavish fears which would use the people, places, things and circumstances of this Age to hinder us from fully obeying God. These men discovered an unswerving principle of discipleship in the Kingdom of God, that Jesus calls each of us to

> *In the Kingdom of God, discipleship is that process by which God raises up a people who fear nothing and no one, save God alone.*

trust Him at that point where our obedience to Him intersects our greatest fear. And having been delivered from our fears of everything but God, a fishing business becomes a small thing to leave behind for the sake of the Kingdom.[62]

And They Dreamt Of A Kingdom

Questions For Reflection

Reflecting on this lesson, what did you learn about discipleship in the Kingdom of God that you did not know before?

How would you describe the difference between a "servile fear" and a "sanctified fear"? How do these two types of fear affect your own discipleship?

Reflect on the following observation: *"Jesus calls each of us to trust Him at that point where our obedience to Him intersects our greatest fear."* What is your greatest fear when it comes to your discipleship and following Jesus? What have you learned from this lesson that could help you confront and deal with those fears?

Reflect on the following observation: *"The opposite of faith is not doubt, but fear."* Explain why you agree or disagree. How is it true or not true in your own discipleship with Jesus?

Key Thought

In the Kingdom of God, discipleship is that process by which God raises up a people who fear nothing and no one, save God alone.

---

20 - A Messianic Miracle And A Claim To Deity

"And the scribes and the Pharisees began to question, saying, 'Who is this who speaks blasphemies? Who can forgive sins but God alone?' When Jesus perceived their thoughts, he answered them, 'Why do you question in your hearts? Which is easier, to say, 'Your sins are forgiven you,' or to say, 'Rise and walk'? But that you may know that the Son of Man has authority on earth to forgive sins' - he said to the man who was paralyzed - 'I say to you, rise, pick up your bed and go home.'" (Luke 5:21-24)

Discipleship Reading: Luke 5:12-26   **When:** Spring, A.D. 28
Contextual Reading: Luke 5; Matthew 9; Mark 2   **Where:** Galilee

Healing A Leper (Luke 5:12-16)

"While he was in one of the cities, there came a man full of leprosy. And when he saw Jesus, he fell on his face and begged him, 'Lord, if you will, you can make me clean. And Jesus stretched out his hand and touched him, saying, 'I will; be clean.' And immediately the leprosy left him." (Luke 5:12-14)

Following the renewed call of His disciples, Jesus set off on a ministry tour of neighboring towns. It was a new day in the "School of Jesus," and His disciples had much to learn. His first encounter involved a leper, whom He healed with a touch(Luke 5:12-16). Lepers were social and religious outcasts in Israel. They were banned from participation in the religious life of Israel, and were generally forced to live lives of separation and isolation away from the rest of Jewish society. They were the "untouchables" of the ancient world. Jesus could have healed this person with a spoken word, just as He had done earlier with the Nobleman's son (John 4:43-54). But Jesus chose to demonstrate His compassion for the marginalized by doing what no religious leader in Israel would have done. He touched him . . . and healed him.

Technically, the Law concerning leprosy did not forbid touching a leper. But the Law did require the separation of lepers from the community. Under the Law the ritual uncleanness of the leper transferred to anyone and everyone they touched, or who touched them . . . including Jesus. So, why would Jesus touch him? *"Luke describes Jesus' action as deliberate . . . . human contact that violated the law (since uncleanness was communicable) but also communicated acceptance and reentry into the community. Jesus is presented as one who is both able and willing to cross conventional boundaries in order to bring good news."* [63] Jesus was willing to violate the Law in order to embrace the marginalized and to touch them with the Kingdom of God. But there was more. With Jesus, there always is.

The Old Testament Law provided for the recognition and restoration of a leper (see Leviticus 13-14). But, in the long history of ancient Israel there was no record of a leper ever being healed and restored according to the Law. In fact, throughout Israel's history only two people had ever been healed of leprosy: Miriam the Prophetess (Numbers 12) and Namaan the Syrian (2 Kings 5). And both of these had been supernaturally healed apart from the Law.

Because of such realities, Jewish rabbis over the years had divided miracles into two categories: those that anyone could perform if empowered to do so (people like Moses or Elisha), and those miracles reserved only to Messiah. According to Rabbinic tradition, there were three main miracles reserved for the Messiah, miracles which would help the Jewish people recognize the Messiah when he came.[64] For years the Rabbis had taught that the healing of a leper fell into this special class of "Messianic Miracles." Everyone who witnessed or heard about the healing of this leper knew what it meant, just as they had been taught: the Messiah had arrived. As Thomas and Gundry rightly point out, *"The proper course would have been for the priests to verify the cleansing and announce to the nation the arrival of Messiah."* [65] And this explains why the news of this leper being healed spread like a wildfire among the people, *"now even more the report about him went abroad, and great crowds gathered to hear him and to be healed of their infirmities."* (Luke 5:15)

Healing A Paralytic (Luke 5:17-26)

"On one of those days, as he was teaching, Pharisees and teachers of the law were sitting there, who had come from every village of Galilee and Judea and from Jerusalem. And the power of the Lord was with him to heal. And behold, some men were bringing on a bed a man who was paralyzed, and they were seeking to bring him in and lay him before Jesus, but finding no way to bring him in, because of the crowd, they went up on the roof and let him down with his bed through the tiles into the midst before Jesus.

Jesus' new-found fame resulting from performing a "Messianic Miracle" (i.e., healing a leper) has brought Him to the attention of the religious leadership and has changed the dynamic in His relationship with the institutional Judaism. The *"Pharisees and teachers of the law,"* who have been noticeably absent up to this point (just over a year into His public ministry) have now shown up in force, coming *"from every village of Galilee and Judea and from Jerusalem"* (Luke 5:17). Their attitude of benign neglect toward Jesus has changed. Jesus and His ministry are now the center of their focused attention.

When this passage unfolds, Jesus appears to be ministering in a private home. In the course of events, several men arrive carrying a paralyzed man on his bed. When the crush of people prevents them from bringing the man into the house they come up with a creative alternative: they would lower the paralyzed man into the house, in front of Jesus, through a hole in the roof. Jesus' response to the whole episode takes everyone by surprise. Rather than simply healing the man, Jesus declares, *"Man, your sins are forgiven you."* Such a declaration was guaranteed to create controversy, and it was quick in coming. The Pharisees were quick to point out that only God can forgive sin, *"Who can forgive sins but God alone?"*

These religious leaders had unknowingly stepped into a carefully laid trap. They had undoubtedly sought Jesus out in response to the "Messianic Miracle" which He had performed by healing a leper. Such an event would not go unnoticed. Their plan was to further examine Jesus' credentials as a possible "Messiah." But Jesus had a plan of His own. By declaring this man's sin "forgiven" Jesus' set the stage to present these religious leaders with His ultimate credential. By healing the leper, Jesus had staked His claim to be Messiah. He would now publicly demonstrate that He was both Messiah and Immanuel - "God with us." [66]

Jesus now responded to the challenge presented by His inquirers, *"'Which is easier, to say, 'Your sins are forgiven you,' or to say, 'Rise and walk'?"* The answer, of course, was obvious. It is much easier to say *"your sins are forgiven"* because there is no way of proving or disproving that anything has happened. To be valid, such a claim requires proof, which Jesus now gives. *"But that you may know that the Son of*

Man has authority on earth to forgive sins' - he said to the man who was paralyzed - 'I say to you, rise, pick up your bed and go home.' And immediately he rose up before them and picked up what he had been lying on and went home, glorifying God."

There are moments in the ministry of Jesus which seem to defy description, and this was one of those moments. The Gospel writer put it this way, *"And amazement seized them all, and they glorified God and were filled with awe, saying, 'We have seen extraordinary things today.'"* The Greek text makes it clear that the writer struggled with words to adequately express the response of those present. The Greek word for "amazement" (*ekstasis*) describes an affront to the mind which ranges from bewilderment and astonishment to terror. The Greek word for "awe" (*phobos*) adds to this by communicating the idea of genuine "fear." And the Greek word for "extraordinary" (*paradoxos*) describes something *"wonderful and unexpected."* In simple terms, this was a moment which beggared description.

Jesus' First Claims To Messiahship And Deity

The Scribes and Pharisees had come looking for a potential Messiah who had healed a leper. They had expected to find a Rabbi. What they found was a manifestation of the Kingdom of God in both power (to heal) and authority (to forgive sin). Who they found was Immanuel. They found One Who, by His words and His deeds, demonstrated Himself to be both Messiah and God. There would be more words and deeds from Jesus over the next couple of years. And while this might be the first time Jesus claimed to be God, it would not be the last. There would be more "Messianic Miracles," along with other miracles which the religious leaders of 1st Century Judaism could never have imagined possible. But all of them would do nothing more than confirm what they had discovered on this day. Later in His ministry, when religious leaders challenged His Messiah-ship, Jesus' answer would refer back to days like this and to works like these, *"So the Jews gathered around him and said to him, 'How long will you keep us in suspense? If you are the Christ, tell us plainly.' Jesus answered them, 'I told you, and you do not believe. The works that I do in my Father's name bear witness about me, but you do not believe because you are not part of my flock."* (John 10:24-26)

Both the words and the deeds of Jesus confirm that He is both Messiah and God. But spiritual blindness can blind men to the most obvious spiritual truths. C.S. Lewis summed it up well when he observed that any person who can read the Gospels and not see that Jesus is both Messiah and God could stare into the sky at noon on a cloudless day and not see the sun. It is amazing how many people, both then and now, are blind to the sun.

It is amazing how many people, both then and now, are blind to the sun.

What The Disciples Learned Thist Day

It was a busy time in the discipleship school of Jesus. The learning curve for these six disciples of the Kingdom was undoubtedly steeper than anything they had ever experienced before. Welcome to life in the Kingdom of God, and to what it means to be a disciple of that Kingdom. On some days, it's a challenge just to keep up. So, to prevent falling behind and getting lost, let's summarize some of the lessons the disciples learned on this day.

A Lesson Concerning God's Compassion For The Marginalized. This was not a new lesson. The disciples had witnessed it before during their time in Samaria.

And They Dreamt Of A Kingdom

It would be a recurring theme through Jesus' ministry. But on this day the disciples were reminded that compassion for and ministry to the marginalized lay at the heart of Jesus' ministry and His message of the Kingdom. These were the very people He had come to seek, to find and to redeem. And if the One Who is Messiah, God and King can touch, heal and serve a leper, so could they. They not only could, but they must.

A Lesson Concerning The Transforming Power of the Kingdom. The religion-shaped spirituality of 1st Century Judaism marginalized those it had no power to serve or heal. But the Jesus-shaped spirituality of the Kingdom is different. On this day the disciples watched as the power of the Kingdom healed, transformed and restored what the Law and the religion-shaped spirituality of 1st Century Judaism could not. The Law could identify a leper and provide for his ritual cleansing and restoration to the community. But it could not heal him. Only the power of the Kingdom could do that. One day, Simon Peter would demonstrate the transforming power of the Kingdom to a lame man at the Gate Beautiful. Today sowed the seed for that day.

A Lesson Concerning Messianic Miracles. Throughout their lives, sitting under the teaching of the religious leaders of Israel, the disciples had heard about the three great Messianic Miracles which only the Messiah could perform. On this day, the disciples watched as Jesus, the Rabbi from Galilee whom they had now been following for over a year, performed one of those Messianic Miracles. These were the miracles would enable everyone to recognize the Messiah when He came. This lesson and this miracle embodied a powerful confirmation of everything these five men had learned over the previous year.

A Lesson Concerning Authority, Power And Forgiveness. On this day, the disciples learned that Jesus not only had the power to heal, but He also had the authority to forgive sin. Such power and such authority belonged only to the God of Israel. And this reality led to, perhaps, the greatest lesson of all.

A Lesson Concerning Immanuel. On this day, six Galilean fishermen began to understand a deeper truth of the Kingdom that would expand and grow in their awareness over the months to follow. This Rabbi from Galilee was more than a teacher sent from God; more than religious rabble rouser; more than a miracle worker. The cumulative lessons and experiences of the past year genuinely began to come together on this day as six Galilean fishermen and disciples of the Kingdom began to understand that this Jesus - their teacher - was both Messiah and Immanuel, "God with us."

It was a lot for six Galilean fishermen to absorb. And their discipleship with Jesus was just getting started.

Questions For Reflection

Reflecting on this Lesson, what did you learn about Jesus and His ministry that you did not know before?

How did Jesus demonstrate His compassion for the marginalized (the leper and the paralytic)?

How did Jesus' ministry on this day demonstrate a clear claim to Deity? What difference does a claim to Deity make?

Read Isaiah 7:14 and Matthew 1:23. How did Jesus fulfill this Messianic prophecy on this day? How do you think witnessing the fulfillment of this passage affected the disciples? How does it affect you?

Key Thought

As disciples of the Kingdom, we follow One who by His words and His deeds has demonstrated Himself to be both the promised Messiah and Immanuel, "God with us."

And They Dreamt Of A Kingdom

21 - The Call of Levi

"After this he went out and saw a tax collector named Levi, sitting at the tax booth. And he said to him, 'Follow me.' And leaving everything, he rose and followed him. And Levi made him a great feast in his house, and there was a large company of tax collectors and others reclining at table with them. And the Pharisees and their scribes grumbled at his disciples, saying, 'Why do you eat and drink with tax collectors and sinners?' And Jesus answered them, 'Those who are well have no need of a physician, but those who are sick. I have not come to call the righteous but sinners to repentance.'" (Luke 5:27-32)

Discipleship Reading: Luke 5:27-32   **When:** Spring, A.D. 28
Contextual Reading: Matthew 9; Mark 2; Luke 5   **Where:** Galilee

The Jewish religious leaders of Jesus' day, particularly the Pharisees, frequently accused Jesus of spending too much time with *"tax-gatherers and sinners."*[67] Of course, for the Pharisees, any time spent with such people was too much time. Their religion-shaped spirituality taught them that merely associating with such ceremonially "unclean" people would be enough to "defile" them and render them "unclean." But the situation was actually much worse than even the Pharisees imagined. Jesus didn't just associate and spend time with such people. He specifically sought them out, chose them and called them to be His disciples, and leaders in His nascent church. Why? Because these were the very people He had come to redeem. The least of them would soon be among the greatest in the Kingdom of God. These "unclean" people embodied the inverted values of the Kingdom.

The Inverted Values Of The Kingdom

Throughout His ministry, Jesus had much to say about the inverted values of the Kingdom, including the issue of what it means to be "great." The religion-shaped spirituality of 1st Century Judaism defined greatness by appearances, by self-righteousness, by position, by being "first," and by being served. Jesus rejected all such notions of "greatness." In the Kingdom of God, the least would be great, the last would be first, and the greatest must be the servant of all (see Mark 9:33-37). These were the inverted values of the Kingdom which Jesus taught. But as the wise master teacher He was, Jesus understood that it was not enough to simply teach such values. They also must be authentically lived out and modeled. Jesus made it a point with His disciples to always model what He taught. In our current passage, Jesus takes the opportunity to personally model the inverted values of the Kingdom by intentionally reaching out to "the least of these"; those people who had been marginalized by 1st Century Jewish culture.

Levi - A Man Of Peace

"And Levi made him a great feast in his house, and there was a large company of tax collectors and others reclining at table with them. And the Pharisees and their scribes grumbled at his disciples, saying, 'Why do you eat and drink with tax collectors and sinners?'"

Levi was a tax collector, literally a *telones*, a "collector of tolls." In Capernaum, a "collector of tolls" was responsible for collecting the various taxes imposed by Herod Antipas (with the approval of Rome), particularly customs duties on goods being traded.[68] Mark 2:13-14 suggests that Levi's customs booth was located by the lakeshore where boats would load and unload cargo subject to customs duties. In 1st Century Palestine "collectors of tolls" were particularly odious because they were frequently fellow Jews who worked under contract with unpopular rulers to collect taxes from their fellow Jews. They were regarded as people *"given to dishonesty and abuse of authority"* (as described by John the Baptizer in Luke 3:12-13).[69] As a result, Levi and his fellow "tax collectors" were ostracized and marginalized by their own people who treated them as worse than Gentiles (i.e., non-Jews, who were also to be avoided). In the thinking of 1st Century Judaism, there was no moral difference between a "sinner" and a "tax-collector." Both were to be avoided and shunned as ritually "unclean" by all good religious Jews.

This attitude helps us better understand the story of Zacchaeus in Luke 19. Zacchaeus wasn't just a tax-collector. He was a "chief tax collector." When Jesus spots Zacchaeus and invites Himself over to his house for dinner, the reaction of the crowd is quick and hostile, *"And when they saw it, they all grumbled, 'He has gone in to be the guest of a man who is a sinner.'"* (Luke 19:7) No good religious Jew would ever do that. In fact, most of them wanted to kill Zacchaeus, not eat lunch with him. The same was true of Levi.

But Jesus was different. The inverted values of the Kingdom meant that Jesus sought out and embraced the "unclean" and the marginalized. People like Levi. Where the religion-shaped spirituality of 1st Century Judaism saw an unclean, marginalized tax-collector, Jesus saw a lost sheep of Israel, a potential disciple and a man of peace who would open both his life and his home to Jesus' and the Kingdom.

Like Peter, Andrew, Nathaniel, James and John before him, Levi "left everything" to follow Jesus. The Greek verb "left" (*kataleipo)* is an intensified verb meaning "forsake" or "abandon," and gives an emotional sense of finality to Levi's action.   To celebrate his new-found discipleship, Levi held a great feast in his home for Jesus, His disciples and *"a large company of tax collectors and others."* For His part, Jesus chose to model what He would one day teach. Look for people of peace who will open their hearts and their homes to the good news of the Kingdom. Accept their invitation

In the Kingdom of God, people of peace, like Levi, often start out as the least likely and end up as the most fruitful.

to dinner, call them to be disciples, and encourage them to share the good news of the Kingdom with their friends. How well did that discipleship strategy work out? In the case of Levi, it worked out pretty well. In the New Testament Levi was also known as Matthew. He went on to write the Gospel which bears his name. Not a bad outcome for an "unclean," marginalized and ostracized tax-collector! *In the Kingdom of God, people of peace, like Levi, often start out as the least likely and end up as the most fruitful.* Welcome to the inverted values of the Kingdom of God.

Compassion Versus Sacrifice

"And when the Pharisees saw this, they said to his disciples, 'Why does your teacher eat with tax collectors and sinners?' But when he heard it, he said, 'Those who are well have no need of a physician, but those who are sick. Go and learn what this means, 'I desire mercy, and not sacrifice.' For I came not to call the righteous, but

sinners.'" (Matthew 9:11-13)

For Jesus to dine in the home of a known "sinner" represented a profound departure from social and religious norms and pushed the religion-shaped spirituality of 1st Century Judaism and the Pharisees to its breaking point. In 1st Century Jewish culture, the act of dining in someone's home represented an act of acceptance and close association. The Pharisees were appalled. Rabbinic teaching held that the mere act of entering the home of such an "unclean" individual rendered the visitor ritually unclean as well. No good Pharisee would even consider such an act, and they were stunned that Jesus would.[70]

In his own written account of the events of this day, Levi (also known as Matthew, and author of the Gospel) records the above exchange between Jesus and the Pharisees. Levi remembers Jesus quoting from the Old Testament Prophet Hosea who declared, *"For I desire steadfast love (mercy) and not sacrifice, the knowledge of God rather than burnt offerings."* (Hosea 6:6). Levi understood that the Pharisees (and other religious leaders of Israel) had chosen to "sacrifice" people like himself upon the altar of their religion-shaped spirituality of legalistic adherence to the Law as they understood it. By doing so they had demonstrated that they were strangers

In the Kingdom of God, some lessons are so important that they must be repeated until they are fully embraced, because our fear and our prejudice predispose us against them.

to the heart of God and His compassion toward "sinners." Levi heard Jesus' words and understood what they meant. In the Kingdom of God, the true knowledge of God goes beyond "sacrifice" and "burnt offerings" to manifest compassion toward those we would rather marginalize and reject. It must have been an eye-opening experience for this tax collector turned disciple.

But this lesson was not new. Jesus' disciples had already seen and experienced Jesus' passion for the marginalized. They had witnessed it during their journey through Samaria. They had seen it again in Jesus' interaction with a leper, healing him with a physical touch, when a word at a distance would have been sufficient. But in the Kingdom of God, some lessons are so important that they must be repeated until they are fully embraced, because our fear and our prejudice predispose us against them.

For the sake of world redemption, Peter, Andrew, Nathaniel, Philip, John and James, now found themselves dining in the home of someone more "odious" than a Samaritan: a "collector of tolls" and all his friends! For His part, Jesus needed to free His disciples from the narrow religion-shaped spirituality given to them by 1st Century Judaism. The disciples must take Jesus' yoke of inverted Kingdom values and ministry to the marginalized upon themselves and walk with Him into places where they and their religion-shaped spirituality would rather not go. The change would happen fearfully, hesitatingly and reluctantly at first. But the change would come. And so would the day when the disciples would no longer fear or avoid those who were different from themselves or resist the call to seek them out. Jesus knew that one day these disciples of the Kingdom would be His witnesses not just in Jerusalem and Judea among their own people, but also among the marginalized of Samaria, and even among those Gentiles who live at the farthest ends of the earth (Acts 1:8). But that day would never come if a handful of reluctant disciples did not embrace the lesson of this day, and attend a feast in the home of a despised tax collector.

And They Dreamt Of A Kingdom

Principle and Practice

Jesus' dealings with both Levi and Zacchaeus reveal two important aspects of how Jesus made disciples. First, they reveal Jesus' most basic *operating principle*, expressed in verse 32, *"I have not come to call the righteous but sinners to repentance."* Jesus' *operating principle* was to seek out the very people whom most good religiously observant Jews spent their lives trying to avoid. Second, if seeking the marginalized was Jesus' *operating principle*, then spending extended time with them was His *operating practice*. Jesus saw all of life through the eyes of the Kingdom of God. He saw Levi's feast for what it was, an opportunity to spend extended time with the very people who needed Him the most and to tell stories about the Kingdom of God.

But there was more. With Jesus, there always is.

As the disciples discovered on their journey With Jesus through Samaria, certain lessons simply cannot be taught. They must be caught. It wasn't enough to simply teach His disciples to *"love your enemies"* from the comfort of a mountain side or from a boat with no enemies in sight. Jesus understood that if you and I are going to call sinners to repentance, we can not do it from a distance. We must be willing to go where they and their friends live. Jesus understood that if the religion-shaped spirituality of the disciples - a spirituality which divided people into the "clean" and the "unclean" - was ever to be transformed into a spirituality sufficient for the demands of life in the Kingdom, it would require more than instruction. Such a radical transformation required confrontation. Just as He had demonstrated in Samaria, such a transformation required bringing the disciples face to face with those people whom their religion-shaped spirituality had taught them to avoid. Their transformation required dinner in the home of Levi and his friends. And our transformation requires nothing less.

Jesus understood that you cannot successfully change a behavior without first changing the values which produced that behavior. And in order for that to happen, a profound personal transformation was needed in these men. It was not enough to merely teach the inverted values of the Kingdom. They must be modeled, seen, experienced and eventually embraced. Jesus knew that without the lesson of this day in the home of Levi, there would be no future ministry, no tomorrow. There is no Kingdom ministry tomorrow if we fail to embrace the Kingdom lessons of today. This was a day for challenging the values of His disciples in the hope of eventually changing their behavior.

> *Jesus understood that you cannot successfully change a behavior without first changing the values which produced that behavior.*

Epilogue: And Then There Were Seven

At this point, in the Spring/Summer of A.D. 28, Jesus is roughly one year into His public ministry. His disciples now number seven. Five of them (John, Peter, Andrew, Philip and Nathaniel) have been with Jesus for roughly 18 months. A sixth (James, brother of John) has been with them roughly a year. Levi now joins them for a total of seven. Over the next six months or so Jesus will call five more (although we have no record of their individual calls), bringing the final number to twelve (See Mark

3:13-19; Luke 6:12-16). Jesus has much to teach them over the next two years.

Questions For Reflection

Reflecting on this Lesson, what did you learn about Jesus and His ministry to the marginalized that you did not know before?

Reflecting on Jesus' ministry with Levi, how would you define or describe a "person of peace"? Based on Jesus' calling of Levi, what did you learn about the importance of seeking out and spending time with such people?

Who are the marginalized people you have spent more than casual time with over the past month? Who are the marginalized people in your sphere of influence you could reach out to? How could they fulfill the role of being a "person of peace"?

How would you describe the "inverted values" of the Kingdom? What situations have arisen in your own life recently which have challenged you to demonstrate the inverted values of the Kingdom?

Reflect on this statement: *"There is no Kingdom ministry tomorrow if we fail to embrace the Kingdom lessons of today."* What is God teaching you today about ministry to the marginalized that you must learn in order to move forward with your discipleship?

Key Thought

As disciples of the Kingdom, you and I are called to embrace and live out the inverted values of the Kingdom by seeking out the marginalized with the good news of the Kingdom of God.

And They Dreamt Of A Kingdom

22 - Fasting, Garments And Wineskins

"Then the disciples of John came to him, saying, 'Why do we and the Pharisees fast, but your disciples do not fast?' And Jesus said to them, 'Can the wedding guests mourn as long as the bridegroom is with them? The days will come when the bridegroom is taken away from them, and then they will fast. No one puts a piece of unshrunk cloth on an old garment, for the patch tears away from the garment, and a worse tear is made. Neither is new wine put into old wineskins. If it is, the skins burst and the wine is spilled and the skins are destroyed. But new wine is put into fresh wineskins, and so both are preserved.'" (Matthew 9:14-17)

Discipleship Reading: Matthew 9:14-17   **When**: Summer, A.D. 28
Contextual Reading: Matthew 9; Mark 2; Luke 5   **Where:** Galilee

Fasting And Mourning

At some point, an issue arose in the ministry of Jesus and His disciples. We can watch it unfold in the above passage where the disciples of John the Baptist pose a question to Jesus: *"Why do we and the Pharisees fast, but Your disciples do not fast."* The question probably arose on one of the two regular Rabbinical "fast-days" when the religion-shaped spirituality of the Pharisees called people to fast. Although it was not required anywhere in the Law, the Pharisees fasted on Mondays and Thursdays because, according to tradition, Moses went up on Mt. Sinai to receive the tablets of the Law on a Thursday and returned on a Monday. Chances are good that John's disciples were also fasting on one of those days, while Jesus and His disciples were not (see Mark 2:18: *"And John's disciples and the Pharisees were fasting"*).

As was often the case in Jesus' ministry, this violation of contemporary Judaism's religion-shaped spirituality created an opportunity for the religious leadership (especially the Pharisees) to criticize Jesus and His disciples (*"Why aren't you religious like us?"*). Jesus did not fast like the Jewish religious leaders for a simple reason. Unlike them, He did not regard fasting as a means of earning either favor with God or approval with men (Matthew 6:1, 16). This didn't mean that Jesus didn't fast. He certainly fasted as commanded by the Law on the Day of Atonement. And He began His earthly ministry by fasting for forty days. Jesus was no stranger to fasting, nor was he opposed to fasting. He simply refused to do it for the wrong reasons.

Jesus answered their question with a question of His own, which cut to the heart of the matter, *"Can the wedding guests mourn as long as the bridegroom is with them?"* What did this mean? In John 3:29, John the Baptizer had described Jesus as "the Bridegroom." Responding to this question from John's disciples, Jesus now continues that analogy. Jesus is, indeed, the bridegroom, and His presence marks the symbolic beginning of the "marriage-week." According to Rabbinic law, the marriage week was to be a time of unmixed festivity. Even on the holiest day of the Mosaic Law, the Day of Atonement, when fasting was specifically commanded by the Law, a bride was allowed to relax one of the requirements of that strictest fast. During the marriage week all mourning was to be suspended. It was regarded as a religious duty to cheer the bride and bridegroom. Fasting, with its Old Testament implications of mourning, would be inappropriate and out-of-place during such a festive time. But Jesus knew that the time would soon come when He, the Bridegroom, would be violently taken away, and that would be the time for fasting, and even mourning, *"The days will come when the bridegroom is taken away from them, and then they will fast."*

And They Dreamt Of A Kingdom

This passage offers two important lessons for every disciple of the Kingdom. The first lesson has to do with fasting. There are appropriate times to fast, and there are inappropriate times to fast. For disciples of the Kingdom, seeking God through fasting and prayer is not an "if" but a "when," as Jesus Himself taught elsewhere:

"And when you fast, do not look gloomy like the hypocrites, for they disfigure their faces that their fasting may be seen by others. Truly, I say to you, they have received their reward. But when you fast, anoint your head and wash your face, that your fasting may not be seen by others but by your Father who is in secret. And your Father who sees in secret will reward you." (Matthew 6:16-18)

In both Matthew 6 and 9, Jesus clearly teaches that it is appropriate for disciples of the Kingdom to fast today during the absence of our heavenly bridegroom. We mourn His absence and we long for His soon return. Beyond that, as disciples desiring to fast *"unto the Lord,"* we need to be sensitive to the leading of the Holy Spirit as we fast. As with all spiritual disciplines, we need to ask Him to show us when it is appropriate and when it is not. And this speaks to us concerning God's holiness. One aspect of biblical holiness is doing what God desires both for the right reason and at the right time. A religion-shaped spirituality often takes root when right things are done for the wrong reasons or at the wrong time. The Pharisees did the right thing, but they did it for the wrong reason. They fasted to be seen by men as righteous before the Law. John's disciples did the right things, but at the wrong time. They failed to understand that because Jesus was present, this was the season to rejoice with the Bridegroom. The time for fasting would come later, when the Bridegroom was taken away. But there was more. With Jesus, there always is.

> *A religion-shaped spirituality often takes root when right things are done for the wrong reasons or at the wrong time.*

The Old And The New

This lesson on fasting was important. Disciples of the Kingdom must be sensitive to God's times and seasons, and the leading of the Holy Spirit. But there was a second, more critical lesson embodied in this episode, which Jesus now brought into focus, *"No one puts a piece of unshrunk cloth on an old garment, for the patch tears away from the garment, and a worse tear is made. Neither is new wine put into old wineskins."*

> *Disciples of the Kingdom must be sensitive to God's times and seasons, and the leading of the Holy Spirit.*

Jesus understood that His disciples faced a very real, subtle and powerful danger. They faced the daily on-going pressure exerted by 1st Century Judaism to pull them back into its religion-shaped spirituality. Jesus was bringing the new wine of the Kingdom, and the old wineskin of 1st Century Judaism's religion-shaped spirituality was unable to receive that new wine without either destroying the wine . . . or being destroyed by it.

The coming of the Kingdom, in the person of Jesus, the King, had changed everything. And the new wine of the Kingdom must be placed into new wineskins which could contain it because they were created for it. What were those wineskins? Disciples of the Kingdom and the new *ekklesia* they would form when they met together. These disciples of the Kingdom would soon take the message of the Kingdom far beyond the boundaries of 1st Century Judaism. Would those Kingdom disciples practice fasting? Of course they would, but not out of any sense of religious obligation imposed by 1st Century Judaism. They wouldn't fast because the old wineskin prescribed it, or to please the Pharisees. They would fast in ways, at times and in places appropriate to their situations, their needs and their ministries. They would fast in order to worship God, to wait upon God and to seek Him for His Kingdom purposes and instructions (Acts 13:1-2). They would manifest the new wine of the Kingdom in the new wineskin of Kingdom disciples and the new *ekklesia* (or "churches") they established, unfettered by the constraints of any religion-shaped spirituality left over from religious Judaism.

But such things are easier said than done. Old religion-shaped spiritualities tend to actively resist their own God-appointed demise. In the book of Acts, as the early church proclaimed the good news of the Kingdom, the disciples found themselves in a growing conflict with those who wanted to take the new wine of the Kingdom back into the old wineskins of the old covenant and religious Judaism. This conflict soon became so unavoidable that the leaders of the early church were forced to gather together and hammer out a response. The conflict, the gathering of leaders and the resolution are all recorded in Acts 15.

Old religion-shaped spiritualities tend to actively resist their own God-appointed demise.

A critical moment had arrived for both the message of the Kingdom and for those Kingdom disciples who would carry it to the ends of the earth. Would the new wine of the Kingdom be pulled back into the religion-shaped wineskin of traditional Judaism as some demanded, *"It is necessary to circumcise them and to order them to keep the law of Moses"* (Acts 15:5). Or would the new wine be poured into the new wineskin of a Jesus-shaped spirituality lived out by disciples of the Kingdom gathering as "churches"? Simon Peter expressed what all of the apostles were thinking, *"Why are you putting God to the test by placing a yoke on the neck of the disciples that neither our fathers nor we have been able to bear?"* (Acts 15:10)

The old covenant and wineskin had performed the task assigned to it by God. It had *"imprisoned everything under sin, so that the promise by faith in Jesus Christ might be given to those who believe. Now before faith came, we were held captive under the law, imprisoned until the coming faith would be revealed. So then, the law was our guardian until Christ came, in order that we might be justified by faith. But now that faith has come, we are no longer under a guardian, for in Christ Jesus you are all sons of God, through faith."* (Galatians 3:22-26) The "guardian" (Greek: *paidagogos*, "tutor" or "school guardian") of the old covenant wineskin had brought both Jew and Gentile to Christ and the good news of the Kingdom which He proclaimed.

But the guardianship of the old was now finished. Now, the new wine of the Kingdom must go into new wineskins, unencumbered by the old covenant or the religion-shaped spirituality of old wineskins and 1st Century Judaism, *"For it has seemed good to the Holy Spirit and to us to lay on you no greater burden than these requirements: that you abstain from what has been sacrificed to idols, and from blood, and from what has been strangled, and from sexual immorality. If you keep yourselves*

And They Dreamt Of A Kingdom

from these, you will do well. Farewell." (Acts 15:28-29)

Religion-shaped spiritualities are timeless. Some are old. Others are new. Some begin innocently. Others are more intentional. Even today there are people seeking to pour the new wine of the Kingdom of God into religious wineskins of their own design in the hope of creating their own religion-shaped spirituality fashioned around themselves rather than around Jesus and His Kingdom. All of these present the same danger, namely, the danger of destroying the wineskin and losing the wine.

Questions For Reflection

Reflecting on this Lesson, what did you learn about Jesus and His attitude toward the religion-shaped spirituality of 1st Century Judaism?

Reflecting on this Lesson, how did the Pharisees do "the right thing" for "the wrong reason"? What are some ways in which we do the same thing today?

Describe a "religion-shaped spirituality" you have personally been involved with that didn't work well. What did you learn from that experience that you can apply in your walk as a disciple of the Kingdom?

Describe some ways you have seen people or organizations try to pour the new wine of the Kingdom into old wineskins? What is the impact of those efforts on both the wine and the wineskin?

Key Thought

Disciples of the Kingdom, gathering as the Church, are the new wineskin into which Jesus is pouring the new wine of the Kingdom of God.

---

23 - Healing At The Pool of Bethesda

"Jesus said to him, 'Get up, take up your bed, and walk.' And at once the man was healed, and he took up his bed and walked. Now that day was the Sabbath." (John 5:8-9)

Discipleship Reading: *John 5:1-18*　　　　　**When:** *Fall, A.D. 28*
Contextual Reading: *John 5*　　　　　　　　**Where:** *Jerusalem*

Something on the order of six months have elapsed since the call of Levi. An unrecorded Passover in the Spring of A.D. 28 has come and gone. Jesus and the disciples have spent this intervening time ministering in Galilee, but we have no record of it. Now, it is the Fall of A.D. 28 in the Jewish month of *Tishrei* (somewhere between late September and late October). Jesus and his disciples have made the journey from Galilee to Jerusalem to celebrate the great Fall Feast of Booths (also known as "Tabernacles" or *Sukkot*). A year of teaching, healing and performing Messianic miracles in the Synagogues of Galilee - particularly in Capernaum and particularly on the Sabbath - has brought Jesus and His ministry to the official attention of the religious authorities of 1st Century Judaism. They are now watching Him closely, and it would not be long before a full-blown controversy would emerge. That's what happens when the Kingdom of God confronts our religion-shaped spiritualities. The resolution of all such conflicts reveals the priorities of our hearts. Are the priorities of our hearts those of the Kingdom of God, or are they the priorities of our religion-shaped spirituality?

The Pool of Bethesda (John 5:1-4)

"After this there was a feast of the Jews, and Jesus went up to Jerusalem. Now there is in Jerusalem by the Sheep Gate a pool, in Aramaic called Bethesda, which has five roofed colonnades. In these lay a multitude of invalids--blind, lame, and paralyzed [waiting for the moving of the water; for an angel of the Lord went down at certain seasons into the pool, and stirred the water: whoever stepped in first after the stirring of the water was healed of whatever disease he had]." (John 5:1-4)[71]

The writer John knows that a little context is in order, and so He provides it for us in these opening verses. The "sheep gate" is the place in Jerusalem where sheep were sold for sacrifice in the Temple. It is mentioned two other times in Scripture (Nehemiah 3:32 & 12:39). It was located on the north east side of Jerusalem, a short walk from the Temple proper. In 1888, an archaeologist named Schick excavated a site not far from the Crusader Church of St. Anne and found twin pools, one fifty-five feet long and a second sixty-five feet long. The second one was arched in by five arches with five corresponding porches. The Crusaders believed this to be the site of John 5 and so they built a Church over it. [72]

Challenging Religious Tradition (John 5:5-9)

"One man was there who had been an invalid for thirty-eight years. When

And They Dreamt Of A Kingdom

Jesus saw him lying there and knew that he had already been there a long time, he said to him, 'Do you want to be healed?' The sick man answered him, 'Sir, I have no one to put me into the pool when the water is stirred up, and while I am going another steps down before me.' Jesus said to him, 'Get up, take up your bed, and walk.' And at once the man was healed, and he took up his bed and walked. Now that day was the Sabbath." (John 5:5-9)

In the midst of this religious tradition and lore lay a man who had been lame for 38 years. In other words, basically all of his life. Jesus approached this man with a simple question, *"Do you want to be healed?"* It was a simple question, and yet the man never gave Jesus an answer. Instead, he responded to Jesus by explaining why he couldn't get healed based on local religious traditions (the whole angel-stirring-the-water thing) and his own limitations.

John Calvin observed, *"This sick man does what we nearly all do. He limits God's help to his own ideas and does not dare promise himself more than he conceives in his mind."* Not only was the man physically crippled, but he was also spiritually crippled by his religion-shaped spirituality of traditions and expectations which prevented him from imagining that God could heal him in any other way, or by any other means. Jesus, for His part, simply healed the man, irrespective of any religious tradition, limitation or even the man's lack of faith. Jesus simply ignored all of the prevailing traditions and expectations, including the greatest tradition of all, namely, that no one should heal or be healed on the Sabbath.

The Crisis (5:10-15)

"So the Jews said to the man who had been healed, 'It is the Sabbath, and it is not lawful for you to take up your bed.' But he answered them, 'The man who healed me, that man said to me, 'Take up your bed, and walk.'" They asked him, 'Who is the man who said to you, 'Take up your bed and walk'?' Now the man who had been healed did not know who it was, for Jesus had withdrawn, as there was a crowd in the place. Afterward Jesus found him in the temple and said to him, 'See, you are well! Sin no more, that nothing worse may happen to you.' The man went away and told the Jews that it was Jesus who had healed him." (5:10-15)

As events unfold, the newly healed man is confronted by the Jewish religious authorities who ignore the fact that a miraculous healing has taken place. They only note the fact that the man is violating the Sabbath by carrying his bed (pallet). Rather than asking who healed him, they want to know who told him to violate the Sabbath by carrying his bed. A religion-shaped spirituality doesn't like to have its rules interrupted by the miraculous, or disobeyed . . . even by God!

For his part, the newly healed man hadn't learned Jesus' identity before He slipped away in the crowd. Later (we don't know how much later), Jesus finds the man in the Temple and says, *"See, you are well! Sin no more, that nothing worse may happen to you."* It is a curious statement which suggests that the newly healed man is not yet a believer in Jesus. He has been healed, but he remains a spiritually blind sinner. Unless he repents of his sin and believes, something far worse than any physical affliction awaits him: eternal death.

In the Kingdom of God, miracles, such as this man's healing, evoke one of two basic responses. On the one hand, miracles cause some to believe and to follow Jesus. This happened at the wedding in Cana where the miraculous transformation of water into wine causes the disciples to believe in Jesus. It happened again in Cana when Jesus healed the Nobleman's child who lay dying in Capernaum. On the other hand, miracles cause some people to question what they have seen or experienced, and to turn Jesus in to the authorities. The newly healed man gave no evidence of faith in Jesus, but he did return to the religious leaders,

In the Kingdom of God, miracles, such as this man's healing, evoke one of two basic responses.

"The man went away and told the Jews that it was Jesus who had healed him." The stage was now set for a confrontation between Jesus and "the Jews" over the issue of the Sabbath, and that is where we need to go next.

The Sabbath

In a previous Lesson we discovered how teaching in the Synagogues of Galilee on the Sabbath was Jesus' regular practice (see Lesson 18). Throughout His ministry Jesus used His Sabbath teaching and healing to directly challenge the religion-shaped spirituality of 1st Century Judaism. Starting with this incident at the Pool of Bethesda, Jesus' Sabbath activities now become a point of controversy between Himself and the religious authorities. Their priority was to maintain their religion-shaped spirituality (which Jesus now threatened). Jesus' priority was to manifest the life transforming power of the Kingdom of God. The stage was now set for both a confrontation and a lesson in Kingdom discipleship. But to better understand both the confrontation and the lesson we need to take a moment and briefly review the nature of the Sabbath, both in Scripture and in 1st Century Judaism.

The Hebrew word "sabbath" means "cessation" or "rest." The first mention of a Sabbath day occurs in Exodus 16:23ff (prior to the giving of the Law) where the Israelites were forbidden from gathering or preparing manna on the Sabbath. The Fourth Commandment of the Decalogue says, *"Remember the sabbath day, to keep it holy. Six days you shall labor and do all your work, but the seventh day is a Sabbath of the Lord your God; in it you shall not do any work, you or your son or your daughter, your male or your female servant or your cattle or your sojourner who stays with you. For in six days the Lord made the heavens and the earth, the sea and all that is in them, and rested on the seventh day; therefore the Lord blessed the Sabbath day and made it holy."* (Exodus 20:8-11) No work was to be done on the Sabbath on penalty of death (See Exodus 31:12-17; Numbers 15:32-36).

But there's a problem. What constituted work? After all, there is no biblical prohibition anywhere in the Law against carrying one's bed.[73] If someone gathering manna or firewood on the Sabbath could be subject to death (see Numbers 15:32-36), what other activities might bring a similar punishment? In order to solve this problem of defining what constituted "work" the Rabbis over the centuries had created 39 categories of prohibited activities which were regarded as work and were not to be performed on the Sabbath, including carrying an item from one domicile to another (i.e., the bed). Over time, all of these "traditions of the elders" came to be regarded as Law. This was the history and the context when "the Jews" (i.e., John's name for the Jewish religious leaders) told the formerly lame man that he was violating the Sabbath, because *"it is not lawful for you to take up your bed."* No such biblical prohibition existed, but by Jesus' day it didn't matter. Why? Because the Rabbis taught that it existed, and for a religion-shaped spirituality, that was sufficient.

Beyond this profound biblical disconnect, something else was noteworthy by its absence. Absent from the exchange is any recognition by the religious leaders that a significant miraculous sign has taken place, that a son of Abraham has been healed, and that God has been at work in their midst, calling them to repentance and faith. They have become so entrenched in the religion-shaped spirituality of their regulations and traditions that they are now

Their religious regulations and traditions have become more important to them than either God's activity or people's needs.

spiritually blind to the reality of God working in their midst. Their religious regulations and traditions have become more important to them than either God's activity or people's needs. And for Jesus, such willful spiritual blindness could not go unchallenged.

Six Sabbath Controversies

Throughout His ministry Jesus relentlessly challenged the spiritual blindness of this religion-shaped spirituality. It would be a mistake for us to read this passage and to conclude that this Sabbath controversy was a minor issue, or a "one off" (as our British friends might say). It was neither. The nature of the Sabbath lay at the heart of 1st Century Judaism. But from within the spiritual blindness of its religion-shaped spirituality, 1st Century Judaism had come to regard the Sabbath as a taskmaster rather than as a servant; a Law to be obeyed, rather than a rest to be enjoyed. In order to set people free from the servile fear such spiritual blindness creates, Jesus used six Sabbath encounters with Jewish religious leaders to challenge their religion-shaped spirituality to its breaking point.

1.   Healing A Crippled Man At The Pool of Bethesda (John 5:1-18)
2.   Picking Grain On The Sabbath (Matthew 12:1-8; Mark 2:23-28; Luke 6:1-5)
3.   Healing a Man With A Withered Hand (Matthew 12:9-14; Mark 3:1-6; Luke 6:6-11)
4.   Healing A Woman With A Disabling Spirit (Luke 13:10-17)
5.   Healing A Man With Dropsy (Luke 14:1-6)
6.   Healing A Man Born Blind (John 9)

Jesus had no desire - and made no effort - to uphold the erroneous teachings of the Rabbis concerning the Sabbath. From the perspective of the Rabbis, man was made for the Sabbath. Contrary to the teaching of the Rabbis, Jesus understood that the Sabbath was made for man, to give him freedom and rest. And what better freedom and rest could there be for someone who has been lame for 38 years than to be healed. And what better day for such a healing and such a gift of freedom than the Sabbath. But there was more. With Jesus, there always is.

The Sabbath And The Kingdom

Jesus' message went deeper than explaining which activities could or could not be performed on this day versus that day. Jesus had come to bring the Kingdom, and the Kingdom transforms everything it touches, including the Sabbath. The Sabbath was to the Kingdom what the Passover was to the sacrificial death of Jesus - a prophetic type and shadow of things to come. Up until the coming of Jesus, the people of God had experienced the type and the shadow every Sabbath Day. All of that was about to change under the fulfilling and transforming power of the Kingdom.

In the Kingdom of God, the Sabbath would no longer be a day to be religiously observed on pain of death. In fact, in the Kingdom of God, the Sabbath would no longer be a day at all, but a spiritual rest of faith, *"So then, there remains a Sabbath rest for the people of God, for whoever has entered God's rest has also rested from his works as God did from His."* (Hebrews 4:9-10) To enter into the Kingdom of God by faith and the new birth is to enter into God's true Sabbath rest for His

> *To enter into the Kingdom of God by faith is to move from type and shadow to fulfillment and substance.*

people. In the Kingdom of God the Sabbath would no longer be observed on *a* day, but on **every** day. To enter into the Kingdom of God by faith is to move from type and shadow to fulfillment and substance.[74] To be a disciple of the Kingdom is to enter in to God's Sabbath rest, because the Kingdom *IS* the Sabbath. And this was the greater lesson Jesus wanted His disciples to understand and embrace.

When it comes to our discipleship in the Kingdom of God, some lessons must be repeated to be learned. A religion-shaped spirituality which challenged Jesus and openly declared, *"There are six days in which work ought to be done. Come on those days and be healed, and not on the Sabbath day"* (Luke 13:14) would not yield itself easily to the transforming truth of the Kingdom. And so this Sabbath lesson must be repeated (six times). As a wise master sculptor, Jesus would chisel away on His disciples and their religion-shaped spirituality, eventually replacing it with a spirituality molded and shaped around Jesus Himself, and fit for life in the Kingdom of God. But there was more. With Jesus, there always is.

A Claim To Deity (John 5:16-18)

"And this was why the Jews were persecuting Jesus, because he was doing these things on the Sabbath. But Jesus answered them, 'My Father is working until now, and I am working.' This was why the Jews were seeking all the more to kill him, because not only was he breaking the Sabbath, but he was even calling God his own Father, making himself equal with God." (John 5:16-18)

The religious leadership of Jesus' day had a problem, which Jesus now made the effort to point out. The Rabbis had consistently taught that God maintains the universe without breaking the Sabbath. Jesus now appealed to that teaching to explain His own Sabbath activity. Jesus' argument was a simple one: Only God could work without violating the Sabbath. Jesus was working on the Sabbath without violating it, just as God, His Father, does. Conclusion: Jesus was *"calling God his own Father, making himself equal with God."* To claim the ability to work on the Sabbath just as God does is to claim equality with God. This was a direct claim to deity by Jesus, and the religious leaders understood.

Jesus, the Rabbi from Nazareth, was working on the Sabbath and claiming equality with God, disrupting all of their carefully constructed religious regulations and traditions in the process. If His claims were true, then the Messiah was truly among them with divine authority, not merely to work on the Sabbath, but to re-interpret the meaning of the Sabbath in terms of the Kingdom of God. If His claims were true, then many things - if not everything - in 1st Century Judaism would have to change. But people who hold tightly to their religion-shaped spirituality don't like to be challenged with change. Not even by God. And so, the religious leaders responded to Jesus' Sabbath working with unbelief and hostility. They continually sought to persecute Him for healing on the Sabbath. And they continually sought to kill him for blasphemy; for claiming equality with God. [75]

What The Disciples Learned That Day

At moments like this it is important to remember that everything Jesus did He did with an eye toward the training and equipping of His disciples. They were His audience for this lesson. The religious authorities who questioned Him, or the multitudes which followed Him, might provide the backdrop for a lesson on the Kingdom, but they were never His primary audience, or even His target. The disciples were His focus, and what they learned from each encounter was His primary concern. And that included the lessons of this day at the Pool of Bethesda. On this day the disciples found themselves confronted with several lessons at once.

A Lesson Concerning Unbound Compassion. On this day the disciples undoubtedly learned something about the compassion of Jesus for those who are suffering, along with His power to heal. This was not a new lesson. They had seen it before, and would see it again. But on this day the disciples discovered that Jesus would not allow His power or His compassion to be bound by men's religious rules and traditions, or by their misunderstanding of Scripture. Jesus was bringing the Kingdom to set men free, not to allow Himself - or them - to be bound by myths about angels, or by the religious rules and regulations of men concerning the Sabbath.

A Lesson Concerning Jesus Deity And Authority. At the height of this confrontation with the religious authorities, the disciples heard Jesus openly claim what they had already come to believe, or at least to suspect. Jesus was God-incarnate, possessing and exercising full equality with the Father. And as God-incarnate, Jesus the Creator was unwilling to allow the creature to tell the Creator what His Laws - particularly concerning the Sabbath - did or did not mean. Jesus could have demonstrated His compassion by healing this paralytic at the Pool of Bethesda on any day of the week. After all, the man had been there a long time, and Jesus knew it. Chances were good he would be there tomorrow, or next week. So, why heal him on the Sabbath? Jesus healed him on the Sabbath because of the challenge it would present to the religion-shaped spirituality of 1st Century Judaism, and for the lesson His disciples would learn as a result of that challenge.

A Lesson Concerning The Kingdom And The Sabbath. On this day the disciples began to discern the outline of a lesson which would grow and mature in their awareness as they witnessed Jesus' ministry. Jesus and the Kingdom are the substance of which the Sabbath and the Law were the type and the shadow. The Kingdom *IS* the Sabbath. Jesus *IS* our Sabbath rest. Jesus is both King and Lord of the Sabbath. He alone possesses both the authority and the power to fulfill and re-define the true meaning of the Sabbath and to transform crippling Sabbath traditions and regulations into health, freedom and rest. Jesus embodies the substance and the fulfillment of everything the Law and the Prophets had promised, but were unable to deliver. Until

> *The Kingdom IS the Sabbath. Jesus IS our Sabbath rest. Jesus is both King and Lord of the Sabbath.*

now.

A Lesson Concerning Religious Power And Authority. For the disciples much of this day must have felt like *"de ja vu all over again."* It wasn't the first Sabbath Day they had spent With Jesus, watching Him heal the sick and deliver the demonized. Now it was happening again. And once again, Jesus' disciples found themselves confronted with a profound contrast. The religious leaders of Jesus' day possessed a pseudo-authority given to them by their religious position, but they lacked the supernatural, spiritual power which Jesus demonstrated. The religious authorities could condemn a man for carrying his pallet on the Sabbath, but they had no power to heal him of the affliction that imprisoned him on the pallet in the first place. Religious authority without spiritual power creates a religion-shaped spirituality with the power to imprison those who are free, but no power to free those who are prisoners (Matthew 23:13ff). This was a lesson which the disciples needed to learn, again. Which explains why this particular lesson in Kingdom discipleship was not yet over. There was more. With Jesus, there always is.

Questions For Reflection

Reflecting on this Lesson, what did you learn about Jesus, the Sabbath and the Kingdom of God that you did not know before?

Reflecting on this Lesson, how do we allow misplaced religious authority and religious traditions to cripple our relationship With Jesus, and the Kingdom?

Key Thought

To enter the Kingdom of God by faith is to move from type and shadow to fulfillment and substance. It is to enter into God's Sabbath rest, because the Kingdom is the Sabbath.

And They Dreamt Of A Kingdom

24 - By What Authority?

"So Jesus said to them, 'Truly, truly, I say to you, the Son can do nothing of his own accord, but only what he sees the Father doing. For whatever the Father does, that the Son does likewise. For the Father loves the Son and shows him all that he himself is doing. And greater works than these will he show him, so that you may marvel. For as the Father raises the dead and gives them life, so also the Son gives life to whom he will." (John 5:19-21)

Discipleship Reading: *John 5:19-47*　　　　　　**When:** *Fall, A.D. 28*
Contextual Reading: *John 5*　　　　　　　　　　**Where:** *Jerusalem*

A Lesson Continued

　　　　Jesus was not yet finished with either His disciples or the religious leaders who had questioned His Sabbath "work." The lesson at hand was so important that Jesus extended it beyond what we would have expected. Having claimed equality with the Father and the right to work on the Sabbath, just as the Father does, a claim which the religious leaders rejected, Jesus now addressed the underlying question which would follow His ministry for the next two years, reaching its climax in a confrontation with the religious rulers of Israel during the week of His crucifixion, *"And when he entered the temple, the chief priests and the elders of the people came up to him as he was teaching, and said, 'By what authority are you doing these things, and who gave you this authority?'"* (Matthew 21:23)

By What Authority?

　　　　The question of authority wasn't new. It didn't even begin with Jesus. It had started with John the Baptizer when the religious leaders from Jerusalem sent representatives to question John about his ministry, *"And this is the testimony of John, when the Jews sent priests and Levites from Jerusalem to ask him, 'Who are you?'"* (John 1:19) To ask *"Who are you?"* is to ask *"What is your authority?"* because authority is "positional." It's like asking *"What position do you hold that gives you the authority to do what you are doing?"* The question first arose in earnest in Jesus' ministry in Luke 5 (which we examined earlier) when Jesus forgave the sins of the paralytic brought to Him for healing, *"And the scribes and the Pharisees began to question, saying, 'Who is this who speaks blasphemies? Who can forgive sins but God alone?'"* (Luke 5:21) Jesus proceeded to demonstrate his authority to forgive sins (thereby claiming to be God) by healing the paralytic.

　　　　Now, at the Pool of Bethesda, the issue was arising again. It was implied, but it was there. *"'Who is the man who said to you, 'Take up your bed and walk?'"* That was the question the religious leaders asked the former paralytic. In other words, *"What position gave him the authority to do this?"* Jesus' initial response to this challenge was eloquently simple: *"I am only doing those works which my Father Himself does on the Sabbath."* In one simple response Jesus addressed both the issue of His position and His authority. His position and His authority were those of an obedient Son in perfect submission to His Father. And the Jewish religious authorities understood the meaning of Jesus' response. This represented a claim to equality with the Father. It was a claim to deity. [76]

And They Dreamt Of A Kingdom

Things Only God Can Do

If Jesus had simply stopped at this point and said nothing more, His declaration would have presented a "game changing" moment for the Jewish religious authorities. If Jesus' declaration was true, then the twin issues of His position and His authority - including His authority both to heal on the Sabbath and to re-interpret the meaning of the Sabbath -

If Jesus can do those things which only God Himself can do, then Jesus must be God.

would be definitively settled. But, this was another "teachable moment," particularly in the lives of His watching disciples. So, like the master teacher He was, Jesus pressed the advantage of the moment to underscore a basic point: If Jesus can do those things which only God Himself can do, then Jesus must be God.

The logic of the argument is clear. If the premise is valid (Jesus can do those things which only God Himself can do), then the conclusion must also be true (Jesus must be God). To demonstrate the validity of His claim to equality with the Father, Jesus offers a series of divine attributes and activities which the Jewish religious leaders would all agree could only apply to God, all of which Jesus now claims to share with the Father:

1. Jesus gives eternal life (John 5:21);
2. Jesus has authority to execute judgement (John 5:22);
3. Jesus deserves the same honor as God the Father, failure to honor Jesus is to fail to honor God (John 5:23);
4. Jesus' voice (i.e., hearing His voice) gives eternal life (John 5:24);
5. Jesus' voice (i.e., hearing His voice) is the difference between a resurrection of life and a resurrection of judgment (John 5:28-29);
6. The Scriptures speak of Jesus (John 5:39).

This was a critical moment. The religion-shaped spirituality of 1st Century Judaism, along with the pseudo-authority of its leadership, was being directly challenged by God Himself in the Person of Jesus, the Messiah-King. Jesus now drew the spiritual dividing line which would define His ministry for the next two years, dividing faith from unbelief, divine authority from religious authority, and obedience from rebellion. On one side of the line stands Jesus the Messiah-King and the Kingdom of God. On the other side of the line stands everyone and everything else. Everything the religious leaders of 1st Century Judaism would do in response to Jesus from this point forward would confirm their place on one side

For Jesus, this wasn't about the Sabbath. It was about the Kingdom, and the authority of the Messiah-King to rule His Kingdom on His terms.

of that line or the other. They must now decide whether to fall back on their own religious pseudo-authority, or to acknowledge and submit to the divine authority of the Rabbi from Nazareth who now stands before them, claiming to be God, Messiah and King. At stake is nothing less than their eternal destiny in the Kingdom of God.

For Jesus, this wasn't about the Sabbath. It was about the Kingdom, and the authority of the Messiah-King to rule His Kingdom on His terms. As God-incarnate He has the authority to do what He has been doing on the Sabbath. He has the authority to heal the sick, to deliver the demonized and more. He also has the authority to nullify the "traditions of the elders," and in the process, to re-interpret the Law in terms of the Kingdom of God. For Jesus, this wasn't about the Sabbath. It was about whether or not the religious leaders of 1st Century Judaism were willing to abandon their religious rebellion and pseudo-authority and to submit themselves to the genuine authority of the Messiah-King. In the Kingdom of God, rebellion is like the sin of witchcraft, and to obey is better than all of the sacrifices offered at the Temple (1 Samuel 15:22-23).

A man in rebellion to God's authority may continue to offer sacrifices, or even to "keep" the Sabbath. But such a man (or woman) has lost the meaning of the Sabbath, confusing the type and shadow with the substance. The type and shadow can be controlled and manipulated, but the Substance demands submission and obedience. A man in rebellion keeps the Sabbath on his own terms and in obedience to his own man-made rules and regulations, not God's. Such a religion-shaped spirituality eventually becomes a convenient mask for self-worship and rebellion against God's authority. To truly worship and obey God is to submit to God's authority in our lives, to repent of our sins, and to abandon any religion-shaped spirituality we have created to mask our rebellion.

> *A man in rebellion to God's authority may continue to offer sacrifices, or even to "keep" the Sabbath.*

Five Witnesses

Under Old Testament Law, claims, assertions and accusations were to be confirmed by the testimony of at least two witnesses (primarily in cases of capital murder, see Deuteronomy 17:6-7). Aware of this background, and that He might be accused of making unsubstantiated claims (John 5:31), Jesus offers five "witnesses" which offer "testimony" to confirm His claims to deity. [77]

1. The Testimony of John, the Baptizer (John 5:32-35);
2. The Testimony of the very works He is doing, things only God can do (John 5:36);
3. The Testimony of the Father Himself (John 5:37-38);
4. The Testimony of the Scriptures (John 5:39);
5. The Testimony of Moses (John 5:46-47).

Jesus' argument (a declaration might be a better description) to the religious leaders was simple and profound. He has the authority to heal on the Sabbath because He enjoys equality with God, His Father, Who also works on the Sabbath. His equality with the Father is evidenced by His ability to do those things which only God can do. And His claim to equality (and therefore Deity) is confirmed by multiple witnesses who cannot be impugned. The unavoidable conclusion? Jesus is Messiah, King and God, enjoying equality with the Father. He is Immanuel, "God with us." If this claim is true, then He has the authority to do what He does on the Sabbath. But such a claim is greater than the Sabbath. Such a claim is life encompassing, and life changing. It means that Jesus has authority to re-interpret the Law (which He will soon do) and to fulfill it on His terms, not theirs. He has authority to challenge the religion-shaped spirituality of 1st Century Judaism to its breaking point, and to replace it with a spirituality formed, shaped and modeled around Himself . . . and Him alone.

The spiritual line marking the separation between faith and unbelief has been unmistakably drawn. On one side of that line stands Jesus. On the other side of that line stands everyone and everything else. For the next year and a half, Jesus' public ministry would represent the Q.E.D. of His claims to Messiahship, Kingship and Deity, and of His call to *"repent and believe the good news"* of the Kingdom.[78]

A Lesson Concerning Spirituality and Authority

This was a "line in the sand" moment for everyone involved, but especially for Jesus' disciples. Imagine being the disciples at this moment in time, hearing the Teacher you have walked with for more than a year declare that He is Messiah, King and God, enjoying equality with the Father. This Rabbi with whom you have shared days, nights, meals and journeys now claims the authority of the Father to judge all men and to determine their eternal destiny. The growing crowds surrounding Jesus would prove themselves fickle and their belief in Jesus would ebb and flow with the tide of popular events and religious opinion. The Jewish religious leaders, for the most part, would never "cross the line" from unbelief to faith, if doing so jeopardized their religious or political authority over the masses. But neither the crowds nor the religious leaders were the real the focus of Jesus' declaration on this day. The disciples were His audience. Forsaking all other authorities, they must embrace Jesus' authority, allowing Him and Him alone to shape their spirituality from this day forward.

Each of us lives out a spirituality which has been shaped by whatever or whoever exercises authority over us. If religious men and religious organizations are our spiritual authority, then we will walk in a religion-shaped spirituality which reflects those people and those organizations. If Jesus is our spiritual authority, then at the end of the day our obedience to Him will manifest a Jesus-shaped spirituality which reflects Him. In the Kingdom of God, our discipleship expresses who or what exercises spiritual authority over our lives. This is as true of us as it was of Jesus' disciples.

In the Kingdom of God, our discipleship expresses who or what exercises spiritual authority over our lives.

We are never told how the disciples responded to the lesson of this day. We simply know that they did respond, and that Jesus became the sole spiritual authority in their lives. We know this for two reasons. **First**, we know it because they continued on in their discipleship with Jesus. It would have been all but impossible to do so without acknowledging both His claim and His authority. **Second**, we know it because others saw it and commented on it. The day would soon come, following Jesus death, resurrection and ascension, when the Jewish religious authorities would challenge the disciples with the same question they had posed to Jesus, *"And when they had set them in the midst, they inquired, 'By what power or by what name did you do this?'"* (Acts 4:7). In other words, *"What is your authority?"*

After a moment of reflection, the truth dawned on the religious leaders, *"Now when they saw the boldness of Peter and John, and perceived that they were uneducated, common men, they were astonished. And they recognized that they had been with Jesus"* (Acts 4:13). The focus and foundation of their authority had profoundly changed, from institutional religious Judaism and its religion-shaped spirituality to Jesus. He had become their authority in all things. *"But Peter and John answered them, 'Whether it is right in the sight of God to listen to you rather than to God, you must judge, for we cannot but speak of what we have seen and heard'"* (Acts 4:19-20). Welcome to the heart of biblical discipleship in the Kingdom of God. Jesus is King. He is our authority.

Questions For Reflection

Reflecting on this Lesson, what did you learn about the claims of Jesus that you did not know before? How have you responded to those claims?

Reflecting on this Lesson, who exercises spiritual authority over your life? Who shapes your spirituality? Jesus the King, or someone else?

Key Thought

In the Kingdom of God, our discipleship expresses who or what exercises spiritual authority over our lives.

And They Dreamt Of A Kingdom

25 - Two Sabbath Confrontations

"At that time Jesus went through the grainfields on the Sabbath. His disciples were hungry, and they began to pluck heads of grain and to eat. But when the Pharisees saw it, they said to him, 'Look, your disciples are doing what is not lawful to do on the Sabbath.'" (Matthew 12:1-2)

Discipleship Reading: *Matthew 12:1-12*   **When:** *Spring, A.D. 29*
Contextual Reading: *Matthew 12; Mark 2-3; Luke 6*   **Where:** *Galilee*

The Feast of Booths and the incident with the lame man at the Pool of Bethesda have passed. It is now sometime in the Spring of A.D. 29, and Jesus and His disciples have returned to Galilee. We discovered earlier in Lesson 18 that Jesus' normal, on-going practice was to teach and heal in the Synagogues of Galilee on the Sabbath. This teaching and healing ministry eventually brought Him to the attention of the Pharisees, the religious leaders who oversaw Synagogue activities. By the time Jesus healed the lame man at the Pool of Bethesda on the Sabbath, Jesus' Sabbath activities had already been reported to the authorities in Jerusalem (which helps explain why their interactions with Jesus in that episode were so contentious). Now, back in Galilee, Jesus has two more Sabbath Day encounters with the Pharisees.

We need to be reminded of just how important the Sabbath Day observance was to ancient Israel. Judaism regarded Sabbath observance as one of its defining characteristics, setting Israel apart from other peoples in New Testament times. Leon Morris points out, *"The Jews took the Sabbath observance very seriously. Thus when the enemy attacked on the Sabbath in the days of the Maccabees they, they let themselves be slaughtered, men, women, and children, rather than break the Sabbath by defending themselves (1 Macc. 2:31-38). At a later time Pompey was able to erect the earthworks that made his siege of Jerusalem successful quite unhindered by the defenders because he did it on the Sabbath (Josephus, Ant. 14.63). The Jews were ready to suffer rather than break the Sabbath."*[79]

Jesus' Authority Challenged (Matthew 12:1-8)

Our present passage finds Jesus and the disciples walking through a grain field on the Sabbath, probably on their way to the local Synagogue where Jesus intended to teach (see 12:9). Along the way, the disciples pluck some heads of grain, rub it in their hands (to remove the chaff) and begin to eat the grain because they are hungry. A contingent of Pharisees (who were apparently shadowing and observing Jesus) confront Jesus and accuse the disciples of violating the Sabbath laws. All acts of preparing food on the Sabbath were prohibited, including the reaping, threshing, and winnowing of grain.

In the prior incident involving the healing of the lame man at the Pool of Bethesda, Jesus had claimed equality with God. By doing so He also claimed authority over the Sabbath, including the authority to decide both its meaning and its proper observance in terms of the Kingdom. That incident represented the beginning of Jesus' Sabbath confrontations with the Pharisees. It is difficult to imagine that the news of that incident had not spread through the community of Pharisees. It is quite possible (although we cannot say for certain) that some of the Pharisees following Jesus around now in Galilee had witnessed the incident at the Pool of Bethesda. They had rejected His claim to authority over the Sabbath then, and were challenging His authority now. Rather than simply reasserting His claim to authority over the Sabbath, Jesus responds to this challenge by offering a five part rebuttal to their accusation.

1. The Example Of David (12:3-4). *"He said to them, 'Have you not read what David did when he was hungry, and those who were with him: how he entered the house of God and ate the bread of the Presence, which it was not lawful for him to eat nor for those who were with him, but only for the priests?'"* Jesus begins by accusing the Pharisees of ignorance concerning biblical history, *"Have you not read what David did?"* Jesus was referring to the incident found in 1 Samuel 21. When fleeing from King Saul, David had taken the "Bread of the Presence" from the tabernacle for his men who were hungry. According to the Law of the Tabernacle, this bread was "holy" (i.e., set apart for God's purposes) and could only be eaten by the Priests (see Leviticus 24:5-9). But David and his men had taken and eaten this bread without condemnation either by Ahimelech, the Priest (who knew the Law), or by the writers of Scripture. If David's authority and the need of his men were sufficient to suspend the regulations concerning the "Bread of the Presence," how much more are Jesus' authority (as the Davidic Messiah) and the need of His disciples sufficient to suspend the Law regarding the Sabbath.

2. The Teaching Of The Law (12:5). *"Or have you not read in the Law how on the Sabbath the priests in the temple profane the Sabbath and are guiltless?"* Jesus' next step in His rebuttal is to accuse the Pharisees of not knowing the Law, an accusation that must have stung! Jesus is referring to the fact that on the Sabbath the Priests who serve in the Temple continue the duties assigned to them by the Law, including the sacrificial services, without violating the Sabbath. Simply put, the Law itself provided for exceptions to Sabbath observance. The Pharisees knew this, but they ignored it. [80]

3. The Arrival of "Something Greater" (12:6). *"I tell you, something greater than the temple is here."* This next step in Jesus' rebuttal represented nothing less than a "bombshell" for His listeners. As France observes, *"It is hard to overestimate the shock value of this pronouncement. The tabernacle set up under God's directions in the wilderness, and the fixed temple which had succeeded it, were understood to be the focus of God's relation with his people. The temple was more than a place of worship. It was a symbol of nationhood."* [81] Jesus' ongoing challenges regarding the temple come to symbolize His challenge to the status quo of 1st Century Judaism. In His "Olivet Discourse" (Matthew 24) Jesus will explain how the future destruction of the temple embodies God's judgment on the religion-shaped spirituality of the old status quo. And it will be Jesus' attitude toward the temple which will form the primary charge brought against Him at His trial (Matthew 26:59-61).

Jesus' declaration concerning "something greater" begs for a question and an answer. *Question:* What could possibly be greater than the temple or the Sabbath? *Answer:* the Kingdom of God. As we noted earlier in Lesson 11, *"The 'jealous zeal' of Jesus was not for a building, and certainly not for a Temple building which He knew would be reduced to a pile of rubble not many years later."* In the person of Jesus, a "greater than David" had arrived, namely, the long-promised Davidic Messiah-King. And He brought with Him

The arrival of the Kingdom transforms everything it touches, including both the Temple and the Sabbath.

something greater than the temple, namely, the long-promised Kingdom of God. The arrival of the Kingdom transforms everything it touches, including both the Temple and the Sabbath. The presence of God would no longer dwell in or be confined to a Temple made with hands (Acts 7:48). The Kingdom transforms the temple from a physical building made of stones to a spiritual building built with "living stones," disciples of the Kingdom, who embody a "spiritual house" and "a holy priesthood," as Peter would later describe, *"As you come to him, a living stone rejected by men but in the sight of God chosen and precious, you yourselves like living stones are being built up as a spiritual house, to be a holy priesthood, to offer spiritual sacrifices acceptable to God through Jesus Christ"* (1 Peter 2:4-5). And the coming of the Kingdom of God transforms the Sabbath from a day to be religiously observed on pain of punishment, to a spiritual rest of faith to be experienced and enjoyed every day. The Kingdom *IS* the Sabbath; the spiritual fulfillment of everything promised by the type and shadow of the Law.

4. The Purpose of The Sabbath (12:7). *"And if you had known what this means, 'I desire mercy, and not sacrifice,' you would not have condemned the guiltless."* Jesus continues His rebuttal by accusing the Pharisees of failing to understand the words of God to His people through the Prophet Hosea, *"For I desire steadfast love and not sacrifice, the knowledge of God rather than burnt offerings"* (Hosea 6:6). Jesus accuses the Pharisees of failing to understand the heart of God and the purpose of the Sabbath. He declares them guilty of the same sin which God condemned in the leaders of ancient Israel: substituting religious ritual (sacrifice and offerings) for the true knowledge of God, and failing to understand His mercy.

> *A religion-shaped spirituality finds guilt and disobedience where none exists.*

A religion-shaped spirituality finds guilt and disobedience where none exists. In their religious zeal the Pharisees were willing to ignore human need and condemn seven hungry men for plucking, crushing and eating a handful of grain on the Sabbath. In sharp contrast, the Jesus-shaped spirituality of the Kingdom finds need and extends mercy. The Jesus-shaped spirituality of the Kingdom emphasizes the mercy of God over all such misplaced religious observances. With the arrival of the Kingdom, God will no longer dwell in a physical temple made of stones. No. He will now dwell but in a spiritual temple made of "living stones," disciples of the Kingdom, who will experience the true knowledge of God and will understand His great mercy toward those in need.

5. The Messiah As Lord Of The Sabbath (12:8). *"For the Son of Man is lord of the Sabbath."* Jesus' rebuttal of the Pharisees now reaches its culmination as He revisits a point which He had made during the healing of the lame man at the Pool of Bethesda. Equality with the Father, which Jesus claimed and explained at length during that episode, means that Jesus is "lord of the Sabbath." Lordship over the Sabbath means that Jesus, not the Rabbis, the Scribes or the Pharisees, has the authority to determine the true meaning of the Sabbath.

Jesus' Authority Demonstrated (Matthew 12:9-14)

"He went on from there and entered their synagogue. And a man was there with a withered hand. And they asked him, 'Is it lawful to heal on the Sabbath?'—so that they might accuse him. He said to them, 'Which one of you who has a sheep, if it falls into a pit on the Sabbath, will not take hold of it and lift it out? Of how much

And They Dreamt Of A Kingdom

more value is a man than a sheep! So it is lawful to do good on the Sabbath.' Then he said to the man, 'Stretch out your hand.' And the man stretched it out, and it was restored, healthy like the other. But the Pharisees went out and conspired against him, how to destroy him." (Matthew 12:9-14)

Jesus' confrontation with the Pharisees now moves from the field to the Synagogue. And the demonstration of His authority over the Sabbath now moves from the theological to the practical. Some twenty-five years after the events of this day, the Apostle Paul will write to the disciples in the Greek city of Corinth and tell them that the Kingdom of God does not consist simply of words, but of power (1 Corinthians 4:20). On this Sabbath day in a Synagogue in Galilee, Jesus will demonstrate the truth of what the Apostle Paul will later teach.

Having rejected Jesus' claim to authority, the Pharisees are not done challenging Jesus concerning the "lawfulness" of His healing activity on the Sabbath. They are stuck in their religion-shaped spirituality and refuse to let it go, even when challenged by the Messiah-King. Using the presence in the Synagogue of a man with a withered hand, they challenge Jesus directly, *"Is it lawful to heal on the Sabbath?"* Earlier, in His rebuttal of the Pharisees, Jesus had argued that God is more concerned with mercy than religious ritual. Now, Jesus applies that principle, comparing the mercy the average person would show toward a distressed sheep on the Sabbath to the mercy God would show toward a distressed man on the Sabbath. Jesus' conclusion reflects God's mercy: *"So it is lawful to do good on the Sabbath."* Doing good on the Sabbath, by healing someone with a withered hand (or a man who had been lame for 38 years), expresses both the goodness and the mercy of God.

Jesus' appeal to mercy and doing good did not go over well with the Pharisees. Luke tells us that the Pharisees were "furious" (Luke 6:11). The Greek word (*anoia*) literally means to be "without understanding." Here, it describes being "out of one's mind" or "beside oneself" with anger. The ESV renders it as "fury." In his account of this incident, Mark tells us that Jesus, for His part, was both angered and grieved by their lack of responsiveness, *"And he (Jesus) looked around at them with anger, grieved at their hardness of heart"* (Mark 3:5).[82] What does it say about us when our religious hardness-of-heart earns Jesus' anger and grief? Are we so spiritually blind that we are unwilling and unable to let go of our religion-shaped spirituality and to embrace the mercy of God in doing good toward those in need?

This encounter ends on a disturbing note that foreshadows things to come. Rather than approving of the healing, celebrating God's mercy and acknowledging Jesus' authority, the Pharisees begin to plot Jesus' demise, *"the Pharisees went out and conspired against him, how to destroy him."*

Epilogue (Matthew 12:15-21)

"Jesus, aware of this, withdrew from there. And many followed him, and he healed them all and ordered them not to make him known. This was to fulfill what was spoken by the prophet Isaiah: 'Behold, my servant whom I have chosen, my beloved with whom my soul is well pleased. I will put my Spirit upon him, and he will proclaim justice to the Gentiles. He will not quarrel or cry aloud, nor will anyone hear his voice in the streets; a bruised reed he will not break, and a smoldering wick he will not quench, until he brings justice to victory; and in his name the Gentiles will hope.'" (Matthew 12:15-21)

The biblical writer could have ended his account of this day at verse 14 with the plotting of the Pharisees to destroy Jesus. But, instead, Matthew offers us some perspective regarding Jesus' ministry. **First,** Matthew wants us to see that Jesus' ministry of healing on the Sabbath fulfills the prophetic promise of Scripture given through Israel's greatest prophet, Isaiah. By both word and deed on this day, Jesus has demonstrated Himself to be God's chosen servant; beloved and well-pleasing to God and anointed with His Spirit, just as Isaiah had promised 700 years earlier.

Second, Jesus has demonstrated Himself to be the hope of the Gentiles (all non-Jews). Jesus brings the Kingdom. And the hope of the Kingdom is not circumcision, temple worship or Sabbath-keeping. While such things may be distinctive characteristics of God's Old Testament people, the Jews, such things mean nothing to the Gentiles. The Kingdom of God is not about offering the Gentiles the Law and a religion-shaped spirituality on steroids. The Kingdom of God is about the true knowledge of God, expressed through His love and mercy toward those in need, and embraced by faith by all who trust in His Name as disciples of the Kingdom. The Kingdom of God is not about ritual religious observances, but about righteousness, peace and joy in the Holy Spirit (Romans 14:17).

What The Disciples Learned This Day

Jesus' disciples undoubtedly learned several important lessons on this day. They certainly experienced the next installment of a continuing lesson concerning Jesus' authority, a lesson which had begun during the episode of the lame man at the Pool of Bethesda. On this day the disciples also learned a lesson concerning God's mercy toward those in need, even on the Sabbath. And on this day the disciples learned a lesson concerning the genuine characteristics of all who profess to be disciples of the Kingdom. The disciples learned that those things which historically set Israel apart from the other nations, things such as circumcision, Temple worship, dietary laws and Sabbath observance, would no longer define the true people of God. In as little as 40 years the Temple

> *The true lesson of this day was about the Kingdom of God, and the power of the Kingdom to transform everything it touches, and every person who embraces the Kingdom by faith.*

would be gone, along with temple worship. Sabbath observance would steadily decline in the life of the church, especially among Gentile believers.[83] Disciples of the Kingdom would gather for worship in diverse places (frequently in private homes), and they would gather on the first day of the week (rather than the seventh or Sabbath) in honor of the Resurrection (see Acts 20:7; 1 Corinthians 1:2).[84]

But, perhaps the greatest lesson of this day wasn't about temples, Sabbath rules or anything else that religious men understand and value. The true lesson of this day was about the Kingdom of God, and the power of the Kingdom to transform everything it touches, and every person who embraces the Kingdom by faith. The Kingdom of God has the power to transform the type and shadow of the Sabbath into a genuine spiritual rest, characterized not by weekly religious rule-keeping, but by daily good works of mercy toward those in need. The Kingdom of God has the power to transform ordinary people into living stones in a spiritual temple where God Himself dwells by His Spirit and produces springs living water, welling up to eternal life. And the Kingdom of God has the power to produce in every disciple a Jesus-shaped

And They Dreamt Of A Kingdom

spirituality, which will set them apart as the defining characteristic of the new people of God. And that was a lesson which would change their lives . . . forever.

Questions For Reflection

Reflecting on this Lesson, what did you learn about Jesus and the Sabbath that you did not know before?

Spend some time reflecting on this passage from Paul's letter to the disciples in Galatia.

"But when Cephas [Peter] came to Antioch, I opposed him to his face, because he stood condemned. For before certain men came from James, he was eating with the Gentiles; but when they came he drew back and separated himself, fearing the circumcision party. And the rest of the Jews acted hypocritically along with him, so that even Barnabas was led astray by their hypocrisy. But when I saw that their conduct was not in step with the truth of the gospel, I said to Cephas [Peter] before them all, 'If you, though a Jew, live like a Gentile and not like a Jew, how can you force the Gentiles to live like Jews?'" (Galatians 2:11-14)

How do Paul's words here reflect Jesus' teachings in our current Lesson? How do our behavior and attitudes affect others around us (for good or bad)?

Reflect on this observation: *"The Kingdom of God is about the true knowledge of God, expressed through His love and mercy toward those in need, and embraced by faith by all who trust in His Name as disciples of the Kingdom."* How does your personal walk as a disciple of the Kingdom reflect this truth?

Key Thought

The Kingdom of God is not about ritual religious observances, but about righteousness, peace and joy in the Holy Spirit.

---

26 - And Then There Were Twelve

"In these days he went out to the mountain to pray, and all night he continued in prayer to God. And when day came, he called his disciples and chose from them twelve, whom he named apostles: Simon, whom he named Peter, and Andrew his brother, and James and John, and Philip, and Bartholomew, and Matthew, and Thomas, and James the son of Alphaeus, and Simon who was called the Zealot, and Judas the son of James, and Judas Iscariot, who became a traitor." (Luke 6:12-16)

Discipleship Reading: Luke 6:12-16   **When:** Spring, A.D. 29
Contextual Reading: Mark 3; Luke 6   **Where:** Galilee

The Spring of A.D. 29 is underway, along with a busy season of itinerant ministry throughout Galilee. Jesus' ministry is growing, along with the size of the crowds which now follow Him, coming from every part of Israel and beyond. The time has now arrived for His circle of disciples to grow, too.

A Foundation For the Journey Ahead

Roughly two years into His public ministry, Jesus' circle of disciples numbers seven.[85] Jesus has spent the preceding months laying a spiritual foundation of Kingdom truth which these seven men - and others to come - could build upon as they moved forward. Their journey together began with a faith borrowed from John the Baptizer on the shores of the Jordan River. It had grown to a faith of their own possession at the Wedding in Cana. In Jerusalem, at the beginning of His public ministry, the disciples had witnessed Jesus' passionate zeal for the Kingdom of God, and had learned the necessity of a new birth for entry into that Kingdom. On a personal journey of necessity through Samaria, they had experienced first-hand Jesus' passion for the marginalized and His unwillingness to allow either personal or religious prejudice to stand in the way of the message of the Kingdom. Returning to Galilee, they had heard Jesus' message of repentance and faith, and had watched Him perform miraculous - even "Messianic" - signs.

When Jesus came to challenge them with a call to "follow me," they had seen and heard enough to know that such a call was more of a command to obey than an invitation to consider. But obedience comes at a price. Their experiences with Jesus had opened their eyes to the reality of persecution by those whose religious authority and spiritual powerlessness were now being challenged by the power and authority of the Kingdom. The disciples understood that the religion-shaped spirituality, ingrained in them all of their lives by 1st Century Judaism, was wholly inadequate to receive the new wine of the Kingdom. They must be willing to allow Jesus to set them free and to re-mold them with a spirituality shaped around Jesus and Jesus alone. His yoke must replace all others. In addition, they must confront those servile fears which threatened to keep them bound to their old life; fears of daily provision as they traded the stability of a fishing business for the unpredictability of an itinerant life of fishing for men.

All of these lessons (and more) Jesus had taught these men over the preceding months. But as important and attention-grabbing as these lessons might be, such lessons by themselves were not sufficient for what lay ahead. If these seven men were to uproot their lives, confront their fears, endure persecution and more, they needed something greater than the visionary promises of an itinerant, miracle-working

And They Dreamt Of A Kingdom

Rabbi. Jesus understood that these seven men needed an encounter which would bring all of these lessons to a resolution far greater than the sum of its parts. And that is what Jesus provided by healing the lame man at the Pool of Bethesda. Through this miraculous sign, and the confrontation which followed, Jesus proclaimed what the disciples needed to hear to solidify their commitment as disciples of the Kingdom. This Jesus whom they follow is more than a rabble-rousing Rabbi from Galilee. He is even more than a gifted teacher sent from God (as Nicodemus had described Him). This Jesus whom they follow is Messiah, King and God, sharing equality with the Father and holding life, death and judgment in His hands. His words give eternal life and His voice will one day raise the dead. In short, He is Immanuel, "God with us." And that represents a foundation as deep as the Eternal God Himself. That is a foundation sufficient to build one's life upon, and more than sufficient for the journey of Kingdom discipleship which lay ahead. And their journey was just getting started.

And Then There Were Twelve

The text from Luke makes it clear that among the crowds of people following Jesus there was a group of people generically referred to as "disciples" who had followed Jesus and the others for some time. Their ranks numbered in the dozens, not in "multitudes."[86] From this group of other "disciples," Jesus now chooses five additional individuals to join the seven in close association with Himself.[87]

The appointing of the twelve as recorded by Mark and Luke lends itself to a handful of observations which are relevant both to our own discipleship and to those we seek to disciple in the Kingdom of God. *First,* Jesus did not take the choice of these five men lightly. Humanly speaking, the success or failure of Jesus' earthly mission would rest upon these twelve men and their willingness to learn, to grow, to change, to obey, to trust and to bear fruit. The Scriptures tell us He spent all night in prayer before taking this step (Luke 6:12). Jesus understood that a commitment to discipleship without

Jesus understood that a commitment to discipleship without a commitment to prayer is an exercise in futility.

a commitment to prayer is an exercise in futility. If that was true of Jesus and His disciples, how much more is it true of us? Who are the disciples we are praying for?

Second, Jesus called and chose the disciples. They didn't call and choose themselves. In retrospect, Jesus' call to "Follow Me" was more profound than the disciples understood. It was a call rooted in eternity and played out in time. Shortly before His crucifixion Jesus would remind them of this truth, *"You did not choose me, but I chose you and appointed you that you should go and bear fruit and that your fruit should abide."* (John 15:16). Jesus reminds His disciples and us that our discipleship in the Kingdom is not a casual or haphazard affair. It is the result of God's prevenient grace in our lives, stretching back into eternity past. He calls. He chooses. We follow. Or, as Mark describes it in Mark 3:13, *"And he . . . . called to him those whom he desired, and they came to him."*

Third, Jesus' call to discipleship came with a two-fold purpose, *"so that they might be with him and he might send them out to preach and have authority to cast out demons."* The call to discipleship comes as a call to fellowship, offering both an opportunity and a requirement to spend extended time with Jesus. To accept the yoke of discipleship is to enter into an intimacy with Jesus which requires that we re-prioritize all other relationships and fellowships. But Jesus' call to discipleship also comes as a call to obedience. To accept the yoke of discipleship is to accept a call to go wherever Jesus might send us, to proclaim the good news of he Kingdom and to exercise that same authority over the demonic realm which Jesus exercised. The call to discipleship is a two-fold call. It is a call to be with Jesus, and it is a call to be sent out by Jesus.

Fourth, and finally, Jesus' call to discipleship is also a call to disciple others. The seven would now disciple the five, because that's how discipleship works. The seven would now tell the five newcomers about their experiences with Jesus. They would share what they had learned in His company over the past several months and explain the conclusions they had come to regarding the Teacher, His claims and His authority. And Jesus would disciple them all, because that is how discipleship works in the Kingdom of God. Jesus disciples us while we disciple others.

> *The call to discipleship is a two-fold call. It is a call to be with Jesus, and it is a call to be sent out by Jesus.*

Twelve Disciples Of The Kingdom

"For consider your calling, brothers: not many of you were wise according to worldly standards, not many were powerful, not many were of noble birth. But God chose what is foolish in the world to shame the wise; God chose what is weak in the world to shame the strong; God chose what is low and despised in the world, even things that are not, to bring to nothing things that are, so that no human being might boast in the presence of God." (1 Corinthians 1:26-29)

When Paul wrote these words to describe the church in the Greek city of Corinth, he could just as easily have been writing about Jesus' disciples. All but one of them hailed from Galilee in northern Israel. To hail from Galilee was not exactly a résumé builder. Galilee was regarded as the rural, uneducated, unsophisticated "hinterlands" of Israel. But the unsophisticated Galileans also had their strengths. The Talmud said of the Galileans, *"They were more anxious for honor than for gain, quick-tempered, impulsive, emotional, easily aroused by an appeal to adventure, loyal to the end."* Those qualities would serve them well as disciples of the Kingdom.

Before they became disciples of Jesus, the twelve were so non-noteworthy that we know very little about them. In some cases, we know nothing at all. Peter and Andrew were brothers from the small village of Bethsaida on the northern shore of the Sea of Galilee, now living in Capernaum. James and John were brothers who worked with their father (Zebedee) in a fishing business. They fished alongside Peter and Andrew, indicating that they, too, now lived in Capernaum. Philip, like Peter and Andrew, was from Bethsaida. We do not know what he did there, although some have suggested that he, too, was a fisherman. Bartholomew is a surname, meaning "son of Tolmai or Talmai." His given name appears to have been Nathaniel. He came from Cana, where Jesus performed His first miraculous sign, but beyond that we know little about him. Matthew (Levi) was a Jew under public contract with the Romans to collect taxes for the Empire from his fellow Jews. This made him a non-fisherman, reasonably literate (record keeping and all that), and widely hated by his fellow Jews. Thomas is an enigma about whom little is known other than he came from Galilee. James, the son of Alphaeus, lived in Galilee and appears to have been the brother of Thaddaeus.

And They Dreamt Of A Kingdom

Apart from that, nothing is known about him. Thaddaeus was described by St. Jerome as *"Trinominous"* meaning *"a man with three names."* (In Mark 3:18 he is called Thaddeus. In Matthew 10:3 he is called Lebbeus. Apparently, his surname was Thaddeus. In Luke 6:16 and Acts 1:13 he is called Judas the son of James). His given name appears to have been Judas. Apart from his three names, we know nothing about him. Simon the Zealot (also called "the Cananaean") appears to have been a political radical. The Zealots were an organized "sect" that could be accurately described as "Pharisees with knives." In matters of religion they agreed with the Pharisees, but were politically motivated by a "zeal" for Jewish independence and a hatred of Rome. They were feared by the Romans as assassins and rebels. Finally, Judas Iscariot came from the small town of Kerioth in southern Judah, making him an outsider, the only non-Galilean in the group.

This was all that was known about these twelve men when Jesus called them and set them apart as His disciples. They are notable, not for who they were before they met Jesus, but for who they became as a result of their discipleship with Him. In the Kingdom of God, what distinguishes each of us is not who we were before our deliverance from the domain of darkness, but who we become under the Kingdom's transforming power. Some of the twelve would be called to both notoriety and profound ministry. Most would find themselves called to that profound service found only in obscurity. Peter, the volatile and impetuous fisherman, whose own

> *In the Kingdom of God, what distinguishes each of us is not who we were before our deliverance from the domain of darkness, but who we become under the Kingdom's transforming power.*

discipleship included a profound personal failure and four separate calls to "follow me," would become a leader of the early Church, a "rock" of faith for others, an Apostle to the Jews and, eventually, a martyr for what he believed. John, the fisherman, would become the most prolific writer and the theologian of the twelve, writing the most theologically profound of the four Gospels, along with three more letters plus the book of Revelation. John's brother, James, would see his discipleship cut short roughly 15 years after Jesus resurrection, martyred in Caesarea at the hands of Herod Agrippa (ca. 44 B.C.). Matthew (Levi), the despised tax-collector, would one day write a Gospel account specifically tailored to share the good news of the Kingdom of God with his fellow Jews who had so despised and ostracized him. Philip would find brief notoriety in the book of Acts for his ministry in Samaria and to the Ethiopian eunuch. After a final brief meeting in his home (Acts 21:8), he would disappear from the biblical record. But the disciple who would become the most well known of all is *"Judas Iscariot, who became a traitor."* His name and his life would become a symbol and a metaphor for personal betrayal and failed discipleship. The remaining six disciples would quickly disappear from the biblical record following Jesus' resurrection and ascension, with their profound ministries and martyrs' deaths veiled in obscurity, tradition and lore.

Reflection Versus Resolution

The biblical record often frustrates us by denying us the very information and resolution we so often seek. And after denying us what we want, the biblical writers offer us what we need; a personal challenge to reflect on our own journey of discipleship.

Resolution wants to know why anyone who spent prolonged time with Jesus, experienced His love, witnessed His miracles and sat under His teaching could betray Him, or experience such a profound failure of personal discipleship. Reflection asks, *"Am I any different from Judas? What makes my discipleship in the Kingdom any better, stronger or more lasting than His?"*

Resolution wants to know why God calls such spiritually gifted people to experience early deaths, or to spend their lives serving in obscurity and ministering to people who reject them and their message, even to the point of martyrdom. Reflection asks, *"Am I willing to go wherever Jesus sends me, even if it means a life of obscurity spent among people who may never appreciate me? Am I willing to be the insignificant mustard seed of the Kingdom from which great things grow, but not in my lifetime?"*

Resolution seeks a promise that our faithful obedience will result in personal success for ourselves and our ministry. Reflection is willing to embrace the insignificance of being a mustard seed, and the simple assurance that whatever God organically sows and plants through us will one day grow to greatly exceed us.

Questions For Reflection

In Plato's "Apology" the philosopher Socrates observed that *"the unexamined life is not worth living."* The same can (and should) be said about our discipleship in the Kingdom of God. It's time to reflect on your own journey of discipleship in light of the lessons we have seen so far. Before moving forward, it's time to look back . . . and reflect.

Reflecting on this Lesson, what did you learn about Jesus call to discipleship that you did not know before? How have you answered His call to discipleship in your own life?

Reflect on this statement: *"To accept the yoke of discipleship is to enter into an intimacy with Jesus which requires that we re-prioritize all other relationships and fellowships."* How has your discipleship caused you to re-prioritize your other relationships?

How have you embraced the lessons concerning discipleship in the Kingdom of God which Jesus has taught His disciples up to this point? How does your own discipleship in the Kingdom of God rest upon the foundation embodied in these lessons?

Key Thought

In the Kingdom of God, our ability to move forward in our discipleship demands a willingness to reflect upon what we have learned and to allow God to build upon the foundation which He has laid in our lives.

And They Dreamt Of A Kingdom

27 - The Values Of The Kingdom

"Seeing the crowds, he went up on the mountain, and when he sat down, his disciples came to him. And he opened his mouth and taught them" (Matthew 5:1-2)

Contextual Reading: *Matthew 5-7; Luke 6*

As we observed in the previous lesson, Jesus has spent the past 18 months laying a foundation in the lives of His disciples that He is Messiah, King and Immanuel with authority to exercise the transforming power of the Kingdom in all things. He will spend the next year building on that foundation, beginning with a group of lessons delivered to all twelve disciples on a mountain side in Galilee. These lessons, spanning three chapters in the Gospel of Matthew, were not so much a sermon delivered to the crowd as a workshop on discipleship taught by Jesus for the benefit of His disciples. They were His audience. The crowds could benefit from what Jesus was about to teach, if they had ears to hear. But these lessons were intended for the disciples, who must embrace them and allow themselves to be transformed by them. The long-term success of both their personal discipleship, and the mission Jesus would soon give them, depended upon their understanding of the Kingdom of God and how it transforms everything it touches. This is the new wine. They are the new wineskins. And it is time to pour.

> *"A rigid matter was the law,*
> *demanding brick,*
> *denying straw,*
> *But when with gospel*
> *tongue it sings,*
> *it bids me fly and gives me*
> *wings."*
> -Ralph Erskine-

The Transforming Power of The Kingdom

"Do not think that I have come to abolish the Law or the Prophets; I have not come to abolish them but to fulfill them." (Matthew 5:17)

Jesus understood a simple spiritual reality that we frequently miss. You never change a structure before you change the underlying values which created the structure in the first place. The transformation from the religion-shaped spirituality of 1st century Judaism to the Jesus-shaped spirituality of the Kingdom of God required a profound change in values. The coming of Jesus and the arrival of the Kingdom in the person of the King represented a transformational moment in the life of God's people. Jesus Himself acknowledged the change when He declared, *"The Law and the Prophets were until John; since then the good news of the kingdom of God is preached, and everyone forces his way into it."* (Luke 16:16).

The Law of Moses, which had guided and shaped the daily spiritual life of Israel for a millennium, had fulfilled its intended purpose, holding them in captivity to sin and serving as a tutor in righteousness, a *paidagogos*, to lead God's people to their need for a Redeemer- Messiah.[88] The Law was holy, righteous and good (Romans 7:12), but it was an insufficient foundation for the Kingdom Jesus now proclaimed. At its best, the Law was a type and a shadow of what was now unfolding in the Kingdom, *"For since the law has but a shadow of the good things to come instead of the true form of these realities, it can never, by the same sacrifices that are continually offered every year, make perfect those who draw near"* (Hebrews 10:1; see

And They Dreamt Of A Kingdom

also Hebrews 8:5 and Colossians 2:16-17). Outward obedience to the requirements of the Law was insufficient for entry into the Kingdom, just as Nicodemus had discovered. If salvation and the Kingdom could have been achieved by keeping the Law, heaven and the Kingdom would have been filled with Pharisees who, like Nicodemus and Paul, were legendary for their devotion to keeping the Law, *"a Hebrew of Hebrews; as to the law, a Pharisee . . . . . as to righteousness under the law, blameless"* (Philippians 3:5-6). Jesus understood that the Kingdom of God offered more than *"the Law on steroids."* It offered the fulfillment of all of God's promises. It offered spiritual transformation. The Kingdom of God transforms everything it touches. And it begins by transforming hearts, just as the Prophet Jeremiah had promised 580 years earlier. And that reality invites a closer look.

> *If salvation and the Kingdom could have been achieved by keeping the Law, heaven and the Kingdom would have been filled with Pharisees . . .*

The Promise of Inward Spiritual Transformation

"Behold, the days are coming, declares the LORD, when I will make a new covenant with the house of Israel and the house of Judah, not like the covenant that I made with their fathers on the day when I took them by the hand to bring them out of the land of Egypt, my covenant that they broke, though I was their husband, declares the LORD. But this is the covenant that I will make with the house of Israel after those days, declares the LORD: I will put my law within them, and I will write it on their hearts. And I will be their God, and they shall be my people. And no longer shall each one teach his neighbor and each his brother, saying, 'Know the LORD,' for they shall all know me, from the least of them to the greatest, declares the LORD. For I will forgive their iniquity, and I will remember their sin no more." (Jeremiah 31:31-34)

The Old Testament was all about promise, whereas the New Testament is all about fulfillment. The Old Testament promised spiritual transformation. The New Testament fulfills that promise in the arrival of the Kingdom. The above passage from the Old Testament book of Jeremiah represents one of the greatest and most important Old Testament promises regarding the people of God, the Law of God and "true spirituality." Under the Old Testament covenant "true spirituality" was primarily defined as outward personal conformity to the 613 commandments of the Law (no, not just the 10 Commandments).

The history of ancient Israel can be summarized as the story of Israel's consistent failure to keep those 613 commands. That failure culminated during the ministry of the Prophet Jeremiah, the "Prophet of the Covenant," who prophesied the destruction and captivity of God's people for their continued unfaithfulness to the Covenant and its requirements. Yet, in the midst of this 52-chapter-long condemnation of the people for their "spiritual adultery" Jeremiah offers this stunning promise: A day is coming when God will replace the Old Covenant of outward conformity with a NEW covenant of inward transformation: *"I will put My law within them, and on their heart I will write it; and I will be their God, and they shall be My people."* God, through Jeremiah, promised a coming day when outward religious conformity to a set of external rules would be replaced with the "true spirituality" of a transformed life whose highest desire will be to obey God because His Law will be written on their hearts.

Jesus and Spiritual Transformation

If the Old Testament was the record of the promise of a New Covenant, the New Testament is the record of the unfolding fulfillment of that New Covenant. Jesus highlighted this difference between outward religious conformity to the Law and inward spiritual transformation in His encounter with the rich young ruler in Luke 18:18-23. This young man had dedicated his life to outward religious conformity to the requirements of the Law, *"All these things I have kept from my youth,"* he declared in response to Jesus. Perfect conformity to all the rules. Jesus never corrected the young ruler's

. . . the New Covenant isn't about the requirements of the Law, it's about the condition of the heart.

self assessment. He never said, *"No, that's not true."* But Jesus did see things differently. Jesus saw a heart bound by religious legalism and self-righteousness. Jesus saw a heart in desperate need of spiritual transformation. So, to highlight that need Jesus asked him to do the one thing an untransformed heart could not do, *"One thing you still lack, sell all that you possess, and distribute it to the poor, and you shall have treasure in heaven; and come, follow me."* There was nothing in the Law which required such an action. But the New Covenant isn't about the requirements of the Law, it's about the condition of the heart. Jesus exposed a condition of the heart which the Law simply couldn't address. The Law could condemn an action, but it could not transform a heart. And this highlights the conflict between outward religious conformity to rules (such as the 613 commandments of the Law) and inward spiritual transformation. A religious person can keep all of the Law yet never experience genuine spiritual transformation. But a spiritually transformed person will want to obey - even exceed - all of Jesus' commandments, and to do so for love's sake, if for no other reason.

Paul And Spiritual Transformation

As a former Pharisee - someone who once dedicated himself to outward obedience to the Law - the Apostle Paul had come to understand the difference between the Old Covenant of outward religious conformity and the New Covenant of inward spiritual transformation. Writing to the disciples in the church at Corinth, Paul explained that the promise of Jeremiah Chapter 31 was now being fulfilled in the lives of believers through the ministry of the Holy Spirit, *"you are a letter of Christ, cared for by us, written not with ink, but with the Spirit of the living God, not on tablets of stone, but on tablets of human hearts"* (2 Corinth. 3:3). The Kingdom of God has arrived. And in the Kingdom of God, stone tablets have been replaced with human hearts.

*Run, John, and work,
the law commands,
yet finds me neither
feet nor hands,
But sweeter news the
gospel brings,
it bids me fly and lends
me wings!*
John Berridge
(1716–1793)

Paul offers a series of contrasts between the Old Covenant of outward conformity to the Law and the New Covenant with its promise of inward spiritual transformation. The Old Covenant was a *"ministry of death"* which offered only a fading glory, whereas the New Covenant represents a *"ministry of the Spirit"* which offers a greater glory. The Old Covenant was a ministry of *"the letter"* which killed, whereas the New Covenant is a ministry of the Spirit which gives life. The Old Covenant was a *"ministry of condemnation"* (i.e., because the Law condemns us for our unrighteousness) whereas the New Covenant is a *"ministry of righteousness,"* giving us the very righteousness - the righteousness of Christ - which the Old Covenant demanded but could not provide. The Old Covenant represented a fading glory whereas the New Covenant represents a glory which "abides" and "abounds."

But Paul isn't done, yet. The climax of his explanation comes in 2 Corinthians 3:17-18: *"Now the Lord is the Spirit; and where the Spirit of the Lord is, there is liberty. But we all, with unveiled face beholding as in a mirror the glory of the Lord, are being transformed into the same image from glory to glory, just as from the Lord, the Spirit"* (NASB). In the Kingdom of God, the Spirit of God transforms human hearts and brings liberty, not legalism. It sets people free from the impossible demands of outward religious conformity and religious legalism. Under this new and glorious Covenant, the Spirit of God brings about something the Law never could - inward spiritual transformation, resulting in our being transformed into the very image of God in Christ!

> *In the Kingdom of God, the Spirit of God transforms human hearts and brings liberty, not legalism.*

The arrival of the Kingdom in the person of Jesus, the King, changed everything. The Law and the Prophets have not been destroyed, abolished or set aside. They have been fulfilled. And a new "law" has been introduced: The Law of Christ, *"Bear one another's burdens, and so fulfill the law of Christ"* (Galatians 6:2). To be a disciple of the Kingdom is NOT to be subjected to the Old Covenant on steroids. It is to be transformed and set free (Romans 8:2) to truly love the Lord our God with all our heart, mind, soul, and strength, and to love our neighbor as ourselves:

"Owe no one anything, except to love each other, for the one who loves another has fulfilled the law. For the commandments, 'You shall not commit adultery, You shall not murder, You shall not steal, You shall not covet,' and any other commandment, are summed up in this word: 'You shall love your neighbor as yourself.' Love does no wrong to a neighbor; therefore love is the fulfilling of the law." (Romans 13:8-10; see also Galatians 5:14 & 6:2)

As we saw earlier in Lesson 22, the early Church in the book of Acts understood the profound change which the arrival of the Kingdom had brought about. When the good news of the Kingdom began to spread beyond Israel into predominantly Gentile (non-Jewish) lands, the Church was confronted with a basic question. Should these Gentile disciples be told that *"It is necessary to circumcise them and to order them to keep the law of Moses."* (Acts 15:5). The resounding answer of the assembled Church was "No." Their written response to the Gentile disciples was simple and clear: *"For it has seemed good to the Holy Spirit and to us to lay on you no greater burden than these requirements: that you abstain from what has been sacrificed to idols, and from blood, and from what has been strangled, and from sexual immorality. If you keep yourselves from these, you will do well. Farewell."* (Acts 15:28-29) [89] The early Church of the book of Acts understood an important spiritual reality: *the coming of the Kingdom in the Person of the King changed everything.*

Jesus And A "High" View Of The Law

In the three Chapters we are about to examine, Jesus offers His disciples (and us) what can best be described as a "high" view of the Law. Its demands are so thorough-going that it brings us to our knees and to the realization that satisfying its demands - in thought, word and deed - is completely beyond any ability we might possess. It demands internal and external perfection which no man can deliver. If you and I fail to understand this reality, we will become frustrated Christian legtalists, and will completely miss the "rest" offered by Jesus and the Kingdom. Legalism knows no rest. It demands that we make bricks, but provides no straw. It demands that we run and work, but gives us neither feet nor hands with which to obey. It is a tutor in righteousness whose instructions bring us to a point of personal despair, crying out with the Apostle Paul, *"Wretched man that I am! Who will deliver me from this body of death?"* (Romans 7:24).

But 1st Century Judaism suffered from something different. The Scribes and Pharisees, the religious leaders and even Jesus' own disciples labored under a "low" view of the Law. A low view of the Law produces legalism by deceiving people into believing that, if they work hard enough, they can please God by fulfilling the demands of the Law. But legalism is what remains of the Law and of God's holiness after the Spirit of God departs. It is the "fools gold" of religion, promising wealth but bringing only disappointment and spiritual poverty. It is true of the unbeliever seeking salvation through obedience.

> *. . . legalism is what remains of the Law and of God's holiness after the Spirit of God departs.*

It is also true of the disciple of the Kingdom who mistakenly believes that he can please God and find sanctification (spiritual growth in Christ-likeness and maturity) by keeping the Law.

Twelve Transformed Kingdom Values

The Kingdom of God transforms everything it touches. And the lessons on transformational Kingdom values which Jesus is about to teach His disciples in these three Chapters (Matthew 5-7) can be grouped and summarized in twelve basic lessons. We will begin by summarizing all twelve lessons here, and then expand on seven of them in separate lessons.

1. The Blessings of Discipleship (5:3-12). The Kingdom God redefines and transforms what it means to be "blessed." In the Kingdom of God, blessing is not defined in terms of wealth, political power, outward success, social standing or any of the standards men use to measure success. The twelve men who now sat listening to Jesus expound on the values of the Kingdom had left everything in order to follow Him, a fact not lost on them as time went on (see Matthew 19:27; Mark 10:28). In the coming years they would experience poverty, hunger and thirst, persecution, insults and even death. This is what it means to be a disciple of the Kingdom. But Jesus tells them that they are "blessed," and He admonishes them to *"Rejoice and be glad, for your reward is great in heaven"* (Matthew 5:12). To be a

> *The Kingdom God redefines and transforms what it means to be "blessed."*

And They Dreamt Of A Kingdom

disciple of the Kingdom is to be "blessed" beyond anything the world has to offer.

2. Salt, Light and Good Deeds (5:13-16). In the Kingdom of God, the transformed life of a disciple is known by the fruit which it bears, the light which it shines, the salt which it provides (to flavor and preserve) and the good deeds it performs. We will examine this more closely in Lesson 28.

3. Law, Righteousness, and the Kingdom (5:17-20). The Kingdom of God transforms the _locus_ of our righteousness, relocating it from outward conformity to the Law to inward transformation by the Spirit of God. Everyone knew that the Pharisees were legendary for their efforts to keep the Law and to achieve that outward "righteousness" which Paul later described to the Philippians: *"as to righteousness under the law, blameless"* (Philippians 3:5-6). Listening to Jesus, the disciples had to be asking themselves, *"How is it possible to be more righteous than those guys?"* How is it possible to exceed a righteousness which is "blameless"? Answer: you can't. The only possibility of exceeding the righteousness of the Scribes and Pharisees lay in sharing the righteousness of the One Who was greater and more righteous than every Scribe and Pharisee who ever lived. We share the blameless righteousness of very Son of God Himself. And that is transformational. The Jews of Jesus' day never imagined the possibility of being clothed in someone else's righteousness, or that the Messiah Himself would one day indwell every believer by the Holy Spirit. And, yet, that was the mystery which lay ahead in the near future: Christ in us, the hope of glory (Colossians 1:27). In the Kingdom of God, discipleship isn't about working harder to be righteous. In the Kingdom of God discipleship is about being born again by the Spirit of God and living out a transformed life that even the most righteous of Pharisees could neither imagine nor experience. If outward conformity to the requirements of the Law is your measure of spirituality, you do not understand what it means to experience a transformed life in the Kingdom of God.

> In the Kingdom of God, discipleship isn't about working harder to be righteous.

4. Six Contrasts and Transformations (5:21-48). The Kingdom of God transforms everything it touches, including our relationship to the Law. To make this point Jesus offers six examples to contrast the requirements of the Law with the transformational values of the Kingdom: Murder, adultery, divorce, oaths, justice and loving your neighbor. **Murder.** The Law could tell a man not to commit murder, and could punish him for the crime (Exodus 20:12; Deuteronomy 5:17). But it had no power to address the condition of the heart, or to cleanse it from the sin of anger. To transform a man with murderous rage in his heart into a man of peace and reconciliation required more than the Law could provide. **Adultery.** The Law could warn a man against committing the physical act of adultery, while prescribing punishments for disobedience (Exodus 20:14; Deuteronomy 5:18). But it was powerless to address the lust of the human heart which gives birth to adultery. **Divorce.** The Law could (and did) grant a man a certificate of divorce to end an apparently failed marriage (Deuteronomy 24:1-3). But it was powerless to heal a broken heart or a broken marriage. It was powerless to restore God's ideal or to transform a man into a loving husband who loved and desired His wife above all others. **Oaths.** The Law could regulate the use of oaths, warn a man against bearing false testimony and punish him for disobedience (Leviticus 19:12; Numbers 30:2; Deuteronomy 23:31). But it could not transform his heart and make him a person of integrity whose word can be trusted. **Justice.** The Law could provide for reciprocal justice ("eye for an eye") to suppress men's tendency toward revenge (Exodus 21:24; Leviticus 24:20; Deuteronomy 19:21). But the Law was powerless to transform a man's heart and to make him willing to patiently endure injustice, or to respond to evil with good. **Love.** The Law could command a person to love his (or her) neighbor (Leviticus 19:18). But it was powerless to transform a person's heart, causing them to love their enemies or the marginalized - people like lepers, tax collectors, Romans or Samaritans or Gentiles in general.

In short, the Law and the Old Covenant sought to regulate behavior and control sin by addressing issues of outward obedience, condemning sinful behavior and proscribing punishments for disobedience. But it was powerless to transform the fallen heart which produced the behavior in the first place. We sin because we are sinners, and the Law was powerless to change that. Not even a Law on steroids. The perfection of which Jesus spoke (*"You therefore must be perfect, as your heavenly Father is perfect."* - Matt. 5:48) required something which the Law had never been able to provide. Such genuine change requires a personal transformation. And only the Kingdom of God offers such a radical, personal transformation. In the Kingdom of God, transformed men will perform greater exploits of obedience in the name of Love, than they would ever have performed in the name of the Law.

> *In the Kingdom of God, transformed men will perform greater exploits of obedience in the name of Love, than they would ever have performed in the name of the Law.*

5. Transforming Charity, Prayer and Fasting (6:1-18). The Kingdom of God transforms our spiritual values, which in turn transforms our spiritual disciplines. Prayer, fasting and charity were spiritual values and religious activities the disciples had grown up with all of their lives. They embodied the three pillars of Jewish piety, to be practiced by all religiously observant Jews. But the religion-shaped spirituality of 1st Century Judaism had turned these spiritual disciplines into public spectacles. The Pharisees valued public show and the admiration of the masses. They offered long and eloquent prayers in public to impress the masses, but they prayed to a closed heaven. They fasted twice a week, made certain that everyone knew they were fasting and frowned on anyone who didn't join with them. They also made a public spectacle of their acts of charity, so that everyone but God was aware of their generosity. The Kingdom of God rejects all such public displays of piety and transforms them from public spectacles of no value (*"Truly, I say to you, they have received their reward."* - Matthew 6:2) into personal spiritual disciplines which God Himself sees, blesses and rewards (*"And your Father who sees in secret will reward you."* - Matthew 6:4).

6. The Priority of the Kingdom (6:19-34). The Kingdom of God transforms our priorities from those of earth to those of heaven. We are all anxious about those things of this world which touch our hearts and lives. By transforming hearts and our priorities the Kingdom gives us a "clear eye" which can see heaven and its priorities when others cannot. In the process, the Kingdom challenges our faith to believe God for greater things and to make our pursuit of the Kingdom our greatest single priority. We will examine this more closely in Lesson 29.

171

And They Dreamt Of A Kingdom

7. *Specks, Logs And Measuring Cups (7:1-5).* The Kingdom of God transforms the values by which we judge both others and ourselves. In the Kingdom of God, the transformed life of a disciple means that we abandon any masks of religious play acting and examine our own fruitfulness before we examine someone else's fruitfulness (or lack thereof). In the Kingdom of God our discipleship requires us to remove the "wood beam" from our own eye before we make any attempt to remove the "wood chip" from someone else's eye. We will examine this more closely in Lesson 30.

8. *Dogs, Pigs & Pearls (7:6).* The Kingdom of God challenges the spiritual blindness of "this present age," transforming spiritual blindness into spiritual sight for those who believe. As disciples of the Kingdom we have been given spiritual truth which, in past ages, has been hidden from prophets and men of God. It remains hidden from those outside the Kingdom, who are spiritually blind to its truth. How we share that truth with those who are spiritually blind presents a challenge for our walk as disciples of the Kingdom. We will examine this more closely in Lesson 31.

9. *Ask, Seek, Knock (7:7-12).* The Kingdom of God transforms the spiritual discipline of prayer from a religious ritual to a personal relationship. In the Kingdom of God, our discipleship rests upon a personal discipline of on-going, persistent prayer, because we have the privilege of addressing God as "abba," Father; and God responds to us as a Father responds to a child.

10. *Broad Ways And Narrow Gates (7:13-14).* The Kingdom of God transforms our understanding of entry into that Kingdom. It teaches us, just as it taught Nicodemus, that entry to the Kingdom of God is not the birthright of any people or group. Rather, it is God's gift to those who by faith have been transformed - born again - by the Spirit of God. Entry to the Kingdom must be diligently pursued in this life, and the narrow path into the Kingdom of God must be the intentional pursuit of every would-be disciple of the Kingdom. We will examine this more closely in Lesson 32.

11. *False Prophets And Fruit (7:15-23).* The Kingdom of God transforms our understanding of the relationship between spiritual power and spiritual fruit. In the Kingdom of God, false prophets and genuine disciples are distinguished from each other, not by their profession or by their power, but by their fruit. We will examine this more closely in Lesson 33.

12. *The Wise And The Foolish (7:24-27).* The Kingdom of God transforms our understanding of wisdom and foolishness. In the Kingdom of God, the wise and the foolish are distinguished from one another by how they respond to the words and teachings of Jesus. The wise man listens and obeys. The fool does not. The words and teachings of Jesus are the foundation upon which our discipleship is built. We will examine this more closely in Lesson 34.

Questions For Reflection

Reflecting on this Lesson, what did you learn about the transforming power of the Kingdom that you did not know before?

Reflect on this statement by St. Augustine of Hippo (circa A.D. 400): *"Love God and do whatever you please: for the soul trained in love to God will do nothing to offend the One who is Beloved."* How does St. Augustine's declaration reflect what we have learned in this Lesson about how the message of the Kingdom transforms the life of the believer?

Reflect on this statement: *"Legalism is the 'fools gold' of the Kingdom of God, impoverishing everyone who clings to it and tries to spend it."* How have you discovered this to be true in your own discipleship?

Key Thought

The Kingdom of God transforms everything it touches, including the values upon which our discipleship is built.

And They Dreamt Of A Kingdom

28 - Salt, Light And Good Works

"You are the salt of the earth, but if salt has lost its taste, how shall its saltiness be restored? It is no longer good for anything except to be thrown out and trampled under people's feet. You are the light of the world. A city set on a hill cannot be hidden. Nor do people light a lamp and put it under a basket, but on a stand, and it gives light to all in the house. In the same way, let your light shine before others, so that they may see your good works and give glory to your Father who is in heaven." (Matthew 5:13-16)

Discipleship Reading: Matthew 5:13-16
Contextual Reading: Matthew 5-7; Luke 6

When: Spring, A.D. 29
Where: Galilee

The Kingdom of God transforms everything it touches. And the first thing it transforms is us. Or, at least it is supposed to. Contemporary Christianity appears to have made peace with a practical and biblical contradiction, namely, "professing" disciples of the Kingdom whose lives give no evidence of having ever been transformed. We have come to accept as normal a type of salt that has no flavor, doesn't preserve anything and makes no one thirsty.

> *The Kingdom of God transforms everything it touches. And the first thing it transforms is us.*

We have come to accept as normal a curious kind of lamp that is perfect in every way but one: it produces no light. To change metaphors, we now believe in assembling a collection of can openers which are perfect in nearly every detail, except one. They can't, don't and won't open any cans. Apart from that one "flaw," they're excellent. Contemporary Christianity has come to an awkward accommodation with the phenomena of professing believers with unchanged lives. Jesus understood. He talked about it with His disciples two thousand years ago. Unfortunately, much of the contemporary church today may not want to hear what He had to say.

The Realities Of A Changed Life

As we have already seen in the ministry of Jesus, the New Testament portrays our entrance into the Kingdom of God as a life-changing experience - a "transformation." It is so life-altering that Jesus, describing it to Nicodemus, compared it with re-entering a mother's womb and being "born again." Simply stated, our faith in Jesus and our entrance into the Kingdom of God transforms who we are, just as the Apostle Paul would later explain to the believers in the Greek city of Corinth, *"Therefore, if anyone is in Christ, he is a new creation. The old has passed away; behold, the new has come."* (2 Corinthians 5:17). Our entrance into the Kingdom alters our very existence. For this reason, it is "existential." From that moment on, for as long as we live, life as a disciple of the Kingdom defines who and what we are, not something we may or may not become. Like newborn babies, it may require an entire lifetime to fully manifest this new existential reality, but the change is real - even if it is immature at first.

This is the transformational Kingdom value Jesus wants His disciples to embrace as they listen to Him on this Spring day. In the above passage Jesus offers His disciples two life-changing "existential realities." As disciples of the Kingdom, their lives are being transformed and will now be defined by these two existential realities:

And They Dreamt Of A Kingdom

salt and light.

Reality # 1: You Are the salt of the earth (Matthew 5:13). The history of salt is the history of civilization from its earliest days. The availability of salt as a preservative eliminated dependence on the seasonal availability of food and allowed people to travel and transport food over long distances. Because salt was often difficult to obtain in the ancient world, it quickly became a highly valued trade item and "salt routes" were quickly established. Salt was so valuable that it was even used as money from time to time. Roman soldiers were sometimes paid with salt, and soldiers who did their job well were described as "worth their salt." Our modern word "salary" is derived from the Latin word *salārium*, which originally meant: *"a soldier's allowance for the purchase of salt."* In the world of Jesus' day, salt functioned primarily as a preservative for food. Meats, fish, poultry and more were packed and cured in salt or salt brine for long-term preservation. Salt meant that food would last, and that meant life. In addition to functioning as a preservative, salt also functioned as a spice and flavor enhancer. But it was as a preservative that salt found its primary value in the ancient world. For more centuries than we can count, "salt" meant "life." And the very idea of throwing salt away and trampling it underfoot was, well, unimaginable.

> *Simply put, either you are "salt" - and everything that means - or you are not a disciple of the Kingdom.*

Jesus offers His disciples (and us) a contradiction. Salt that is not salty. *Question:* How could salt lose its "saltiness" (i.e., it's ability to preserve and flavor)? *Answer:* It can't. Salt that isn't "salty" - that won't preserve or flavor - is a contradiction in terms. Whatever else "it" might be, it isn't salt. It has become something worthless that deserves to be thrown out and trampled underfoot, something an ancient believer would NEVER do with salt. And that's Jesus' point. A disciple of the Kingdom who isn't "salty" - who doesn't impact, preserve or flavor his or her immediate environment for the Kingdom of God - is a contradiction in terms. Simply put, either you are "salt" - and everything that means - or you are not a disciple of the Kingdom.

Reality # 2: You Are the light of the world (Matthew 5:14) This second reality is closely related to the first. In the true fashion of Hebrew parallelism (the repetition of an idea in a related form in order to make a single point), Jesus changes metaphors from salt to light to make His point. In the ancient world of Jesus' day, lamps were simple things, usually consisting of a bowl or reservoir of oil and a wick. The wick absorbed oil from the reservoir and burned to provide light. No decorative frills or fancy lampshades. Just a bowl, oil, a wick and light. In the world of Jesus and His disciples, a lamp which didn't provide light was as useless, and as much a contradiction in terms, as salt which wasn't salty and didn't flavor or preserve.

> *A lamp that does not give light is a contradiction in terms, like salt which isn't salty.*

Jesus point is simple. As disciples of the Kingdom, you and I are lamps created for a purpose: to give light. This is why Jesus can declare without equivocation that you and I "*are the light of the world.*" Please note. This isn't a promise for the future, but a statement of present reality. He doesn't say that you and I *could* be the light of the world or *should* be the light of the world or *will* be the light of the world. No. He says that you and I *ARE* the light of the world. Being a lamp is an "existential reality" of our life as a disciple of the Kingdom. And what does a lamp do? It shines and *"gives light to all who are in the house."* A lamp that does not give light is a contradiction in terms, like salt which isn't salty. Either you are a lamp which shines, or you are not a disciple of the Kingdom.

Salt, Light And Good Deeds

At this point the natural question for each of us should be, *"How do we do this? How do we preserve and flavor the world around us? How do we let our light shine before men?"* Fortunately for us, and for all who claim to be His disciples, Jesus gives us a clear and practical answer: Through our good deeds, *"let your light shine before others, so that they may see your good works and give glory to your Father who is in heaven."* [90]

According to Jesus, our good deeds represent the outward manifestation of our Jesus-shaped spirituality. Through our good deeds people can "taste the flavor" of the Kingdom of God. Through our good deeds our unbelieving world will "see the light" of our Jesus-shaped spirituality and glorify God as a result. Our good deeds make us "salt" and "light" to an unbelieving world.

> *According to Jesus, our good deeds represent the outward manifestation of our Jesus-shaped spirituality.*

Have you ever wondered how Jesus' teaching on this principle affected His own disciples? It would appear from Scripture that Jesus' words here in Matthew 5 had a profound impact on at least one of His disciples: Simon Peter. How do we know this? Because years later, writing to churches and young believers in Asia Minor, Peter refers to Jesus words from Matthew 5 , saying, *"Beloved, I urge you as aliens and strangers to abstain from fleshly lusts, which wage war against the soul. Keep your behavior excellent among the Gentiles, so that in the thing in which they slander you as evildoers, they may on account of your good deeds, as they observe them, glorify God in the day of visitation."* (1 Peter 2:11-12). Did you catch it there at the end of verse 12? Peter tells his readers that through their excellent behavior *"among the Gentiles"* unbelievers will see their good deeds and will glorify God. Isn't that what Jesus had taught His disciples so many years before? And isn't that what it means to be salt and light as disciples of the Kingdom? Peter got the point. Do we?

In the Kingdom of God, good deeds cannot be reverse engineered. You and I cannot begin with good deeds and work our way back to the Kingdom of God. Acting like a Christian doesn't make anyone a Christian. Our new birth into the Kingdom transforms us into people of salt and light. And through our good deeds we manifest that salt and light to the world around us. Our Postmodern culture has concluded that it can manifest 'good deeds' without Jesus. The church of our generation has concluded that it can manifest Jesus without 'good deeds'. Our Postmodern culture's plan appears to be working. The Church's plan is a disaster. What's your plan?

And They Dreamt Of A Kingdom

Questions For Reflection

By now you have undoubtedly noticed that I have not provided a list of things which might constitute "good deeds," or anecdotal stories of people doing good deeds. As someone who has worked among the marginalized of our city I could certainly tell stories and offer lists, but I have chosen not to do so for a couple of reasons. *First,* any list I might offer or stories I might tell would quickly become set in stone or criticized as if that list was either exhaustive or not inclusive enough. *Second,* I want to challenge your thinking about what good deeds done in the name of the Kingdom might look like in your own life, your neighbor or your city. Nothing squelches creativity or imagination like a pre-digested list of ideas.

The following 15 passages from the New Testament all speak to the importance of good deeds in the life of the believer. Spend some time reading and reflecting on what these mean for your discipleship and your calling to be salt and light in the world. Try writing your own one line summary of each passage.

1.	John 5: 38	Our Works Are Our Witness
2.	Matthew 5:14-26	Be A Light
3.	Ephesians 2:8-10	Find Your Purpose
4.	2 Corinthians 9:7-9	Learn To Overflow
5.	Romans 2:5-10	Judgment Day Is Coming
6.	Romans 13:3	Make Yourself Valuable
7.	John 10:32-33	Prepare To Be Stoned
8.	Colossians 1:9-10	Be Careful How You Walk
9.	Titus 3:14	Learn To Be Fruitful
10.	1 Timothy 5:24-25	You Can't Hide
11.	Titus 1: 15-16	Do Our Deeds Match Our Words
12.	Titus 2:6-8	Be A Model
13.	Titus 2:11-14	Be Zealous
14.	Titus 3:8	Set The Tone
15.	Hebrews 10:23-25	Stimulate One Another

Key Thought

As Disciples of the Kingdom, our good deeds represent our salt and light, the outward manifestation of our new birth, our Jesus-shaped spirituality and our commitment to the Kingdom of God.

---

29 - The Priority Of The Kingdom

"But if God so clothes the grass of the field, which today is alive and tomorrow is thrown into the oven, will he not much more clothe you, O you of little faith? Therefore do not be anxious, saying, 'What shall we eat?' or 'What shall we drink?' or 'What shall we wear?' For the Gentiles seek after all these things, and your heavenly Father knows that you need them all. But seek first the kingdom of God and his righteousness, and all these things will be added to you." (Matthew 6:30-34)

Discipleship Reading: *Matthew 6:19-34*   **When:** *Spring, A.D. 29*
Contextual Reading: *Matthew 6-7; Luke 6*   **Where:** *Galilee*

On this Spring day of A.D. 29 the truths of the Kingdom are being freely poured out by the Messiah-King as He instructs His disciples concerning the transformational values of the Kingdom. In sixteen brief verses, Jesus now communicates a life-time of truth for every disciple of the Kingdom. His message is simple: The Kingdom of God transforms the priorities of our life. And that transformation begins with a transformed heart.

"The eye is the lamp of the body. So, if your eye is healthy, your whole body will be full of light, but if your eye is bad, your whole body will be full of darkness. If then the light in you is darkness, how great is the darkness!" (Matthew 6:22-23)

In the idioms of Hebrew thought and literature the "eye" was synonymous with the "heart" as an expression of the inner man. To have a transformed heart is to have a "clear" eye, able to see the reality of heavenly treasure as clearly as everyone else sees the reality of earthly treasure. Only a fool would give up the tangible reality of earthly treasure for an intangible promise of heavenly treasure, unless, with a transformed heart and a clear eye, that "fool" could see the spiritual reality of the Kingdom God - that "pearl of great price" - which is hidden to those who are still spiritually blind.

In the span of fifteen verses Jesus uses the word "anxious" (Greek: *merimnao*) five times. Since ancient times this word described a mental burden which occupied the mind to the point of distraction. Jesus understood that His disciples - like all of us - would be anxious about those things which touched their lives and their hearts: food, clothing, money, work, family, making earthly treasure all the more attractive as the answer to all those anxieties. But Jesus knew better. Jesus understood that if His disciples were to avoid the ongoing distractions which the treasures of this world offer, they needed a transformed heart with transformed priorities which would enable them to see the reality of the Kingdom with a "clear eye."

When Life "Squeezes" Our Priorities

Apart from Jesus' words on this day, the New Testament has much to say about the importance of proper spiritual priorities - knowing how to put "first things first." In Revelation 2:4 the Risen Christ rebukes the Church of Ephesus for losing their spiritual priorities and abandoning their "first love." This emphasis upon spiritual priorities began during Jesus' earthly ministry. Jesus turned away would-be disciples who refused to submit their personal priorities to those of the Kingdom (Luke 9:59-61). The priority of the Kingdom of God means that we give Jesus and the demands of the Kingdom exclusivity when it comes to setting the other priorities of our lives: money, work, family, everything. To be a disciple of the Kingdom requires a personal

And They Dreamt Of A Kingdom

willingness to embrace the priorities of the Kingdom in everything we do.

Fans of action movies will quickly recognize a basic principle for manipulating people which frequently finds its way into Hollywood movie plots. The principle works something like this: *"If you want to get someone's attention, find what is important to that person, and squeeze."* You might find it difficult to believe, but this is actually a biblical principle. We find it at work in the book of Job, *"Then Satan answered the LORD and said, "Skin for skin! All that a man has he will give for his life. But stretch out your hand and touch his bone and his flesh, and he will curse you to your face."* (Job 2:4-5). Satan - the great Adversary of our souls - understood that the quickest and most effective way to reveal the true motives and priorities of the human heart is to touch us where we live and to "squeeze" the things which are important to us. And that is precisely what he did with Job. Satan "squeezed" Job by attacking his family and taking away his possessions (Job 1:9-22). Next, Satan "squeezed" Job by attacking his health (Job 2:3-10). The ultimate result of all this "squeezing" was that Job repented of a false understanding of God and came to a new understanding of God and His "priorities" (Job Chapter 42).

> *To be a disciple of the Kingdom requires a personal willingness to embrace the priorities of the Kingdom in everything we do.*

Now for the paradigm bender. Satan is not the only one who "squeezes" our circumstances in order to reveal our priorities. So does God. Someone once observed that Satan and God both want the same thing. They both want to "kill" us, but for different reasons. Satan is a thief who comes to steal, kill and destroy everything God loves (see John 10:10). For His part, God has a different motivation and plan. God wants to "kill" everything in us that He cannot use for His Kingdom purposes. To use a frequent metaphor of Scripture, God sits as a refiner of metal Who seeks to refine us into a people He can use. *"And I will put this third into the fire, and refine them as one refines silver, and test them as gold is tested. They will call upon my name, and I will answer them. I will say, 'They are my people'; and they will say, 'The LORD is my God'."* (Zechariah 13:9)

> *. . . the Scriptures continually teach us that God is more concerned with our character than He is with our comfort.*

For those with ears to hear, the Scriptures continually teach us that God is more concerned with our character than He is with our comfort. And "squeezing" our circumstances is one of the tools He uses to interrupt our comfort, to "clarify our eyes" concerning His priorities and to perfect our character in Christ-likeness. God's plan for every professing believer is essentially the same. He wants to mold us into committed disciples of His Kingdom. To accomplish His plan God uses the circumstances of our lives as His tool, His "refiner's fire" to reveal the true condition of our hearts and to teach us to replace the priorities of this world with those of the Kingdom of God. This is why the Apostle Paul could confidently declare to disciples in the City of Rome, *"And we know that God causes all things to work together for good to those who love God, to those who are called according to His purpose"* (Romans 8:28 - NASB). In the Kingdom of God, the circumstances of our lives become tools in the hand of God for setting us apart and transforming us into disciples of His Kingdom.

The Things Which Set Us Apart

And this leads us back to Jesus' words to His disciples on a mountain side in Galilee on this day in the Spring of A.D. 29. Jesus confronts His disciples (and us) with a simple but basic question: What sets the disciple of the Kingdom apart from everyone else? According to Jesus, disciples of the Kingdom are set apart by how they respond to the circumstances of life. Our responses reveal who we are, what we believe and who we trust. Do we trust and serve God, or money? And in the process, our responses reveal our true priorities.

When the circumstances of life "squeeze" us, we discover the true nature of our faith. The circumstances of life - such basic issues as *"What shall we eat?"* or *"What shall we drink?"* or *"What shall we wear?"* - force each of us to answer a fundamental question: *"Who do we serve, and who do we trust to meet our needs?"* According to Jesus, a disciple of the Kingdom is someone who has made a choice to serve God, rather than money, and to trust Him to meet their daily needs (Matthew 6:24). We worship whatever we serve, and we serve whatever (or whoever) meets our needs.

We worship whatever we serve, and we serve whatever (or whoever) meets our needs.

At this point Jesus introduces a curious term to describe people who are "anxious" about such things, *"O you of little faith."* The Greek term used here (*oligopistos*) occurs only five times in the New Testament and only on the lips of Jesus (See Matthew 6:30; 8:26; 14:31; 16:8; 17:20). It communicates the idea of *"a person who trusts too little,"* hence, *"a person of small faith."* In addition to the present passage (and its counterpart in Luke 12:28), Jesus uses this word to describe the response of the disciples when they are "squeezed" by various circumstances. For example, in Matthew 8:23-26 the disciples and Jesus get caught in a storm on the Sea of Galilee. For his part, Jesus naps through the whole episode. When the disciples wake Him to express their fear of perishing, Jesus stills the storm and admonishes them for being afraid, describing them as *"men of little faith"* (or *"men who trust too little"*). Again, in Matthew 14:28-31, Peter - at Jesus' invitation - steps out of the boat and begins walking on the water toward Jesus. When Peter begins to sink and cries out *"Lord, save me,"* Jesus rescues him, gets Peter safely back in the boat and then admonishes him with these words: *"O you of little faith, why did you doubt?"* (Matthew 14:31).

When you and I are "squeezed" by the circumstances of life, the true nature of our faith is revealed and we are confronted with a basic question: *"Who am I serving, and who do I trust to meet my needs?"* If the God Who can rebuke the wind and calm the sea is napping in my boat, then the storm can't be that bad, unless I don't really trust Him or unless I think He is indifferent to my situation. If the One I trust has just walked half way across the Sea of Galilee and now invites me to walk with Him on the water, why would I not trust Him to keep me from

Our inability to trust God for the basics of life in the midst of challenging circumstances is a sign of an immature faith.

drowning? And if the One I am following and trusting for my eternal salvation tells me to venture out and serve Him without any visible means of support (Matthew 10:8-10), why would I not trust Him to provide for me along the way? By His use of the word *oligopistos* (*"a person who trusts too little"*), Jesus highlights a spiritual reality. Our inability to trust God for the basics of life in the midst of challenging circumstances is a sign of an immature faith. It is also a sign that our spiritual priorities need adjusting.

When the circumstances of life "squeeze" us, we discover our true priorities. You and I pursue the things which own us, and each of us is owned by the things we pursue. Our pursuit reveals our priorities, and our priorities determine our pursuit. Perhaps this is what Jesus meant when He said, *"the Gentiles seek after all these things."* The Greek word translated "seek after" is an intensified form which carries the sense of *"to seek intensely"* or *"to seek zealously."*[91] The Gentiles (non-Jewish unbelievers) are defined by their intense pursuit of the things of this world: money, food, clothes, houses, etc. They

> You and I pursue the things which own us, and each of us is owned by the things we pursue.

have priorities which are far different from those of the Kingdom of God. They have chosen to serve money rather than God. They now pursue the things which own them, and they are owned by the things they pursue. And the difference between the priorities of unbelievers and those of the Kingdom of God highlights the reality that disciples of the Kingdom march to a different drummer and dance to different music, just as Jesus foretold. *"To what then shall I compare the people of this generation, and what are they like? They are like children sitting in the marketplace and calling to one another, 'We played the flute for you, and you did not dance; we sang a dirge, and you did not weep.'"* (Luke 7:31-32). Jesus understood the priority of the Kingdom. Do we? How "clear" is our "eye" to see the priorities of the Kingdom. Do our priorities set us apart from those around us, and mark us as disciples of the Kingdom?

The Early Church And The Priority Of The Kingdom

The early church outside of the New Testament understood how the priority of the Kingdom and the depth of our faith are expressed through the priorities of everyday life and discipleship. They frequently expressed their understanding through their literature. *"The Epistle of Mathetes to Diognetus"* is one of the earliest pieces of Christian literature outside of the New Testament. In Chapter 5, entitled *"The Manners of the Christians"* the author reveals the "priorities" of those early Christian disciples which set them apart from *"the rest of mankind"*:

(1) For Christians are not distinguished from the rest of mankind either in locality or in speech or in customs. (2) For they dwell not somewhere in cities of their own, neither do they use some different language, nor practise an extraordinary kind of life. (3) Nor again do they possess any invention discovered by any intelligence or study of ingenious men, nor are they masters of any human dogma as some are. (4) But while they dwell in cities of Greeks and barbarians as the lot of each is cast, and follow the native customs in dress and food and the other arrangements of life, yet the constitution of their own citizenship, which they set forth, is marvellous, and confessedly contradicts expectation. (5) They dwell in their own countries, but only as sojourners; they bear their share in all things as citizens, and they endure all

hardships as strangers. Every foreign country is a fatherland to them, and every fatherland is foreign. (6) They marry like all other men and they beget children; but they do not cast away their offspring. (7) They have their meals in common, but not their wives. (8) They find themselves in the flesh, and yet they live not after the flesh. (9) Their existence is on earth, but their citizenship is in heaven. (10) They obey the established laws, and they surpass the laws in their own lives. (11) They love all men, and they are persecuted by all. (12) They are ignored, and yet they are condemned. They are put to death, and yet they are endued with life. (13) They are in beggary, and yet they make many rich. They are in want of all things, and yet they abound in all things. (14) They are dishonoured, and yet they are glorified in their dishonour. They are evil spoken of, and yet they are vindicated. (15) They are reviled, and they bless; they are insulted, and they respect. (16) Doing good they are punished as evil-doers; being punished they rejoice, as if they were thereby quickened by life. (17) War is waged against them as aliens by the Jews, and persecution is carried on against them by the Greeks, and yet those that hate them cannot tell the reason of their hostility." [92]

Questions For Reflection

Reflecting on this Lesson, what did you learn about the priority of the Kingdom?

How would you describe the difference between the priorities of unbelievers and the priorities of a disciple of the Kingdom of God?

How has the priority of the Kingdom of God affected the way you set the other priorities of your life, things such as: money, work, family?

Read: Matthew 8:23-27; 14.25-33; 16:1-12. Jesus used the word *oligopistos* ("men who trust too little") to describe the response of the disciples when they were squeezed by challenging circumstances. How does this word apply to you in the midst of your circumstances today? How are circumstances in your life today revealing your priorities and forcing you to trust God for greater things?

Key Thought

Our single-minded pursuit of the Kingdom of God and His righteousness represents both the outward expression of our faith and the inward priority of our life.

And They Dreamt Of A Kingdom

30 - Specks, Logs And Measuring Cups

"Judge not, that you be not judged. For with the judgment you pronounce you will be judged, and with the measure you use it will be measured to you. Why do you see the speck that is in your brother's eye, but do not notice the log that is in your own eye? Or how can you say to your brother, 'Let me take the speck out of your eye,' when there is the log in your own eye? You hypocrite, first take the log out of your own eye, and then you will see clearly to take the speck out of your brother's eye." (Matthew 7:1 - 5)

Discipleship Reading: Matthew 7:1 - 5   **When:** Spring, A.D. 29
Contextual Reading: Matthew 7; Luke 6   **Where:** Galilee

Jesus understood human nature better than we understand ourselves (John 2:24-25). As He taught His disciples on this day and prepared them for what lay ahead in their individual discipleship and their corporate life together in the Kingdom, Jesus understood that human nature hasn't changed since the days of Adam and Eve. And one of the flaws of our fallen human nature is that we tend to be a "judgmental" people. We take a certain degree of insidious pleasure at pointing the finger at the faults of others while ignoring or excusing our own. We question the motives and spiritual maturity of others while taking offense that anyone would question ours. We condemn the adulteries of others while excusing our own lusts or the "occasional" pornography. We readily repeat gossip about others, but respond with "righteous indignation" when we discover that we are the subject of someone else's gossip. Our human nature - particularly our judgment values - needs the transforming power of the Kingdom of God.

Despite our protests to the contrary, we are like the Pharisee who went up to the temple to pray and spent the whole time thanking God that he was so much "better" than everyone else, particularly the tax-collector who prayed only a few feet away, *"The Pharisee, standing by himself, prayed thus: 'God, I thank you that I am not like other men, extortioners, unjust, adulterers, or even like this tax collector. I fast twice a week; I give tithes of all that I get.' But the tax collector, standing far off, would not even lift up his eyes to heaven, but beat his breast, saying, 'God, be merciful to me, a sinner!'"* (Luke 18:10-14). Like the Pharisee, we easily see the speck of sin in the eye of someone else while ignoring the "log" of pride, judgmentalism and religious self-righteousness in our own eye. In short, we are "hypocrites," and that requires both an explanation and a closer look at Jesus' teaching in this passage.

Jesus' words here offer us an example of Hebrew "parallelism," a literary technique in which a concept is repeated or expressed in two different ways while making the same point:

> with the judgment you pronounce you will be judged, and
> with the measure you use it will be measured to you.

In the Greek text, this couplet literally reads,

> You will be judged by the judgment with which you judge,
> It will be measured to you by the measure with which you measure.

And They Dreamt Of A Kingdom

Contrary to much popular interpretation, this passage isn't about judging or not judging. Surprised? Jesus is emphasizing an idea, namely, that the Kingdom of God operates on a divine principle of "reciprocity." Simply stated, you and I will be treated the way we treat others. You and I will be judged by the same standard we use to judge others. And this brings up the issue of "hypocrisy."

The Greek word translated "hypocrite" (*hupocrites*) originated in ancient Greece as a theatrical term. It originally referred to an actor, someone who *"judged from under the cover of a mask."* The word described an individual who assumed an identity and a character not their own in order to play various roles on stage. It described a "play actor." Later, in the Greek translation of the Hebrew Old Testament (called the "Septuagint" or "LXX") *hupocrites* was used to describe the man with a "double heart" and "false lips" (see Psalm 12:3ff). This is the person who always has God on their lips, but who keeps Him far from their heart (Jeremiah 12:2). This sense of "religious play acting" carried over into the New Testament. In Matthew 15:7-9 Jesus used this word to condemn the "religious play

> *. . . a hypocrite is a "religious play actor" who hides their own sins and faults behind a religious mask while openly judging and condemning the same sins and faults in other people.*

acting" of the Pharisees and Scribes when he declared, *"You hypocrites! Well did Isaiah prophesy of you, when he said: 'This people honors me with their lips, but their heart is far from me; in vain do they worship me, teaching as doctrines the commandments of men.'"* In the New Testament, a hypocrite is a "religious play actor" who hides their own sins and faults behind a religious mask while openly judging and condemning the same sins and faults in other people. They are keenly aware of the flaws and sins of others, however small (even the size of a "wood chip"), while being blissfully ignorant of their own flaws and sins, however large (even the size of a "wood beam").

But Jesus isn't done yet with this lesson. There is more, and we discover it in the parallel metaphor Jesus uses: a measuring cup. A hypocrite is someone with two different measuring cups for measuring out God's grace. According to Jesus, hypocrisy is using one measuring cup to measure out God's grace for ourselves, while using a different measuring cup to measure out God's grace for everyone else. As if "religious play

> *A hypocrite is someone with two different measuring cups for measuring out God's grace.*

acting" wasn't bad enough, hypocrisy is treating someone else differently than we treat ourselves; holding others to a higher standard than the one to which we hold ourselves and measuring out more of God's grace for ourselves than we are willing to measure out for others. A hypocrite is "stingy" when it comes to God's grace for others.

Unlike us, God is no hypocrite in His dealings with men. He consistently judges all men equally and without partiality by the same standard - Himself. God uses one measuring cup for everyone, and He expects disciples of His Kingdom to do the same. And to bring this lesson home to us, God frequently uses the trials, tribulations and circumstances of our lives to teach us not to cheat on our measuring cup. If we want God to give us a full measuring cup of grace during OUR tribulations, then we must be prepared to give others that same full measure of grace during their tribulations. If we want God to be generous to us during our times of financial difficulty, then we must be prepared to be financially generous to others during their time of financial difficulty. *"Do unto others"* is not just a child's Sunday School lesson. This is a principle of discipleship in the Kingdom of God; a principle of divine reciprocity designed to prevent religious hypocrisy, "play acting" and cheating on our measuring cups (see Numbers 10:32; Matthew 7:12; Luke 6:31). The amount of grace you and I want for ourselves from God must be equaled by the amount of grace we are willing to show others. Otherwise, we are hypocrites, and Jesus doesn't like hypocrites, especially religious ones who claim to be His disciples.

There was a rabbinic saying in 1st Century Judaism that ninety per cent of all the hypocrisy in the world was to be found in Jerusalem.[93] Institutional religion has a tendency to breed religious play actors, both then and now, offering a big stage for small actors. We don't know whether Jesus agreed with this piece of rabbinical wisdom or not. What we do know is that Jesus holds His would-be disciples to a higher standard. We miss the point if we conclude that the biblical admonition here is "don't judge" or "don't measure." In the Kingdom of God, genuine discipleship begins by asking better questions of ourselves, not others. Jesus demands that, as His

In the Kingdom of God, genuine discipleship begins by asking better questions of ourselves, not others.

disciples, we abandon any masks of religious play acting and examine our own fruitfulness (or lack thereof) before we attempt to examine someone else's fruitfulness (or lack thereof). He demands that we remove the "wood beam" (of sin, fruitlessness, fear, unbelief, etc.) from our own eyes before they make any attempt to remove any "wood chip" from someone else's eye. And Jesus reminds all would-be disciples that the measuring cup of forgiveness and grace which we desire from God for ourselves must be the same measuring cup of forgiveness and grace which we extend to others. To do otherwise is to be nothing more than a religious play actor. A hypocrite. And Jesus doesn't like hypocrites, especially religious ones who claim to be His disciples.

And They Dreamt Of A Kingdom

Questions For Reflection

The New Testament has quite a bit to say about hypocrisy, or "religious play acting." Spend some time reading and reflecting on the following passages. What warnings or examples do they offer us regarding the hypocrisy of "religious play acting"? How can we apply these lessons to our own discipleship?

1. Matthew 23:27 - 28.

2. Mark 12:13 - 17.

3. Luke 12:1 (Matthew 16:5-12).

4. Galatians 2:11-13.

5. 1 Timothy 4:1 - 3.

6. 1 Peter 2:1 - 3.

Key Thought

Our discipleship in the Kingdom of God calls us to look inward and examine ourselves before we look outward to examine others, and to use the same measuring cup of God's Grace for others as we use for ourselves.

---

31 - Dogs, Pigs And Pearls

"Do not give dogs what is holy, and do not throw your pearls before pigs, lest they trample them underfoot and turn to attack you." (Matthew 7:6)

Discipleship Reading: Matthew 7:6
Contextual Reading: Matthew 7; Luke 6

When: Spring, A.D. 29
Where: Galilee

"For everything there is a season, and a time for every matter under heaven" (Ecclesiastes 3:1).

According to the Old Testament book of Ecclesiastes, there is a time *"for every matter under heaven."* But wisdom, it seems, is knowing when to cast stones and when to gather them; when to plant and when to reap. As the word of God made flesh, Jesus Himself had authored those words (Yes, feel free to take a moment and digest that thought). Now, sitting on a hillside in Galilee, the Word made flesh would explain to His disciples how to apply that wisdom to the truths of the Kingdom of God.

Jesus' declaration here offers a certain intentional "shock value" intended to get the attention of His disciples (and us!). Jesus was being provocative. He wasn't trying to insult his listeners. He wasn't calling people "dogs" or "pigs" (or as the KJV so eloquently renders it, "swine"). No name calling or personal insults were involved here. Jesus was making an important but often overlooked point about spiritual truth. Don't give spiritual truth to people who can't appreciate it.

Don't give spiritual truth to people who can't appreciated it.

When we take a closer look at this passage we see a now-familiar technique at work: Hebraic "parallelism" for the purpose of emphasis.

> *Do not give dogs what is holy, and*
> *do not throw your pearls before pigs*

The first metaphor ("dogs") gets our attention and sets us up for the second metaphor, which develops the point and drives it home. Everyone in Jesus' audience understood certain realities. They understood that both dogs and pigs were "unclean" animals under the Old Testament Law. They also understood that no one in their right Jewish mind would ever give "holy" things to dogs, or pearls to pigs. Why? Because, in addition to being unclean, neither animal had the ability to appreciate what was being offered to them. Dogs can't appreciate "holy" things, and pigs would simply trample pearls underfoot like so many rocks, unaware of the treasure they are rejecting. As far as the pigs are concerned, you and I might as well be throwing worthless stones at them, and they just might respond by turning and attacking you! They just don't get it!

There is a spiritual principle at work here that Jesus wants His disciples to understand. As disciples of the Kingdom they have been given spiritual truth which had been hidden for ages from prophets and men of God. And, according to Jesus, it remains hidden from those outside the Kingdom of God. Simply stated, people outside of the Kingdom of God are spiritually blind to the truths of the Kingdom.

Simply stated, people outside of the Kingdom of God are spiritually blind to the truths of the Kingdom.

And They Dreamt Of A Kingdom

When confronted with spiritual truth concerning the Kingdom, they are unable to see or appreciate it. They don't "get it." The disciples had already witnessed this spiritual blindness first hand in the response of the Jewish religious leaders to Jesus' ministry. By both word and deed Jesus had demonstrated that He was the promised Messiah, Immanuel, "God with us." But the religious leaders didn't "get it" and they chose to oppose His ministry. They were spiritually blind.

"How Can These Things Be?"

"Good beats upon the damned incessantly as sound waves beat on the ears of the deaf, but they cannot receive it." - C. S. Lewis

Let's daydream for a moment. Let's daydream about sitting on the beach on the west shore of Maui at sunset. Sunset in the islands is an almost daily spectacle of low clouds, fading light and indescribable colors. And imagine enjoying this sensory spectacle while seated next to a blind person. You can attempt to describe the changing colors as they reflect upon clouds and water, growing in intensity one moment and fading the next. You can attempt to communicate the sublime moment when the sun slips below the horizon - and perhaps even catch the elusive "green flash" created by the fading sunlight refracted by the ocean. But all you can really do for your blind companion is to provide "facts" for someone who cannot see what you are describing. Their physical blindness prevents them from experiencing the sunset. They simply cannot appreciate what you are offering them. *"How can these things be"* is the cry of blind eyes to a sunset they cannot see.

A similar reality exists when it comes to the Kingdom of God and the things of the Spirit. People in their natural condition are spiritually blind to the truths of the Kingdom. Apart from the work of the Holy Spirit through faith to bring about a new birth, the reality of the Kingdom of God is like our sunset on Maui to a blind person, or as the sound waves of a symphony upon the ears of a deaf person. It is a pearl of great beauty and value which they simply cannot see or comprehend, regardless of how accurate our attempted description might be. *"How can these things be"* is the cry of the blind heart and the deaf ear to the good news of the Kingdom of God.

"How can these things be" is the cry of the blind heart and the deaf ear to the good news of the Kingdom of God.

I came to faith during the summer between my Junior and Senior years of High School. One week after experiencing my new birth I left home for a six week summer school with the National Science Foundation at Virginia Polytech in Blacksburg, Virginia. I was surrounded by very bright high school students in math, chemistry and physics. Word quickly spread that I was a Christian. Things culminated one evening when my dorm room filled with inquiring young minds who wanted to talk faith and theology. We talked into the wee hours of the morning with no visible results (although I made many new friends). Like a shaken Nicodemus working to come to terms with a new spiritual reality, *"How can these things be"* seemed to be the dominant question of the evening.

The summer school eventually ended and I returned home to enjoy the rest of my summer. Several weeks later I received a letter in the mail from an individual who had been a silent participant in our dorm room discussion that evening. In the course of our discussion, he recalled, I had commented that the things I was saying that night might not make sense. But a day would come when they would make sense (I honestly don't remember anything I said that night). He was writing to let me know that things now made sense and that he had become a believer. In terms of our present discipleship discussion, his spiritual blindness concerning the Kingdom of God had lifted. His spiritual eyes had been opened by God, and he could now see and appreciate the pearl of great price which he had neither seen nor appreciated before. No longer spiritually blind or deaf, he now understood how these things could be.

This would not be the last time Jesus would raise the issue of spiritual blindness with His disciples. Certain recurring themes emerge in Jesus' ministry with His disciples, and spiritual blindness is one of them. We will see it again. For now, we need to embrace a basic principle of discipleship which reminds us that spiritual blindness prevents people from appreciating the truths of the Kingdom of God. In the Kingdom of God, the purpose of discipleship is not to learn how to do a better job of casting pearls and giving spiritually blind and deaf people truths they can neither see nor hear. In the Kingdom of God, the purpose of biblical discipleship is to allow the Holy Spirit to shine the light of truth into our own lives, illuminating our blindness and challenging us to ask better questions of ourselves, before we go about asking questions of others.

> *In the Kingdom of God, the purpose of discipleship is not to learn how to do a better job of casting pearls and giving spiritually blind and deaf people truths they can neither see nor hear.*

And They Dreamt Of A Kingdom

Questions For Reflection

Ask Yourself: How am I spiritually blind to what God wants to show me about His Kingdom?

Ask Yourself: How am I spiritually blind to my own faithlessness, to my own fruitlessness, or to the reality that I am serving Mammon (money & lifestyle) rather than God?

Reflection: Scripture is clear that people are, in fact, spiritually blind to the good news of the Kingdom. But people don't like being told that they are spiritually blind. Reflect on how people responded to Jesus when He challenged their spiritual blindness:

1. Concerning God's Kingship and Rule over them (John 19:15);

2. Concerning their own sin and rebellion against the King (John 9:39-41);

3. Concerning their need for repentance and deliverance from their present condition (John 8:31-41);

4. Concerning the reality that their blindness makes them blind to other spiritual truth as well (John 8:42-59).

For Further Reflection: How did Jesus communicate truth while avoiding casting pearls before swine or giving holy things to dogs?

Key Thought

Spiritual blindness prevents people from grasping the truths of the Kingdom of God that we want to share with them.

---

32 - Broad Ways And Narrow Gates

"Enter by the narrow gate. For the gate is wide and the way is easy that leads to destruction, and those who enter by it are many. For the gate is narrow and the way is hard that leads to life, and those who find it are few." (Matthew 7:13-14)

Discipleship Reading: Matthew 7:13-14   ***When:*** *Spring, A.D. 29*
Contextual Reading: *Matthew 7; Luke 13*   ***Where:*** *Galilee*

Apparently, this lesson was important to Jesus. How do we know? Because He taught it at least twice. We find the first recorded instance here in Matthew 7:13-14. The second instance took place roughly 18 months later toward the close of Jesus ministry in Luke 13:23-30. In the account from Luke, Jesus was on the road, traveling between villages on his way to Jerusalem, *"He went on his way through towns and villages, teaching and journeying toward Jerusalem."* (Luke 13:22). Since the disciples had heard Jesus teach on this issue before, perhaps when it arose again here in Luke one of the disciples finally decided to ask the obvious question, *"Lord, will those who are saved be few?"* That's a good question, which needs to be explored.

We need to pause for a moment and reflect on why this passage represents a transformational value in the Kingdom of God, as well as in the lives of these disciples. Every religiously observant Jew in 1st Century Israel believed that the Kingdom of God was their national birthright, and that they were destined for eternal life in "the age to come." In other words, the disciples - along with national Israel - believed they were on the narrow path which leads to life. Conversely, that meant that all non-Jews, or "Gentiles," were on the broad way to destruction. Jesus' declaration here in Matthew, along with His teachings in Luke 13, calls that national assumption into question. Jesus understands that, like Nicodemus before them, the disciples need a transformation of their understanding concerning entrance to the Kingdom of God.

But there's more. With Jesus, there always is.

How Narrow Is The Door To The Kingdom?

Jesus' teaching on this subject forces us to ask a basic question: Are His words to be taken at face value? The importance of this question is underscored by the fact that Jesus makes this same basic point on two separate occasions. If we are to take Jesus' words seriously and accept the plain meaning of Scripture, then we are confronted with an uncomfortable truth. While there is indeed a wideness in God's mercy by which He offers the good news of the Kingdom to "all who believe," the practical and theological reality is that the number of people who actually respond to the good news and enter into the Kingdom of God is "few" when compared with the number of those who perish. And that reality begs us to dig deeper into this passage in order to understand exactly what this means for all would-be disciples of the Kingdom. For the sake of simplicity, I want to organize my observations under four basic summary points, combining observations from both the Luke and the Matthew passages.

1. Entrance To The Kingdom Of God Is Restrictively Narrow. Any objective reader of these passages should be struck by an overall impression that Jesus is giving an affirmative answer to the question, *". . . are there just a few who are being saved?"* If this impression were not genuine and wide spread, this passage wouldn't even raise an eyebrow, and we wouldn't be discussing it. But because this impression is both genuine and widespread, it forces us to stop, to take notice and to ask, *"What does Jesus mean?"* What strikes me about the Matthew passage is not its length but its details. Jesus uses several descriptive Greek words to portray how broad and spacious the pathway is which leads to ruin or destruction, and how many people are there.[94] Jesus wants His listeners to understand a simple truth: *"The pathway to ruin is spaciously broad, and the masses are entering into it."*

Next, Matthew gives us equal detail regarding the pathway to life. The two Greek words he uses combine to communicate a sense of difficulty which requires effort; a sense of being *"hemmed in, like a mountain gorge."* The pathway into the Kingdom of God is "restrictively narrow," like a narrow path through the mountains which takes work.[95] Jesus underscores this point - ease versus difficulty - by using the contrast between the two verbs which dominate this passage. On the

You and I don't need to go looking for spiritual ruin or destruction. It will find us.

one hand, those on the pathway to ruin simply "enter in." It's an easy entrance. No effort required. On the other hand, the pathway to life is accessible only by those who "find" it .[96]

The point is so simple as to be easily overlooked. You and I don't need to go looking for spiritual ruin or destruction. It will find us. The "road to ruin" is a broad and spacious place, populated by the masses and not easily missed. Follow the crowd, and you'll get there. Just keep doing what you're doing. But the road to eternal life and the Kingdom is different. It is a small and restrictively narrow path through the mountains which is easily missed by those unwilling to make the effort (*"strive"*) to discover it. In the Kingdom of God, spiritual laziness is as deadly as spiritual blindness.

In the Kingdom of God, spiritual laziness is as deadly as spiritual blindness.

Spiritual blindness causes people to mistake the broad way for the right way, if for no other reason than there are so many people on it. Spiritual laziness causes people to miss the narrow path into the Kingdom due to their unwillingness to make the effort o find it.

As disciples of the Kingdom, part of our calling is to understand that the crowds are frequently wrong, especially regarding the things of the Kingdom. Every would-be disciple of the Kingdom must exercise a conscious choice to ignore the pull of the crowd to join them on their journey on the broad path, choosing instead to pursue the restrictively narrow path which leads to the Kingdom of God.

2. Entrance To The Kingdom Of God Requires Intentionality. The Kingdom of God will not be found by those who are unwilling to make the effort to pursue it. The idea of intentionality jumps out at us from the Luke passage where Jesus uses the word "strive" (Greek: *agonizomai*) which communicates the sense of *"to engage in a contest, to fight or to struggle or to agonize."* It's as if Jesus is addressing all of His disciples as a group and giving them a command: *"All of you (plural), strive to enter the narrow door."* That, friends, is intentionality writ large. Paul uses the same word in 1 Corinthians 9:25 in the context of an athletic competition, describing the intentional self-discipline an athlete must exercise in order to win. Paul uses it again in 1 Timothy 6:12 where he admonishes his young protégé to *"fight the* good fight of faith" in order that he might *"take hold of the eternal life to which you were called."* To rephrase, Paul tells Timothy that, if he wants to lay hold of the Kingdom of God he must *"struggle (agonizomai) the good struggle (agona)."* And any such struggle requires intentionality on our part (See also 2 Timothy 4:7). All the occurrences of this word-group have something in common. They all communicate the idea that salvation, eternal life and entrance into the Kingdom of God are to be diligently

The narrow path into the Kingdom of God must be the intentional focus and daily pursuit of every would-be disciple of the Kingdom.

sought after and fought for in this life. They all require intentionality on our part. The narrow path into the Kingdom of God must be the intentional focus and daily pursuit of every would-be disciple of the Kingdom.

3. Entrance To The Kingdom Is Surrounded By A Sense Of Urgency. When we read Jesus' words in Luke 13 we cannot escape a genuine sense of urgency surrounding our striving for the narrow way of the Kingdom, *"When once the master of the house has risen and shut the door, and you begin to stand outside and to knock at the door, saying, 'Lord, open to us,' then he will answer you, 'I do not know where you come from.'"* (Luke 13:25) Like the ten virgins awaiting the arrival of the bridegroom in Matthew 25, at some unspecified time which we cannot predict, the master of the house will shut the door and the opportunity to enter the Kingdom will be past. The point of the parable is not to generate fruitless discussion concerning the timing, or even the "fairness" of it all. The point of the parable is to communicate a sense of urgency and to motivate us in our pursuit. All would-be disciples need to understand that life is short, and this can't wait.

4. Entrance To The Kingdom of God Will Be Unexpectedly Denied To Many And Unexpectedly Gained By Others. In Luke's account, Jesus' teaching on this subject comes to an unexpected conclusion. Some people who think they should be granted entrance to the Kingdom won't be there, *"Then you will begin to say, 'We ate and drank in your presence, and you taught in our streets.' But he will say, 'I tell you, I do not know where you come from. Depart from me, all you workers of evil!'"* (Luke 13:26-27) Like Nicodemus, most of 1st Century Judaism thought that their Jewish heritage and their faithful religious observances were enough to gain entrance to the Kingdom. After all, they were God's chosen people. In addition, there may have been some who thought that their casual acquaintance with Jesus, perhaps as "followers," would be enough to grant them entry to the Kingdom. But Jesus dashes all such mis-placed hopes, while raising hopes that others from the four corners of the earth will find a place and join patriarchs and prophets *"at table in the kingdom of God."* That was unexpected. Just ask Nicodemus. Jesus wanted His disciples to understand that no one is entitled to a seat at God's table in the Kingdom. Only those who are willing to seek and pursue. Only those who believe. Only those who have truly experienced the heavenly birth. Only those who have heard and responded to Jesus' call to "follow me."

How Should We Respond To This Reality?

Taken at face value in their context, these passages should challenge all would-be disciples with some sobering truth. According to Jesus, more people will enter into eventual destruction and ruin than will find the Kingdom of God and eternal life. You and I need to allow the full impact of this situation to sink in before attempting any response. But exactly how should we as would-be disciples of the Kingdom respond to this spiritual reality? I want to offer three basic responses. One is to be avoided, while the other two should be pursued.

1. Question God's Fairness And Demand A More Inclusive Interpretation. This is an increasingly common response in many circles today. With an increased frequency I am hearing church leaders engaging in rhetorical attacks on Scripture and God's character in an attempt to moot the impact of these passages. They offer such emotionally-laden declarations as, *"What kind of a God would create billions of people, knowing that the vast majority of them would spend eternity in hell?"* Such attacks have breathed new life into the old-but-rejected doctrine of "Universalism" which maintains that everyone will eventually enter the Kingdom, out of "fairness" and "love," if for no other reason.

I have often wondered if, perhaps, this approach has roots in a uniquely American psyche which wants to "fix the door" (*"It's obviously too narrow"*) while making the whole process more democratic and inclusive. But on a deeper level our responses to this truth reveal something about ourselves. Fallen and spiritually blind people think that they and others are more deserving, or more responsive or less blind than they really are (I call this the *"if only they knew, they would respond"* syndrome). This leads to accusations that God isn't being "fair" or "democratic." Like Abraham arguing with God to spare Sodom and Gomorrah if only ten righteous could be found (Genesis 18:16-33), we think

> *People choose to walk on the broad way to destruction for reasons which are, for the most part, hidden from us but well known to God.*

we have a better understanding of the moral universe than God does, and that the Judge of all the earth would act more justly if only He understood what we claim to understand. But when the truth is revealed we discover that God was both correct and just in His judgments. There were not ten righteous to be found, even among Lot's extended family, and even Lot's wife perished when judgment fell. People choose to walk on the broad way to destruction for reasons which are, for the most part, hidden from us but well known to God.

2. Allow This Truth To Motivate Us To Proclaim The Message Of The Kingdom. The spiritual reality that the pathway to salvation, eternal life and the Kingdom of God is narrow and that the masses of people will miss it (or reject it) should motivate every disciple of the Kingdom to share the good news of the Kingdom with those around us, just as it motivated Jesus. And that is the relevant point in this conversation. Jesus Himself was fully aware of people's spiritual blindness and the narrowness of the gate when He began His ministry of proclaiming the good news of the Kingdom. We shouldn't allow those realities to deter us any more than Jesus allowed them to deter Him. We are not responsible for either their blindness or their response, but we are responsible for proclaiming the good news of the Kingdom.

3. Allow This Truth To Motivate Us In Our Personal Pursuit As Disciples Of The Kingdom. Jesus taught in a manner intended to cause people to ask questions, particularly of themselves. The disciples initiated this conversation by asking Jesus a question about the fate of the masses, *"Lord, will those who are saved be few?"* Jesus answered them with a command concerning their own personal situation, *"(You) Strive to enter through the narrow door."* This represents an imperative, a command requiring personal obedience. Jesus' response was intended to motivate and provoke, not to soothe and comfort by offering simplistic answers to hard spiritual questions. The primary calling and foremost responsibility of every disciple of the Kingdom is *"to seek the Kingdom of God and His righteousness."* You and I cannot lead others into that Kingdom if we do not know the way, or if we do not understand the profound difference between the broad way which leads to destruction and the narrow way which leads to the Kingdom of God. Do you?

Questions For Reflection

Reflecting on this Lesson, what did you learn about entry into the Kingdom of God that you did not know before?

How do you find yourself responding to this truth that the masses of people today are on the broad road to destruction?

How has your own discipleship and pursuit of the Kingdom required "striving" and "intentionality"? How would you communicate that need for "intentionality" to someone else?

Read Genesis 18:16 - 19:24. Reflect on how Abraham mis-understood God's dealings with Sodom, the moral situation involved and God's response to it? How do we do the same thing today?

Key Thought

As disciples of the Kingdom we understand that the path into the Kingdom of God is narrow and requires intentional effort on our part both to pursue and to find . . . and to continue pursuing.

And They Dreamt Of A Kingdom

33 - False Prophets And Fruit

"Beware of false prophets, who come to you in sheep's clothing but inwardly are ravenous wolves. You will recognize them by their fruits." (Matthew 7:15)

Discipleship Reading: Matthew 7:15-23   ***When:*** *Spring, A.D. 29*
Contextual Reading: *Matthew 7; Luke 6*   ***Where:*** *Galilee*

First, Some Background

False prophets were nothing new. Over the centuries, from the days of Balaam the son of Beor (Numbers 22-24) to Hananiah the son of Azzur who opposed the prophet Jeremiah, the people of God had been plagued by false prophets who claimed to speak for God, but didn't. Conversely, they were also blessed by many prophets who did speak for God. To speak for God was an awesome privilege and responsibility. To speak lies and deception in God's name was an unforgivable sin. Over the centuries God had made it clear that He actively opposed false prophets who promoted their "false and deceptive visions," but who failed to expose sin and iniquity and to call the people of God to repentance and restoration (Jeremiah 29; Lamentations 2:14; Ezekiel 13:9; Ezekiel 22:28). But there was a basic question which continually confronted God's people, namely, how to recognize a false prophet. How can God's people know if a prophet is truly speaking (or acting) for God, or not? We see this dilemma expressed by Moses in his final instructions to the people of Israel before they entered the land of Canaan:

"And if you say in your heart, 'How may we know the word that the LORD has not spoken?' - when a prophet speaks in the name of the LORD, if the word does not come to pass or come true, that is a word that the LORD has not spoken; the prophet has spoken it presumptuously. You need not be afraid of him." (Deuteronomy 18:21-22)

In Deuteronomy 18 God gave His people the first of two important criteria by which to recognize a false prophet. If he (or she) claims to speak for God, but their word doesn't come to pass, then they don't speak for God. They are a false prophet. But there's an additional problem. What if an alleged prophet performed a miraculous sign or wonder (suggesting God is with them), but by their teaching or example they lead people astray, even to the point of denying the Lord God and following false gods. What then?

"If a prophet or a dreamer of dreams arises among you and gives you a sign or a wonder, and the sign or wonder that he tells you comes to pass, and if he says, 'Let us go after other gods,' which you have not known, 'and let us serve them,' you shall not listen to the words of that prophet or that dreamer of dreams." (Deuteronomy 13:1-3)

This is the second criteria for recognizing a false prophet. Yes, they may speak a true word, and even perform a sign or wonder (again, suggesting that God is with them), but they use these things to promote a false teaching which leads people away from God and away from the truth of His word. In other words, the mark which distinguishes the true prophet from the false is NOT merely the accuracy of the word they speak (although that can certainly be a

In the hands of Jesus, the Kingdom of God transforms the sign of genuine prophecy from words and power to fruit.

And They Dreamt Of A Kingdom

factor), or the miraculous sign they might perform, but the fruit which that word produces in the lives of the hearers. And that brings us to Jesus' teaching on this subject in our passage from the Gospel of Matthew.

Jesus, False Prophets And Fruit Trees

This was the background which laid the foundation for what Jesus wanted to teach His disciples, and us. Beginning with a warning, Jesus proceeds to use a series of word-pictures to describe false prophets. *"Watch out for these people,"* would be an accurate rendering of Jesus' opening words. *"They come to you dressed like sheep, but they are really ravenous robber wolves."* According to Jesus, these people dress, act and talk like "sheep." Outwardly, they look like disciples and talk like disciples. But their behavior is like the religious play acting Jesus warned His disciples about earlier; a mask or a costume ("clothing") worn when convenient but which hides an inward reality that is quite different.

The inevitable question quickly arises, *"How are we to recognize such people for who they really are?"* How do we get behind the religious clothes and mask? Jesus answers this question in no uncertain terms, *"You will recognize them by their fruits."* The word translated "recognize" (Greek: *epiginosko*) represents an intense form of knowledge which enables an individual to "come to a judgment" regarding a situation. Like a judge weighing the evidence presented, we are able to "recognize" what is really going on. When it comes to these false prophets, says Jesus, you and I will be able to come to a judgment concerning them. How? By examining their fruit.

There is a simple but important operative principle at work here. In the hands of Jesus, the Kingdom of God transforms the sign of genuine prophecy from words and power to fruit. We are what we produce, and we produce what we are. When the fruit of a person's life is suspect, his words and his power are suspect, too. Jesus illustrates this basic principle with agricultural illustrations concerning fruit trees which His disciples (and others) would easily understand. John the Baptist, the forerunner of Jesus, had touched on this principle earlier in his own ministry when he declared, *"Even now the axe is laid to the root of the trees. Every tree therefore that does not bear good fruit is cut down and thrown into the fire"* (Luke 3:9). This principle of bearing fruit, and of recognizing the reality that people are what they produce, is so important that Jesus states it twice, first at the beginning of this Lesson (7:16) and again here, at the climax of this lesson (7:20). Jesus even re-iterates this principle during one of His confrontations with the Pharisees when He declares, *"Either make the tree good and its fruit good, or make the tree bad and its fruit bad, for the tree is known by its fruit"* (Matthew 12:33). We are all known by what we produce, not by the outward masks and sheep costumes we may hide behind,

> *We are all known by what we produce, not by the outward masks and sheep costumes we may hide behind.*

"For no good tree bears bad fruit, nor again does a bad tree bear good fruit, for each tree is known by its own fruit. For figs are not gathered from thorn bushes, nor are grapes picked from a bramble bush. The good person out of the good treasure of his heart produces good, and the evil person out of his evil treasure produces evil, for out of the abundance of the heart his mouth speaks." (Luke 6:43-45)

The Fruit Of The Kingdom

"Already the one who reaps is receiving wages and gathering fruit for eternal life, so that sower and reaper may rejoice together" (John 4:36)

Jesus' analogy of bearing fruit only comes into clear perspective when we grasp a simple truth: The Kingdom of God is a fruit bearing tree which produces only good fruit and bears only good seed. And that good seed, when sown into the lives of unbelievers by disciples of the Kingdom, will produce more good trees, more disciples of the Kingdom, who will produce more good fruit and more good seed to be sown by more disciples of the Kingdom into the lives of more unbelievers. And the Jesus-shaped process of creating disciples of the Kingdom repeats itself, from now until He returns. Throughout His ministry, Jesus would use other similar analogies to make the same point: the parable of the sower and seed, the parable of the vineyard, vines and branches. But the operative principle is always the same. We are what we produce. We manifest our relationship to the Kingdom of God through the fruit of our lives.

1. The Kingdom of God Produces Fruit Which Is Different From Our Previous Life. The new, heavenly birth changes us, delivering us from the domain of darkness and transferring us to the Kingdom of God's Son (Colossians 1:13-14). As a result of that personal transformation, the fruit of our new life in the Kingdom of God should be noticeably different from the fruit of our old life in the domain of darkness. This is Paul's point when he writes to the disciples in the church at Rome, *"But what fruit were you getting at that time from the things of which you are now ashamed? For the end of those things is death. But now that you have been set free from sin and have become slaves of God, the fruit you get leads to sanctification and its end, eternal life"* (Romans 6:21-22).

> *The Kingdom of God is a fruit bearing tree which produces only good fruit and bears only good seed.*

2. The Kingdom of God Produces the Fruit of Repentance and Righteousness. Throughout the Scriptures, and in the centuries leading up to the ministry of Jesus, the Kingdom of God had always been about repentance from sin and the pursuit of God's righteousness (or "holiness"). The prophet Jonah had called the people of Nineveh to repent of their sin in order to be spared God's pending judgment. The prophet Jeremiah had proclaimed the same message of repentance to the people of Judah. And the prophet Zechariah explained to the remnant of God's people that their seventy year captivity in Babylon had come about as a consequence of their refusal to repent of their sin and return to the Lord God. Describing the righteous nature of the yet-future Kingdom of God, the prophet Isaiah wrote, *"And a highway shall be there, and it shall be called the Way of Holiness; the unclean shall not pass over it. It shall belong to those who walk on the way; even if they are fools, they shall not go astray"* (Isaiah 35:8).

The Scriptures are clear. If it isn't "righteous," if it isn't "holy," it isn't the Kingdom. The Kingdom of God is a fruit tree of righteousness, the fruit and seed of which are righteous and will produce *"the peaceful fruit of righteousness"* (Hebrews 12:11) in the lives of all who repent of their sins, believe the good news and become disciples of the Kingdom. This is why the Apostle Paul could tell the believers in the Roman colony of Philippi, *"For God is my witness, how I yearn for you all with the affection of Christ Jesus. And it is my prayer that your love may abound more and more, with knowledge and all discernment, so that you may approve what is excellent,*

And They Dreamt Of A Kingdom

and so be pure and blameless for the day of Christ, filled with the <u>fruit of righteousness</u> that comes through Jesus Christ, to the glory and praise of God" (Philippians 1:8-11).

3. The Kingdom of God Produces The Fruit of Salvation. Just as the people of God in the Old Testament understood the reality of the Kingdom, they also understood that the Kingdom of God produces the fruit of salvation, *"Yet God my King is from of old, working salvation in the midst of the earth"* (Psalms 74:12; see also Psalms 44:4). Prophesying the future coming of the Messiah-King, Who would bring the Kingdom, the prophet Zechariah declared, *"Rejoice greatly, O daughter of Zion! Shout aloud, O daughter of Jerusalem! Behold, your king is coming to you; righteous and having salvation is he, humble and mounted on a donkey, on a colt, the foal of a donkey"* (Zechariah 9:9).

When the King brings the Kingdom, He brings salvation with Him. Zechariah, the father of John the Baptist, understood this truth when he prayed and declared, *"Blessed be the Lord God of Israel, for he has visited and redeemed his people and has raised up a horn of salvation for us in the house of his servant David"* (Luke 1:68-69). Jesus, the Messiah-King, described His own ministry in terms of salvation when He declared, *"For the Son of Man came to seek and to save the lost"* (Luke

> When the King brings the Kingdom, He brings salvation with Him.

19:10). Finally, John, the author of The Revelation, heard this truth proclaimed from heaven and wrote, *"And I heard a loud voice in heaven, saying, 'Now the salvation and the power and the kingdom of our God and the authority of his Christ have come, for the accuser of our brothers has been thrown down, who accuses them day and night before our God'"* (Revelation 12:10). The Kingdom of God is a fruit bearing tree which produces the fruit of salvation for everyone who repents of their sins, believes the good news and becomes a disciple of the Kingdom.

4. The Kingdom of God Produces The Fruit of Good Works. The Kingdom of God is a fruit bearing tree which produces the fruit of "good works" in the life of every disciple of the Kingdom. This Kingdom fruit manifests itself in the life of a disciple in a growing desire to please God and to bear fruit "in every good work." This is what Paul meant when he told the disciples in the city of Colossae, *"And so, from the day we heard, we have not ceased to pray for you, asking that you may be filled with the knowledge of his will in all spiritual wisdom and understanding, so as to walk in a manner worthy of the Lord, fully pleasing to him, bearing fruit in every good work and increasing in the knowledge of God"* (Colossians 1:9-10). The Kingdom of God is a fruit

> The Kingdom of God is a fruit bearing tree which produces the fruit of "good works" in the life of every disciple of the Kingdom.

bearing tree. As disciples, if we are the genuine fruit of that Kingdom, then we, too, will eventually bear fruit through our good works.

Fruit Versus Signs And Wonders

On this day on a hillside in Galilee twelve young disciples of the Kingdom listened as the Messiah-King explained the role of professions, signs, wonders and fruit in the life of every disciple of the Kingdom. Neither an outward profession of "Lord, Lord," nor the ability to perform miraculous signs and wonders (prophesying, casting out demons, doing "mighty works") can provide anyone with confirmation regarding their position in the Kingdom of God. Professions of "Lord, Lord" may be nothing more than religious play acting by wolves in sheep costumes (Luke 6:46). Signs and wonders can be the product of Satanic activity (Matthew 24:24; 2 Thessalonians 2:9). But genuine disciples of the Kingdom, like the Kingdom of God itself, are fruit bearing trees, which are not known by either their profession or their power, but by their fruit.[97] Those who believe and act otherwise may one day hear the Messiah-King Himself declare, *"I never knew you; depart from me, you workers of lawlessness."*

Questions For Reflection

The Kingdom of God Produces Fruit Which Is Different From Our Previous Life. Describe how the fruit of your life today is different from the fruit of your life prior to Christ? How has the fruit of your life changed more recently?

The Kingdom of God Produces the Fruit of Repentance and Righteousness. How is your discipleship in the Kingdom producing the on-gong fruit of repentance from sin and the pursuit of "righteousness" or "holiness"?

The Kingdom of God Produces The Fruit of Salvation. How would you describe or explain your own experience of salvation (and discipleship) in the Kingdom to an unbeliever?

The Kingdom of God Produces The Fruit of Good Works. If you were put on trial and accused of **NOT** being a disciple of the Kingdom, what fruit could you point to as evidence of your commitment to Jesus?

Key Thought

In the Kingdom of God, both false prophets and genuine disciples of the Kingdom are known by the fruit they produce, not by the religious masks and sheep costumes they may hide behind.

And They Dreamt Of A Kingdom

34 - The Inverted Values of the Kingdom

"Everyone then who hears these words of mine and does them will be like a wise man who built his house on the rock. And the rain fell, and the floods came, and the winds blew and beat on that house, but it did not fall, because it had been founded on the rock. And everyone who hears these words of mine and does not do them will be like a foolish man who built his house on the sand. And the rain fell, and the floods came, and the winds blew and beat against that house, and it fell, and great was the fall of it." (Matthew 7:24-27)

Discipleship Reading: Matthew 7:24-27   *When: Spring, A.D. 29*
Contextual Reading: Matthew 7; Luke 6   *Where: Galilee*

     Listening to Jesus on this day in the Spring of A.D. 29, the disciples would undoubtedly remember that the Hebrew scriptures had much to say about the "wise" man versus the "fool." The book of Proverbs in particular contained some forty passages which speak to the difference between the wise man and the fool. Since their youth, the disciples had been taught that:

1.   A wise man receives instruction, but a fool does not (Proverbs 10:8).
2.   A fool is right in his own eyes, but a wise man listens to advice (Proverbs 12:15).
3.   A fool is reckless and careless around evil, whereas a wise man is cautious (Proverbs14:16).
4.   A fool couldn't buy wisdom even if he had money (Proverbs 17:16).
5.   A fool is more interested in expressing his own opinion than he is in gaining wisdom (Proverbs 18:2).

     These, along with many more, were the declarations of biblical wisdom which Jesus disciples already knew. What they didn't know was that Jesus was about to transform their understanding of biblical wisdom by applying it in ways they could never have expected. They were about to discover that Jesus' words are wisdom, on an equal level with the wisdom of Proverbs. And the disciple of the Kingdom who hears Jesus' words and acts on them is "wise." [98] The disciple of the Kingdom, hearing and obeying the words of Jesus, is the wise person described in the Book of Proverbs. The life of the disciple of the Kingdom is the house built upon a rock. It will survive, for both time and eternity. On the other hand, the person who hears Jesus' words and chooses not to act on them, who chooses not to become a disciple of the Kingdom, is the "fool" (Greek: *moros*) of Proverbs who refuses to accept wisdom and advice when it is offered to him. This person's life is the house built upon sand. It will not last, either in time or in eternity.

> *The life of the disciple of the Kingdom is the house built upon a rock. It will survive, for both time and eternity.*

     But there's more. With Jesus, there always is.

The Inverted Values of The Kingdom of God

     Even a quick and cursory reading of the Gospels reveals that the Kingdom of

And They Dreamt Of A Kingdom

God is built upon inverted, upside down values. The least will be the greatest. The first will be last. He who saves his life will lose it. He who loses His life will find it. Murder isn't an act, but a hateful thought. Adultery isn't an act, but a lust in one's heart. Love your enemies. Pray for those who mistreat you. If your enemy forces you to carry his belongings one mile, carry them two. Take no anxious thought for tomorrow. Seek first His Kingdom. And deliverance, redemption and salvation will come, not by political posturing, force of arms or intellectual reasoning, but by death on a despised cross. These inverted, upside down values (and there are more) represent the "wisdom" of the Kingdom of God and the "rock" upon which Jesus calls the "wise" man to build the house of his life. From the world's perspective, only a fool would do that. From the perspective of the Kingdom of God, only a fool would not.

The Kingdom of God transforms wisdom by re-defining what it means to be wise. The wisdom of the Kingdom of God is foolishness to those still held captive by the domain of darkness. And the wisdom of the domain of darkness is foolishness to disciples of the Kingdom, or at least it is supposed to be. This conflict between the wisdom of God and the foolishness of men has been a source of on-going tension for disciples of the Kingdom, as the Apostle Paul discovered in his dealings with the disciples in the Greek city of Corinth. Paul had spent no less than 18 months living and ministering among the Corinthian disciples, personally leading most of them to faith in Christ.

The Kingdom of God transforms wisdom by re-defining what it means to be wise.

But after Paul left, false teachers arrived calling into question not only Paul's teaching, but calling into question the "inverted and upside down" values of the Kingdom which Jesus, Himself, had taught. Appealing to human wisdom - which is never far removed from the domain of darkness - they taught the Corinthian believers to justify and tolerate gross immorality in their midst. They ridiculed Paul's simple proclamation of Christ crucified and used their eloquent preaching skills to make Paul's message seem like the ramblings of a second rate "country bumpkin." Neither Paul nor his message of Christ crucified were "wise" by the standards of these false teachers. The situation in Corinth became so bad that Paul was forced to respond aggressively to these false teachers who wanted to use the wisdom of the world to overturn the upside down values of the Kingdom.

"For the word of the cross is folly to those who are perishing, but to us who are being saved it is the power of God. For it is written, 'I will destroy the wisdom of the wise, and the discernment of the discerning I will thwart.' Where is the one who is wise? Where is the scribe? Where is the debater of this age? Has not God made foolish the wisdom of the world? For since, in the wisdom of God, the world did not know God through wisdom, it pleased God through the folly of what we preach to save those who believe. For Jews demand signs and Greeks seek wisdom, but we preach Christ crucified, a stumbling block to Jews and folly to Gentiles, but to those who are called, both Jews and Greeks, Christ the power of God and the wisdom of God. For the foolishness of God is wiser than men, and the weakness of God is stronger than men." (1 Corinthians 1:8-25)

Living Out The Inverted Values Of The Kingdom

Like Jesus, His Master, Paul understood that these Corinthian disciples needed more than correct teaching concerning the inverted values of the Kingdom. Like all would-be disciples, the young Corinthian believers needed correct teaching combined with the personal example of what the inverted values of the Kingdom looked like in the life of a disciple of the Kingdom. That's how Jesus taught His disciples, and that is what Paul knew He must now offer the Corinthians. To accomplish this Paul offered himself as the example, building his teaching around three word pictures: servants, spectacles and fools.

As Disciples Of The Kingdom We Live As "Servants." The first of these word pictures is found in 1 Corinthians 4:1, *"Let a man regard us in this manner, as servants of Christ, and stewards of the mysteries of God."* The Greek word translated "servants" (*huperetes*) originally referred to "an under-rower." The term applied to a rower on the lowest level of a Roman trireme. He was a galley slave whose job was to "row the boat" and whose fate, if the battle went ill, was to perish with the ship, chained to his oar (remember the sea-battle scene from the movie *"Ben Hur"*). Later, the word came to refer to any civil servant or anyone who serves another, but the image of the galley slave would remain. For the disciple of the Kingdom, the upside-down wisdom of God means that each of us - from the least to the greatest - offers ourselves as an under-rower to serve Jesus our King and His Kingdom purposes. Paul gives the Corinthian believers a vivid description of his life as an under-rower, *"To this present hour we are both hungry and thirsty, and are poorly clothed, and are roughly treated, and are homeless; and we toil, working with our own hands; when we are reviled, we bless; when we are persecuted, we endure; when we are slandered, we try to conciliate; we have become as the scum of the world, the dregs of all things, even until now."* (1 Corinthians 4:11-13). This is what it means to live out the inverted values of the Kingdom.

As Disciples Of The Kingdom We Live As "Spectacles." The second word picture which Paul applies to himself is the word "spectacle" found in verse 9, *"For, I think, God has exhibited us apostles last of all, as men condemned to death; because we have become a spectacle to the world, both to angels and to men."* The Greek word here is *theatron* from which we get our English word "theater." Paul likens his life and ministry to playing out a part on a public stage, a divine theater in which both men and angels watch to see how he will acquit himself and play out the role given to him.

Wolfgang Simson suggests that Paul is describing a phenomenon known as the *"meridian gladiators"* (*meridiani gladitorii*) of the Roman arena. The various gladiators of the Roman arena were broken into groups or classes. The gladiators fighting wild beasts appeared in the morning. The *"meridian gladiators"* were the afternoon entertainment, intended to wake up the after-lunch crowd. They were inexperienced, lightly armed, and no match for their opponents. According to some descriptions, their "fights" resembled executions more than gladiatorial competitions. They were "spectacles" before the crowd. And so are we. And that is Paul's point. As disciples of the Kingdom, God's call upon our lives is to live as "spectacles" in God's divine drama for men and angels to witness. Like the *"meridian gladiators"* of the Roman arena, our obedience as disciples is played out in full public display so that others can see what the inverted values of the Kingdom look like when fleshed out in the lives of real people.

As Disciples Of The Kingdom We Live As "Fools." And this third and final

207

And They Dreamt Of A Kingdom

word picture brings us back to where we started, to the word _moros_, to the difference between the wise man and the fool. As disciples of the Kingdom, we are fools for Christ, wise before God but fools before the world. As disciples, we are willing to be regarded by others as engaging in foolishness, staking our lives and reputations on the belief that the foolish things of God are wiser than the greatest wisdom of men. As disciples of the Kingdom, we stand alongside saints who have preceded us, declaring with them that _"He is no fool who gives what he cannot keep to gain that which he cannot lose."_ [99]

Questions For Reflection

Reflecting on this Lesson, what did you discover about the inverted values of the Kingdom and what it means to be "wise" that you did not know before?

Based upon what you have learned so far from the ministry of Jesus, what other inverted values have you encountered in the Kingdom of God?

Reflecting on your walk as a disciple of the Kingdom, how has God called you to live out the inverted values of His wisdom in your daily life 1) as a servant, 2) as a spectacle and 3) as a "fool" in the eyes of those around you?

Key Thought

The wisdom of God means that as disciples of the Kingdom we live our lives by inverted values which make us servants, spectacles and fools before a watching, unbelieving world.

---

35 - A Widespread Ministry

"When he came down from the mountain, great crowds followed him." (Matthew 8:1)

Discipleship Reading: Matthew 8:1　　　　　**When:** Spring, A.D. 29
Contextual Reading: Matthew 8; 11-12; Luke 7　　　**Where:** Galilee

　　　In the Spring of A.D.29 Jesus stood at the zenith of His popularity with the masses, especially in the northern Israel region of Galilee. Such fame and popularity meant a busy season of widespread ministry. So, with a full compliment of twelve disciples in tow, Jesus set out for a ministry tour of Galilee. Once again, it was time to take the good news of the Kingdom to the people who most needed to hear it.[100]

　　　Healing A Leper (Matthew 8:1-4). When Jesus left the mountain side where He had just taught His disciples, He was followed by "great crowds" (Matthew 8:1), and a single leper. Jesus healed this leper with a word and a touch (Matthew 8:2-4). It was a Messianic miracle that passed unnoticed by those who should have noticed. The disciples noticed, and what they undoubtedly saw on this day was the Messiah-King ignoring the "great crowd" and devoting His attention to the healing of a single marginalized leper. That alone was a lesson in Kingdom discipleship that could last a lifetime.

　　　The Faith of a Centurion (Matthew 8:5-13; Luke 7:1-10). Traveling through His adopted home town of Capernaum, Jesus encountered a Centurion whose servant was ill. Jesus offered to come and heal the servant. But the Centurion objected, responding that Jesus only needed to speak a word and his servant would be healed. Had Jesus' disciples not personally witnessed His outreach to the marginalized on other occasions, they might have been stunned by Jesus' declarations. *First,* Jesus declared that in the person of this Roman Centurion, He had found a Gentile who demonstrated greater faith than anyone else in Israel. If you were a Jew living in Israel, that had to hurt. But there was more.

　　　Second, Jesus declared that, in the Kingdom of God, no one is entitled to a seat at the Lord's table. If you were a Jew living in Israel that didn't just hurt. It flew in the face of everything you had been taught all of your life. The Jews of 1st Century Judaism regarded themselves as "sons of the Kingdom," and the Kingdom as their national heritage and spiritual birthright. But Jesus, the Messiah-King, now leveled the playing field for both Jews and Gentiles. There would no longer be a dividing wall between them. On this day, the King Himself declared that the Kingdom of God belongs to all, whether Jew of Gentile, whether from the East or the West, who exercise the same faith as this Gentile Centurion. That, alone, was a "wow" moment.

　　　A Resurrection In Nain (Luke 7:11-17). From Capernaum Jesus made the twenty mile trip south to the town of Nain, followed by twelve disciples and a "great crowd." His arrival at the town gate coincided with the departure of a large funeral procession on its way out of town to bury the young and only son of a widow. Jesus, being deeply moved with compassion,[101] approached the funeral bier, and spoke, *"Young man, I say to you, arise."* And he did. The crowd witnessing this event was overwhelmed. Their first response was profoundly human: Fear. Forget any Sunday School lessons you've heard about "reverential awe." This was raw, genuine fear; the "terror of the Lord." It is the response of the human heart when the God of all creation, the Holy One of Israel, interrupts your funeral procession and raises your son from the dead. The second response of the crowd was both profoundly human and profoundly spiritual. They "glorified" God. The Greek word translated "glorified" (*doxadzo*) is the root from which we get our English word "doxology." Think of it this way. Standing in the middle of the town gate, having just witnessed the Messiah-King raise a local boy from the dead, this "great crowd" did the only thing which seemed appropriate. They broke out in a "doxology" of praise to the God of Israel. Their third response was the unavoidable result of the first two. They acknowledged the undeniable, *"God has visited his people!"* Indeed He had! His name was Jesus, the Messiah-King. Immanuel. "God with us."

John, The Baptizer (Matthew 11:12-19; Luke 7:18-35). The news concerning Jesus ministry activity in Galilee had come to the attention of John the Baptizer languishing in Herod's prison. John had spent a year as Jesus' "forerunner," preparing the way for His ministry by preaching a message of repentance, *"In those days John the Baptist came preaching in the wilderness of Judea, 'Repent, for the kingdom of heaven is at hand'"* (Matthew 3:1-2). It was John who had prepared the way and introduced Jesus to Israel. At least five of Jesus' disciples had begun their journeys into discipleship as disciples of John. But now, after a year of languishing in Herod's prison, John was having a crisis. Not a crisis of faith so much as a crisis of understanding. Why hadn't the Messiah established His Kingdom? Why hadn't He expelled the Romans and called down fire to consume the enemies of Israel? Where was the promised Kingdom? Why the delay? Like many in 1st Century Judaism, John's faith was being challenged and tested by his own misunderstandings regarding God's plans.

To get answers to these questions, John sent two of his remaining disciples to Jesus, *"Are you the one who is to come, or shall we look for another?"* (Luke 7:20) Jesus responded first by performing more miracles, and then by making a stunning pronouncement, *"blessed is the one who is not offended by me"* (Luke 7:23).[102] The ministry of Jesus was scandalous, even "offensive." It presented a genuine stumbling block to 1st Century Judaism's pre-conceived ideas concerning the Messiah and the Kingdom of God. And it would get worse. In spite of prophetic Scriptures portraying the Messiah as a suffering servant (specifically, Isaiah Chapter 53), neither John the Baptizer nor Jesus' disciples nor the leaders of 1st Century Judaism expected a Messiah who would die on a cross for the sin of the world at the hands of their greatest enemies (the Romans). And yet that is precisely what lay ahead.

The ministry of Jesus was "scandalous." It presented a genuine stumbling block to 1st Century Judaism's pre-conceived ideas concerning the Messiah and the Kingdom of God.

But Jesus was not yet done with either John the Baptizer or the reality that religious people are scandalized when others defy popular expectations. People expect to find greatness embodied in soft clothes and King's palaces. But John the Baptizer embodied greatness in a prophet's robe and a life of self-denial. John was a prophet, more than a prophet, and, for those with ears to hear, He was the embodiment of Elijah, whom the prophet Malachi prophesied God would send to Israel *"before the great and awesome day of the LORD comes"* (Malachi 4:5). John's greatness was unmatched by anyone up to his time. While John might be the "greatest" that the Old Covenant would produce, he was among the "least" that the New Covenant would produce. And His ministry was not well received by the leaders of 1st Century Judaism, mainly because it did not meet their expectations. Rather than confronting the Romans, John called Israel and its leaders to repent.

The same was true of Jesus. He was the Messiah-King, but not the Messiah or the King that Judaism expected. Like children in the market place who expect the other children to play the game by their rules, 1st Century Judaism was "scandalized" by Jesus' ministry and His failure to abide by their expectations. That's the problem with the Kingdom of God, and the Jesus-shaped spirituality it produces. The Kingdom challenges, even scandalizes, those who cling to their religion-shaped spirituality of rules and regulations and false expectations. But the wisdom of the Kingdom and its Jesus-shaped spirituality is vindicated by its "fruit."

In the Kingdom of God, the "fruit" of wisdom is found in the disciples of the Kingdom it produces.

The word "fruit" in the ESV is the Greek word _teknon_, meaning "child," rather than _karpos_, the regular Greek word for "fruit." In the world of the 1st Century, disciples were frequently referred to as the "children" of their teachers. In the Kingdom of God, the "fruit" of wisdom is found in the disciples it produces.

Woe! (Matthew 11:20-24). Jesus had one last word for those leaders of 1st Century Judaism who were "scandalized" by both Himself and John, the Baptizer, and their shared message of repentance: *"Woe!"* This is a primary expression of grief in the Gospels, occurring some 31 times. The meaning is clear and simple. The day will come when the towns, the people and the leaders of Israel will all know the personal grief arising from their refusal to repent when the good news of the Kingdom was preached and the miraculous signs of the Kingdom were performed in their midst.[103] In the Kingdom of God, personal "woe" is the price paid for unbelief.

Rest (Matthew 11:25-30). If personal "woe" is the price paid for unbelief, then "rest" is the gift of God to all who believe. The religion-shaped spirituality of 1st Century Judaism was a heavy burden to carry. Those who attempted to meet its demands found themselves "weary and heavy laden." The good news of the Kingdom offers rest to all who are willing to repent of their sins and to accept the yoke of discipleship in the Kingdom, *"Take my yoke upon you, and learn from me, for I am gentle and lowly in heart, and you will find rest for your souls. For my yoke is easy, and my burden is light"* (Matthew 11:29-30). But for those who choose not to repent and not to embrace the yoke of Jesus, the message of the Kingdom will ultimately produce only "woe" and judgment (Matthew 11:21). It was true then. It is still true today.

A Time To Reflect

It is unclear from the biblical narrative how long this ministry tour through Galilee lasted. We can read the record of what happened in a matter of a few minutes, when in reality these events unfolded over several days. As a result, Jesus' disciples had time to absorb and reflect on their experiences with Jesus.

In the Kingdom of God, there is no such thing as instant maturity.

And that's important. In the Kingdom of God, there is no such thing as instant maturity. In the Kingdom of God, spiritual growth and maturity are the result of truth experienced over time. And like the disciples, we, too, need time

And They Dreamt Of A Kingdom

to reflect on and absorb the meaning of these lessons for our own discipleship and ministry in the Kingdom of God.

Questions For Reflection

Spend some time reflecting on the events of this widespread ministry tour with Jesus. Try to summarize each of the six lessons and how you would apply them to your own discipleship in the Kingdom of God.

1. Healing A Leper (Matthew 8:1-4).

2. The Faith of a Centurion (Matthew 8:5-13; Luke 7:1-10).

3. A Resurrection In Nain (Luke 7:11-17).

4. John, The Baptizer (Matthew 11:12-19; Luke 7:18-35).

5. Woe! (Matthew 11:20-24).

6. Rest (Matthew 11:25-30).

Reflect on this passage: *"Take my yoke upon you, and learn from me, for I am gentle and lowly in heart, and you will find rest for your souls. For my yoke is easy, and my burden is light"* (Matthew 11:29-30) To accept or reject the "yoke" of Jesus represents a choice between "rest" and "woe." What do you think this means and how would you explain it to an unbeliever?

Key Thought

The good news of the Kingdom offers rest to all who are willing to repent of their sins, accept the yoke and embrace the Jesus-shaped spirituality of discipleship in the Kingdom of God.

---

36 - She Who Loves Much

"One of the Pharisees asked him to eat with him, and he went into the Pharisee's house and took his place at the table. And behold, a woman of the city, who was a sinner, when she learned that he was reclining at table in the Pharisee's house, brought an alabaster flask of ointment, and standing behind him at his feet, weeping, she began to wet his feet with her tears and wiped them with the hair of her head and kissed his feet and anointed them with the ointment. Now when the Pharisee who had invited him saw this, he said to himself, 'If this man were a prophet, he would have known who and what sort of woman this is who is touching him, for she is a sinner.'
(Luke 7:36-39)

Discipleship Reading: *Luke 7:36-50*   **When:** *Spring, A.D. 29*
Contextual Reading: *Luke 7*   **Where:** *Galilee*

A Pharisee Named Simon

The Spring of A.D. 29 finds Jesus in Galilee at the height of His public ministry. His crucifixion and resurrection now lay just over a year away. Although His ministry and popularity among the masses has grown (particularly in Galilee), so has the opposition by the Pharisees and their religious allies. Their opposition to Jesus would soon culminate in their outright rejection of His claims, His message, His ministry and His teachings. But in the midst of such growing hostility there remained at least one Pharisee willing to invite Jesus over for dinner and a discussion.

We are never told if the disciples accompanied Jesus to this dinner. But given Jesus' commitment to the twelve, and His well-known habit of taking them wherever He went, it seems safe to assume that they joined Him for the evening's festivities. And somewhere in the course of the evening an unexpected dinner guest arrived. *"A woman from the city"* and a *"sinner"* is all we are ever told about her. That's probably Bible-speak for a local prostitute. She obviously hadn't been invited, and she wasn't there to see Simon, the Pharisee. She had come to find Jesus.

There are times when good Greek does not make for good English, and this passage is one of those times. Starting in verse 37, the Gospel writer composes his words as if giving stage instructions for a play. All the characters are on stage except one, who now steps forward, into the gaze of the audience. *"Behold!"* the writer tells the audience, directing their focus to the newcomer on the stage. *"Look, a woman from the city who is a sinner."* Why is she there? What is she going to do? What's her role in this play? And how will Jesus and Simon, the Pharisee, respond? Like a good narrator, the biblical writer offers a series word pictures using four circumstantial participles to set the stage for what this immoral "woman of the city" will do next:

"<u>Knowing</u> that (Jesus) would be reclining in the house of the Pharisee, <u>obtaining</u> a vial of perfume, and <u>standing</u> behind (Jesus) by His feet, <u>weeping</u>, she began to weep tears which fell like rain on Jesus' feet and she dried them with the hair of her head and she kissed His feet and anointed them with perfume" (author's original Greek translation).[104]

This is profound brokenness, contrition and repentance. It is of such a deep and intimate nature that, as the audience to this event, we feel almost embarrassed that we have intruded upon such a moment between a sinner and her Savior. But the events being acted out on this divine stage are not yet done. While the immoral woman has become the unwitting and unintended focus of this play, the scene now changes from a focus upon the woman to a focus upon the responses of the other two primary characters: Jesus and Simon, the Pharisee.

The Pharisees were real people and highly regarded religious leaders, not caricatures or straw-men in anyone's play. Luke understood this. But their religion-shaped spirituality made their reactions and responses very predictable. Because of their commitment to separation from sin, a Pharisee like Simon would never allow himself to be touched, as Jesus now allowed Himself to be touched, by "a sinner" such as this woman. In his inner-most thoughts Simon revealed the judgmental nature of his religion-shaped spirituality. *"Now when the Pharisee who had invited him saw this, he said to himself, 'If this man were a prophet, he would have known who and what sort of woman this is who is touching him, for she is a sinner.'"* (Luke 7:39) Witnessing these events from within the constraints of his religion-shaped spirituality, Simon had arrived at two conclusions. *First,* this woman was an immoral person, a "sinner." *Second,* Jesus was not a prophet. After all, if He were a prophet He would know what sort of person this woman really was, and as a prophet He would never allow such a person to touch Him the way she had.

But Simon, the Pharisee, was wrong. Jesus was a prophet who knew the secret thoughts of both the woman and the Pharisee. Jesus delayed His response to the woman. Simon required His immediate focus. Jesus responded to Simon with a story (a "parable") about a moneylender and two debtors. The first debtor owed the moneylender 500 *denarii*. One *denarius* represented the daily wage of a 1st Century laborer. This debtor owed the equivalent of roughly 16 months' wages. The second debtor owed roughly 50 days wages. Both were extraordinary amounts for an average laborer to owe. When both were unable to repay, the moneylender performed the unprecedented act of forgiving them both. Jesus delivered the moral of the story in the form of a question, *"Now which of them will love him more?"* (Luke 7:42)

For his part, Simon was able to answer the question while missing the point, *"The one, I suppose, for whom he cancelled the larger debt."* (Luke 7:43) Jesus proceeded to make the point for him by comparing Simon's actions (or lack of action) with those of the woman. In 1st Century culture the guest in a home could expect three courtesies upon his arrival. *First*, he could expect to be offered the opportunity to wash his feet. *Second,* he could expect to be greeted and welcomed with a "kiss of peace." *Third,* he could expect to be offered oil to groom and refresh himself if desired. The failure of a host to offer these three courtesies constituted a social snub. In less than subtle language, Jesus pointed out that Simon had "snubbed" Him. But contrary to Simon's snub, the "sinful woman" had washed Jesus feet with her tears, had offered a "kiss of peace" by kissing His feet, and had offered perfume for his feet instead of oil for his head. She had been a far better "host" than Simon had been.

Without giving Simon an opportunity to respond, Jesus drove home the not-so-subtle point of the play, *"Therefore I tell you, her sins, which are many, are forgiven--for she loved much. But he who is forgiven little, loves little."* (Luke 7:47) The actions of this "immoral woman" were those of a hopeless debtor upon learning that her debt had been cancelled. They were the actions of one who loved Jesus "much," because she understood that she had been forgiven "much." Her tears and her actions bore eloquent witness to the depth of her contrition and repentance.

The contrast with Simon could not be more profound. From within the constraints of his religion-shaped spirituality, Simon, the Pharisee, saw no personal debt in need of cancellation, and no great sin in need of either repentance or forgiveness, although he was just as much a debtor as she was. As a result, he had no particular love for Jesus. In fact, Simon was barely tolerating Jesus, as one would tolerate a reluctantly-invited dinner guest in his home. The sooner He left, the better.

Then, for the first time since she had arrived, Jesus addressed the woman directly, *"And he said to her, 'Your sins are forgiven'."* (Luke 7:48) The response of the other actors in this "dinner-theater" were predictable, *"Then those who were at table with him began to say among themselves, 'Who is this, who even forgives sins?'"* (Luke 7:49). Jesus had heard such questions before (See our discussion in Lesson 20). The answer was simple, and should have been obvious by now. Jesus was the Messiah-King. He was Immanuel. He was the very One against whom they had sinned and rebelled. But while they were His audience, these critics were not the focus of Jesus' attention. Turning to the woman again, Jesus spoke to her the words both she and the audience needed to hear, *"Your faith has saved you; go in peace"* (Luke 7:50). Unlike Simon or the audience, the woman, by her actions, had demonstrated genuine contrition, genuine repentance and genuine faith.

A Clash Of Spiritualities

The dinner play at the house of Simon, the Pharisee, now came to an end. The various actors, along with the audience, went their separate ways. The play ended without resolving all of the questions you and I might want to ask. What became of the woman? Did she become a follower of Jesus? What about Simon? Did he ever "get it?" Did the evening have any lasting impact on him? The gospel writer is frustratingly silent when we most want him to speak. But in spite of our unanswered questions, the events of the evening served their purpose, both for us and for Jesus' disciples, who witnessed everything that took place. The events of this evening served to highlight a critical difference; a noticeable and profound clash of spiritualities which must be understood by every disciple of the Kingdom, including the twelve who watched these events unfold.

A religion-shaped spirituality, like that of Simon, sees a sinful - even notorious - woman whose sins are many. A Jesus-shaped spirituality sees a sinful woman who, like the Psalmist, has come to God - in the person of Jesus - with a broken spirit and a contrite heart (Psalm 51:17). A religion-shaped spirituality fears such a person, lest they be "tainted" by contact with her. A Jesus-shaped spirituality loves and embraces such a person, because perfect love casts out all fear. A religion-shaped spirituality sees the law and responds with a lifestyle of sacrificial separation from such sinners and their sin. A Jesus-shaped spirituality sees the law and responds by understanding that the God who wrote the law desires mercy more than sacrifice (Hosea 6:6; Matthew 9:13).

> *A Jesus-shaped spirituality sees the law and responds by understanding that the God who wrote the law desires mercy more than sacrifice.*

On this evening, at a dinner-theater in the home of Simon, the Pharisee, twelve disciples of the Kingdom witnessed a contrast they could not ignore, and discovered what we all must discover. They discovered that our journey into discipleship and the Kingdom of God is defective beyond repair if we are unwilling to shed any religion-shaped spirituality inherited from our past, and to embrace a genuine spirituality fashioned and shaped around Jesus, and Him alone. Whose

215

And They Dreamt Of A Kingdom

spirituality would they choose and embrace; that of Jesus, the Messiah-King, or that of Simon, the Pharisee. The choice was theirs . . . and ours.

Questions For Reflection

Reflecting on this Lesson, what did you discover about Jesus and His ministry to "notorious sinners" that you did not know before?

What did you learn from the parable of the moneylender that applies to you and to your discipleship?

Reflecting on your own responses to "notorious sinners," is the spirituality which you manifest toward others more like that of Simon, the Pharisee, or like Jesus?

Key Thought

As disciples of the Kingdom, our journey into discipleship and the Kingdom of God is defective beyond repair if we are unwilling to shed any religion-shaped spirituality inherited from our past, and to embrace a genuine spirituality fashioned and shaped around Jesus, and Him alone.

---

37 - The Peril of Rejecting Jesus

"Then a demon-oppressed man who was blind and mute was brought to him, and he healed him, so that the man spoke and saw. And all the people were amazed, and said, 'Can this be the Son of David?' But when the Pharisees heard it, they said, 'It is only by Beelzebul, the prince of demons, that this man casts out demons.'" (Matthew 12:22-24)

Discipleship Reading: Matthew 12:22-45   **When:** Spring, A.D. 29
Contextual Reading: Matthew 12; Mark 3   **Where:** Galilee

Following an evening of ministry in the home of Simon, the Pharisee, Jesus and the twelve embarked on another ministry tour of Galilee, *"Soon afterward he went on through cities and villages, proclaiming and bringing the good news of the kingdom of God. And the twelve were with him."* (Luke 8:1) Wherever they went, the popular response was the same, *"a great crowd was gathering and people from town after town came to him . . ."* (Luke 8:4). At some point along the way the crush of the crowds became so great that Jesus and the twelve couldn't even enter a house and eat a meal in peace (Mark 3:20-21). It was the height of Jesus' popularity. But all of that was about to change.

Another Messianic Miracle

Somewhere along the way on this ministry tour, someone brought a "demonized" person to Jesus.[105] Under the influence of this demonic spirit, the man had been rendered blind and a deaf-mute. The Greek word *kophos* is used to refer to someone who is unable to either hear or speak. In simple terms, this man was unable to see, hear or speak.

Earlier, in Lesson 20, we discussed the issue of Messianic Miracles, that class of miracles which the Rabbis taught were reserved exclusively for the Messiah. The purpose of these Messianic Miracles would be to help the Jewish people recognize the Messiah when he came. The three "Messianic Miracles" were: 1) the healing of a leper, 2) the casting out of a mute/dumb demon, and 3) the healing of someone who was blind from birth. Jesus performed the first of the three "Messianic Miracles" when He healed a leper (Luke 5:17-26). As a result, talk was already circulating among the masses (and certainly among the leaders of Judaism) that Jesus might be the Messiah.

According to Rabbinical teaching, it was impossible to cast a demon out of a deaf-mute. In order to cast out any demon, the Rabbis taught that you must first make contact with the demon by addressing it and discovering its name. Knowing the name of the demon gave you power over it to cast it out. But all of this was only possible if the demonized person could hear you and respond to your verbal instructions, including revealing the name of the demon. Since a deaf-mute could neither hear nor respond, it was impossible to cast out such a demon. The conclusion of the Rabbis was simple: only the Messiah would be able to heal such a person and cast out such a demon. Jesus ignored all such teaching and simply "healed" the man. The result was immediate and profound as the blind deaf-mute began to hear, speak and see. The gospel writer tells us that the entire crowd responded with amazed astonishment. Jesus had performed a Messianic Miracle, just as they had been taught by the Scribes and Pharisees.

And They Dreamt Of A Kingdom

And so a question began to circulate through the crowd, *"Can this be the Son of David?"* (Matthew 12:23). Could this be the Messiah-King? The Greek construction suggests that, confronted with this miracle, the crowd was wavering between belief in Jesus as the Messiah-King and rejection.[106] It was a critical - even pivotal - moment. All that was need was someone they respected to push them toward either belief or unbelief. At this critical moment the religious leaders of 1st Century Judaism, who felt increasingly threatened by Jesus and his growing popularity, stepped forward to respond.

By What Authority (Again)?

"But when the Pharisees heard it, they said, 'It is only by Beelzebul, the prince of demons, that this man casts out demons.'" (Matthew 12:24)

Now it began. The official public response of the Pharisees and the religious leaders of Israel to Jesus now began in earnest. And it began by publicly attributing the works of Jesus to Satan (*"Beelzebul, the prince of demons"*). The underlying issue involved here is really quite simple. We saw it earlier in Lesson 24. We can sum it up with a simple question, *"By what authority does Jesus do these things? Where does this power come from?"* That question surrounded Jesus' healing of the lame man at the Pool of Bethesda on the Sabbath. And it is the question now swirling around Jesus and His healing of the blind deaf-mute.

> *Jesus' spiritual authority and power can come from only one of two sources: God or Satan.*

To state the issue simply, Jesus' spiritual authority and power can come from only one of two sources: God or Satan. If it is from God, then Jesus is the Messiah-King, the promised Son of David. If not, then Jesus is a charlatan and a fraud, or worse. When Jesus healed the leper, He established His credentials as the Messiah-King. In the episode of healing the lame man at the Pool of Bethesda Jesus addressed the issue of His authority by claiming equality with the Father. Not only is He the Messiah-King, He is Immanuel, *"God with us,"* possessing both the authority and the power of God-incarnate to heal.

Witnessing Jesus perform what they knew to be a second Messianic Miracle, the Pharisees now make a willful, conscious choice that will have consequences beyond anything they could imagine. Their choice would eventually lead to the crucifixion of Jesus. But it would also lead to the destruction of Jerusalem, the Temple, the Nation of Israel and of 1st century Judaism; God's punishment for the choice made on this day. On this day, the Pharisees chose to push the masses, and eventually the nation, toward unbelief, rejection and hostility toward Jesus, the Messiah-King. Because they must offer an alternative explanation for Jesus' apparent spiritual power, the Pharisees accuse Him of being in league with Satan, of being a sorcerer and practicing sorcery and witchcraft - offenses punishable by death under the Law (Exodus 22:18; Deuteronomy 18:10-11).[107]

Jesus responds to these accusations by agreeing that there are only two sources of such power. But if He is casting out demons by using the power of Beelzebul, then Satan is waging war against himself and is destroying his own kingdom. *"Why would he do that? Your argument makes no sense,"* is Jesus underlying assertion. To counter such an illogical argument, Jesus offers a better explanation. Casting out the demonic is consistent with what they would expect from the Kingdom of God, *"But if it is by the Spirit of God that I cast out demons, then the kingdom of God has come upon you"* (Matthew 12:28).

A quick word is in order concerning verse 29, *"Or how can someone enter a strong man's house and plunder his goods, unless he first binds the strong man? Then indeed he may plunder his house"* (Matthew 12:29). Within the context of the passage (the focus of which is a single demonic deliverance), the meaning appears to be that the demon is the strong man and the "demonized" individual is the house. Jesus has the power to bind the demonic "strong man" and to "plunder his house" by setting

> *Demons are no match for the power of the Kingdom. They can be bound and cast out, and the "demonized" can be delivered.*

the demonized individual free. This more limited and specific interpretation is consistent with the context, where it is never stated that Satan is the strong man or that he has been bound in any universal sense. It is also consistent with other New Testament teaching that Satan is *"the god of this world"* (*aion* - "age") who, along with his demonic hosts, still wields sufficient spiritual power to blind unbelievers and wage spiritual warfare against believers (2 Corinthians 4:4; Ephesians 6:10ff). But demons are no match for the power of the Kingdom. They can be bound and cast out, and the "demonized" can be delivered.

But Jesus is not yet done with the Pharisees and their accusations. He now confronts them with the starkness of the choice before them. Either they are for Jesus, or they are against Him, *"Whoever is not with me is against me, and whoever does not gather with me scatters"* (Matthew 12:30). The sin of "blasphemy" allows for no middle ground. The Greek word for "blasphemy" (*blasphemia*) means *"to speak words which are injurious to another's good name."* The work of the Kingdom in healing and deliverance involves the power of the Holy Spirit.[108] To willfully and knowingly assign the works of Jesus, done under the power of the Holy Spirit, to Satan is to commit "blasphemy" by speaking words which are injurious to the good name of the Holy Spirit.

In an act of profound patience and mercy, Jesus offers the Pharisees a clear warning concerning their words and their choices. *First,* Jesus warns them that their words carry both meaning and consequences. Blasphemy against the Holy Spirit, assigning His work and His power to Satan, is not to be taken lightly. If they persist in doing this, the Pharisees and their followers will be guilty of an "unforgivable sin." Their words and their choices have eternal consequences. *Second,* Jesus warns the Pharisees that because their words proceed from the heart, they reveal something about them - about their inward character.

> *Blasphemy against the Holy Spirit, assigning His work and His power to Satan, is not to be taken lightly.*

Good trees produce good fruit, and bad trees produce bad fruit. Words represent the fruit of our lives and reveal the inner condition of our hearts. By committing the sin of blasphemy the Pharisees have revealed their true character and condition, *"You brood of vipers! How can you speak good, when you are evil? For out of the abundance of the heart the mouth speaks."* (Matthew 12:34) On the day of judgment, their own carelessly spoken words will be used to condemn them.

When Unclean Spirits Return

"Then some of the scribes and Pharisees answered him, saying, 'Teacher, we wish to see a sign from you.'" (Matthew 12:38)

The Scribes and Pharisees responded to Jesus' warnings against blasphemy with a stunning request, *"Teacher, we wish to see a sign from you."* Remember the context of this passage. The Scribes and Pharisees have just witnessed Jesus perform a known Messianic Miracle (the healing of a demonized blind deaf-mute) and have attributed it to the power of Satan. This tells us that they are NOT requesting a "sign." Jesus has already given them two Messianic "signs." Their tongue-in-cheek request represents an out-right rejection of all the signs Jesus has performed up to this point (changing water to wine, healing the nobleman's son, healing a leper, healing the lame man at the Pool of Bethesda, and healing the blind deaf-mute). Their rejection of all these explains Jesus' response: *"But he answered them, 'An evil and adulterous generation seeks for a sign'."* There comes a point when "enough is enough." Jesus felt no obligation to offer more "signs" to people who were spiritually blind because they chose not to see. To perform another sign would be to cast pearls before pigs, or to give holy things to dogs.

Jesus felt no obligation to offer more "signs" to people who were spiritually blind because they chose not to see.

Jesus actually offers three responses to this request for a "sign." *First,* Jesus declares that He will offer no more "signs" for their benefit, except the "sign" of His own death and resurrection. (Matthew 12:39-40). They would eventually reject that sign, too. *Second,* Jesus warns the Scribes and Pharisees that, on the day of Judgment, Gentiles who sought God and repented when confronted with lesser truth will condemn the religious leaders of Israel who witnessed Messianic Miracles and the arrival of the Messiah-King, but refused to repent (Matthew 12:41-42). *Third,* Jesus warns that Israel is like a person ("house") who has been delivered from an unclean spirit. When the unclean demon gets tired of wandering it decides to return. Finding the house cleaned up but empty, the demon invites *"seven other spirits more evil than itself"* to join him. The end result is that *"the last state of that person is worse than the first. So also will it be with this evil generation"* (Matthew 12:43-45).

National Israel is that person, that "house." The arrival of the Kingdom in the person of the Messiah-King has resulted in the house of Israel being "emptied, swept and put in order." The growing rejection of the Kingdom and the Messiah-King by the leaders of Israel now threatens to leave the house of Israel spiritually empty and ready to be re-occupied in a condition that will be worse than before, *"So also will it be with this evil generation."* Rejection of Jesus and the Kingdom comes at a price and brings consequences. Terrible consequences. Over the next forty years that price and those consequences would unfold, culminating in the destruction of Israel in A.D. 70.

Rejection of Jesus and the Kingdom comes at a price and brings consequences.

What The Disciples Learned This Day

"It is enough for the disciple to be like his teacher, and the servant like his master. If they have called the master of the house Beelzebul, how much more will they malign those of his household" (Matthew 10:25).

There are days when being a disciple of the Kingdom and the Messiah-King is a sobering experience. This was one of those days. On this day, the disciples learned that the leaders of 1st Century Judaism, spiritual leaders they had known and respected all of their lives, were now choosing to reject Jesus, the Messiah-King, and to assign His works to Satan. The gravity of this situation could not have been lost on these twelve men. In addition to its implications for Judaism and for Israel, it did not bode well for their own future discipleship. Indeed, Jesus would sum the situation up at a later time with a warning, *"If they have called the master of the house Beelzebul, how much more will they malign those of his household."* Their personal commitment to Jesus as the Messiah-King would soon be challenged, and they themselves would soon be persecuted and tested, by the very leaders of Israel whom they had once followed and respected. This has been true throughout the history of the Church. And the day will come when it will be true of you and me as well.

On this day, the disciples learned that the message and the manifestation of the Kingdom are not passive, static things. They are dynamic, even to the point of being divisive. The message and the manifestation of the Kingdom force people to choose. Like the ancient Ninevites at the preaching of Jonah, there can be no neutrality, only choices. Repent or perish. Are we with Jesus, or are we against Him? Is He the Messiah-King who manifests the power of the Kingdom, or is He a fraud, a magician and a charlatan? Those are the only two choices He allows. If He is, indeed, the Messiah-King, then to be "with" Jesus means we must lay down our preconceived ideas and agendas and pursue the Kingdom on His terms, not ours. We must repent, believe and obey. Or perish.

> *Like the ancient Ninevites at the preaching of Jonah, there can be no neutrality, only choices. Repent or perish.*

On this day, the disciples learned something about words, choices and consequences. They learned that the words of our mouth reveal the condition of our heart. The Pharisees had revealed the true condition of their hearts concerning Jesus by declaring His works and His power to be from Satan (Beelzebul). On the day of judgment God will judge each of us by our own words, like examining the fruit of a tree. The condition of the fruit reveals the condition of the tree. The disciples also learned that words express choices, and choices have consequences. For Israel, assigning the work of Jesus to Satan and rejecting His Kingship and His Kingdom would bring fearful, terrible consequences. The clock of God's judgment was now ticking for Judaism and national Israel. For its part, Israel would reject and crucify God's Messiah. For His part, God would respond in judgment and destroy Israel.

And They Dreamt Of A Kingdom

Questions For Reflection

Reflecting on this Lesson, what did you learn about the ministry of Jesus and the Kingdom that you did not know before? How was your own discipleship challenged by what you learned?

Reflecting on this Lesson, why would respected religious leaders reject the very Messiah-King whom they had taught for generations would one day come? What should disciples of the Kingdom do when confronted with a choice between obeying respected religious leaders and obeying the leading of Jesus?

How have the message and the manifestation of the Kingdom in your own life forced you to make choices regarding your own discipleship?

Reflecting on this Lesson, what did you discover concerning words, choices and consequences in your own life as a disciple of the Kingdom? Would you want God to judge you today based on the words you have spoken and the choices you have made over the past week?

Key Thought

As disciples of the Kingdom, we understand that rejection of Jesus and the Kingdom comes at a price and brings consequences.

---

38 - Why Parables?

"Then the disciples came and said to him, 'Why do you speak to them in parables?'"
(Matthew 13: 10)

Discipleship Reading: *Matthew 13:10-17*   ***When:*** *Spring, A.D. 29*
Contextual Reading: *Matthew 13; Mark 4; Luke 8*   ***Where:*** *Galilee*

This day in the Spring of A.D. 29 found Jesus at a watershed moment that would determine the course of His ministry for the next year. Jesus had spent the preceding two years of public ministry establishing His credentials as the Messiah-King, including two well-known Messianic Miracles. Now, the public response of the Pharisees to one of those Messianic Miracles - the deliverance and healing of the blind deaf-mute - represented the beginning of institutional Judaism's official rejection of Jesus, His claims, His teachings and the Kingdom He proclaimed. Through their influence over the Synagogues and the regular religious life of Israel, the Pharisees would foment a growing hostility toward Jesus among the masses and push them toward unbelief and eventual rejection of Jesus. For His part, Jesus responded by changing the emphasis of His ministry. The first change was to move His teaching ministry from the Synagogues (controlled by the Pharisees) to the open air. The second change was to move the focus of His ministry from establishing His Messianic credentials to telling stories concerning the Kingdom of God. Enter Jesus, the storyteller.[109]

Jesus, The Storyteller

Jesus was a master storyteller. And the type of stories He told were known as "parables." A parable is a story which employs a word-picture or image to illustrate a truth or to impart a lesson. It seeks to draw a likeness between the thing being portrayed and an illustration (e.g. *"the Kingdom of God is like a mustard seed"*).[110] In this way, a parable defines the unknown (i.e., the Kingdom) by using the known (a mustard seed). In addition to such word-picture stories, parables were frequently short stories told to bring out a lesson or a moral. The story of the Good Samaritan is one of those parable short stories. Jesus' parables commonly used illustrations drawn from daily life in 1st Century Israel, things such as fig trees, wineskins, oil lamps, vineyard workers, children's games and more. Jesus' listeners (especially His disciples) would have been very familiar with these illustrations pulled from their daily existence. And all such parables were designed and intended to make a specific point which the teller wanted to communicate. As Barclay notes, Jesus' parables *"were designed to make one stabbing truth flash out at a man the moment he heard it."* [111]

Why Parables?

But parables conceal as much as they reveal, which is exactly what Jesus wanted to do. It was this reality which eventually prompted the disciples to ask Jesus a question, *"Why do You speak to them in parables?"* Like honest questions tend to do, their question created a teachable moment which Jesus used to full advantage by offering insight which the disciples must grasp if they are to understand people and how they respond to the message of the Kingdom.

The disciples had probably heard numerous parables from Jesus prior to this point in His ministry. I suspect they had held onto this question until either their

And They Dreamt Of A Kingdom

frustration or their curiosity got the best of them. You and I can appreciate their dilemma. If Jesus' goal was to communicate truth concerning salvation and the Kingdom of God, why couch that truth in a parable which could be misunderstood? Why not speak plainly? After all, isn't that what you and I would do if we were in Jesus place? Wouldn't we want to give people unvarnished truth clearly presented so they could "make a decision" about what they should do? Yes, that's what we would do. But Jesus' way was different. Jesus wasn't interested in educating the masses. His interest lay in training and equipping the disciples.

Jesus Used Parables To Separate. *"Then the disciples came and said to him, 'Why do you speak to them in parables?' And he answered them, 'To you it has been given to know the secrets of the kingdom of heaven, but to them it has not been given. For to the one who has, more will be given, and he will have an abundance, but from the one who has not, even what he has will be taken away.'"* (Matthew 13:10-12)

Spiritual truth separates people. By their responses to spiritual truth, people reveal the true spiritual condition of their hearts. Spiritual truth separates disciples from everyone else. Listen to what Jesus says, *"To you* (the disciples) *it has been given to know the mysteries of the kingdom of heaven, but to them* (everyone else) *it has not been given."* Jesus used parables to communicate spiritual truth and to separate people into disciples "got it" and everyone else who didn't.

As disciples of the Kingdom, we have been given the Spirit of God and the mind of Christ to understand spiritual truth which is hidden to everyone else. For them, there is no knowledge and no insight. Only a growing spiritual darkness, the consequence of personal choices and decisions not to receive or believe the message of the Kingdom. Once we choose to go down the spiritual watershed toward spiritual darkness, things get increasingly dark. You can not find light by choosing darkness. Spiritual decisions and choices have consequences, like water on the wrong side of a watershed. Water falling on the west side of a watershed can only go one direction - farther west. Likewise, to choose light is to open the way for more light. And to choose darkness is to open the way for more darkness. This is what Jesus meant when He told His disciples, *"For to the one who has, more will be given, and he will have an abundance, but from the one who has not, even what he has will be taken away."* In the Kingdom of God, we lose light by choosing darkness, and we lose truth by embracing error. And this leads us to reflect upon another important reason why Jesus used parables.

> *As disciples of the Kingdom, we have been given the Spirit of God and the mind of Christ to understand spiritual truth which is hidden to everyone else.*

Jesus Used Parables to Reveal. *"This is why I speak to them in parables, because seeing they do not see, and hearing they do not hear, nor do they understand. Indeed, in their case the prophecy of Isaiah is fulfilled that says: 'You will indeed hear but never understand, and you will indeed see but never perceive. For this people's heart has grown dull, and with their ears they can barely hear, and their eyes they have closed, lest they should see with their eyes and hear with their ears and understand with their heart and turn, and I would heal them.'"* (Matthew 13:13-15)

The transition to this discussion is found in verse 13 where Jesus declares,

"This is why I speak to them in parables." [112] In the previous verses Jesus taught that spiritual truth separates people into disciples who "get it" and everyone else who don't. Disciples who "get it" also receive a growing knowledge of the *"mysteries of the Kingdom,"* while everyone else experiences a growing spiritual poverty and darkness, fed by their own choices.

But this separation raises a question. Why would anyone choose spiritual darkness over spiritual light? According to Jesus, the answer is simple and had been prophesied 700 years earlier by the prophet Isaiah, one of ancient Israel's greatest prophets. According to the Prophet Isaiah, people are spiritually blind (and deaf). Jesus used parables to reveal people's spiritual blindness. He wanted to make it clear that spiritual blindness is **both** a condition, *"For this people's heart has grown dull,"* **and** a choice, *"and their eyes they have closed, lest they should see with their eyes."* Spiritually blind people make spiritually blind choices.

> *Spiritually blind people make spiritually blind choices.*

Jesus Used Parables To Avoid Casting Pearls. There is another reason why Jesus used parables to communicate truth, although He doesn't mention it here. We discussed it earlier in Lesson 31. Jesus used parables to avoid casting pearls before swine or giving spiritual truth to people who simply couldn't appreciate it, including the Pharisees and other religious leaders. When we give people raw, unvarnished spiritual truth we increase their accountability without increasing their ability to do anything about it. And when they reject the truth we offer, they incur greater judgment for the rejection, because we are all held accountable for the light we have been given. Jesus knew that we do people no favor by giving them spiritual truth which their blindness will not allow them to understand, but for which they will now be held accountable on the day of Judgment. And so Jesus told parables; truth for disciples who can know the mysteries of the kingdom, and mysteries to the spiritually blind who cannot see the truth. [113]

Parables, Truth And Discipleship

"But blessed are your eyes, for they see, and your ears, for they hear. For truly, I say to you, many prophets and righteous people longed to see what you see, and did not see it, and to hear what you hear, and did not hear it." (Matthew 13:16-17)

In the hands of Jesus, the Parables teach us that the mark of biblical discipleship is not an individual's profession of belief, but their on-going response to the truth of the Kingdom. Professions are helpful indicators, but at best they only represent a beginning. The fruit of an individual's life as they respond to biblical truth is a far better indicator regarding the condition of their heart than any outward profession they might make. And so Jesus used parables to separate and reveal; to separate disciples from everyone else and to reveal the true condition of people's hearts.

In the hands of Jesus, the Parables teach us that, when confronted with spiritual mysteries, disciples get knowledge and understanding, while everyone else gets questions and more mysteries. As disciples of the Kingdom, called to proclaim the good news of the Kingdom, we must understand that people aren't going to "get it" until God reveals it to them. Until that time, people may respond with hostility because spiritually blind people do not appreciate being confronted with their own blindness. Just ask Jesus. In their blindness, they crucified Him. What makes us think

And They Dreamt Of A Kingdom

that we will fare better?

In the hands of Jesus, the Parables reveal something about us as disciples of the Kingdom. Our discipleship is a gift from God, freely given and freely received. It is also a high privilege and a high calling. Jesus spoke of this high calling and privilege when He told His disciples, *"For truly, I say to you, many prophets and righteous people longed to see what you see, and did not see it, and to hear what you hear, and did not hear it."* In the Kingdom of God, privilege and accountability go together. We are all accountable for our responses to the spiritual truth we have been given and for what we do with that truth.

To be a disciple of the Kingdom is to have spiritual sight and knowledge of the mysteries of the Kingdom of God. In the Kingdom of God, "mystery" is not so much secret knowledge which has been withheld, as spiritual truth which must be revealed. Specifically, as disciples of the Kingdom, God has revealed to us His plan to bring in His Kingdom and to secure redemption through His Messiah-King, Jesus. Such knowledge is a gift which must not be taken lightly. As Paul tells the Corinthian believers, *"This is how one should regard us, as servants of Christ and stewards of the mysteries of God."* (1 Corinthians 4:1) We are stewards, "managers," charged with the responsibility of properly managing the spiritual truths of the Kingdom of God which have been entrusted to

> *The spiritual truths and mysteries of the Kingdom constitute a "pearl of great price." A wise man would sell everything he owns to possess it.*

us. These spiritual truths and mysteries, rather than money or any other earthly treasure, are the talents entrusted to us while the master is away, and for which He will hold us accountable when He returns (Matthew 25:14-30). The spiritual truths and mysteries of the Kingdom constitute a "pearl of great price." A wise man would sell everything he owns to possess it.

Questions For Reflection

Reflecting on this Lesson, what did you discover concerning Jesus and His use of parables that you did not know before?

How have you seen the principle of spiritual blindness manifested in the lives of people with whom you have shared the good news of the Kingdom?

As a disciple of the Kingdom, you have been entrusted with a great deal of spiritual truth. What are you doing as a steward of the truth you have received?

Key Thought

As disciples of the Kingdom, we have been given the Spirit of God and the mind of Christ to understand spiritual truth which is hidden to those who are spiritually blind.

And They Dreamt Of A Kingdom

39 - Seed, Soil And Fruit

"That same day Jesus went out of the house and sat beside the sea. And great crowds gathered about him, so that he got into a boat and sat down. And the whole crowd stood on the beach. And he told them many things in parables, saying: 'A sower went out to sow. And as he sowed, some seeds fell along the path, and the birds came and devoured them. Other seeds fell on rocky ground, where they did not have much soil, and immediately they sprang up, since they had no depth of soil, but when the sun rose they were scorched. And since they had no root, they withered away. Other seeds fell among thorns, and the thorns grew up and choked them. Other seeds fell on good soil and produced grain, some a hundredfold, some sixty, some thirty. He who has ears, let him hear.'" (Matthew 13:1-9)

Discipleship Reading: *Matthew 13:1-9, 18-23*   **When:** *Spring, A.D. 29*
Contextual Reading: *Matthew 13; Mark 4; Luke 8*   **Where:** *Galilee*

When Jesus taught this parable, it created somewhat of a crisis for His disciples. We saw that crisis unfold in the previous Lesson when the disciples came to Jesus and asked: *"Why do you speak to them in parables?"* The crisis and the question generated a teachable moment concerning the nature of discipleship. Genuine discipleship begins when, as a result of the message of the Kingdom, the Holy Spirit produces faith in the heart of the individual and they experience the heavenly new birth (as we saw in Lesson 12). At that moment they are delivered from the domain of darkness and the spiritual blindness of this present evil age (2 Corinthians 4:3-4), and are empowered to see and to understand the mysteries of the Kingdom. From that moment on, discipleship becomes a cumulative, line-upon-line experience of growing from the immaturity of spiritual babes to the maturity of spiritual adulthood (1 Peter 2:2-3).

Blindness Versus Immaturity

Jesus' disciples were no longer spiritually blind, but they were spiritually immature. And that is an important distinction. Spiritually blind people aren't immature, they're blind. They don't "get it," although they may think that they do. They don't even get the reality of their own blindness. As we will soon see, spiritually blind people are unable to *"put it all together."* They often respond with hostility when their blindness is confronted and challenged by the truths of the Kingdom.

> *Jesus' disciples were no longer spiritually blind, but they were spiritually immature.*

Jesus' disciples, on the other hand, were no longer spiritually blind. But, they were spiritually immature. They were also teachable. Discipleship is not about being spiritually mature, although maturity is certainly the goal (Luke 6:42). In the Kingdom of God, genuine discipleship is about being teachable at the hands of Jesus. Unteachable people will either not ask questions or will not accept answers when they are given. They make mistakes but, like the fool of Proverbs, they do not learn from them. Jesus' disciples might be spiritually immature, but they were willing to admit their ignorance, ask questions of Jesus and to learn from the answers He gave. They, too, would make mistakes along the way. But Jesus knew His disciples would learn from those mistakes. The lessons they gleaned from those mistakes would make them more fruitful for the Kingdom, and that is what the lesson of this parable was really all about.

Interpreting Roads, Rocks And Thorns

Over the years, this parable has been variously described as *"The Parable of the Sower"* or *"The Parable of the Soils."* But the truth is that this parable isn't about the sower, the seed or the soils. It is about *fruitfulness*, or our lack of fruitfulness. In the Kingdom of God, the only measure of either seed or soil that matters is its fruitfulness. Contemporary Christianity frequently misses the point of this parable. We want to ask questions like *"How can we prepare, improve or fix the soil?"* Answer: You can't. That's not the point of the parable. While such questions might feed our curiosity, they are irrelevant

> *In the Kingdom of God, the only measure of either seed or soil that matters is its fruitfulness.*

to the point Jesus wants to communicate. The question Jesus wants us to ask is *"Which of the four soils am I? Am I fruitful?"* Like the person with a log in their own eye, each of us must begin our journey into this passage with a mirror, the mirror of personal reflection and introspection.

Matthew 13:3-7 depicts seed sown on three types of soil, which we will summarize as 1) Roads, 2) Rocks and 3) Thorns. These three soils depict three basic types of people and their responses to the good news of the Kingdom. All three soils/people share three things in common. *First*, all three hear the message of the Kingdom. *Second*, all three fail to understand the message, thereby reflecting their spiritual blindness. *Third,* all three soils/people produce the same result: no fruit. In the Kingdom of God, all responses to the message of the Kingdom are ultimately measured in terms of their fruitfulness.

Roads. *"When anyone hears the word of the kingdom and does not understand it, the evil one comes and snatches away what has been sown in his heart. This is what was sown along the path."* (13:19) Spiritual blindness is like sowing seed on a roadside path. While the person may "hear" the word, they do not "understand" what they have heard. Literally, they are unable to "put it all together."[114] Why? Because they are spiritually blind.

Rocks. *"As for what was sown on rocky ground, this is the one who hears the word and immediately receives it with joy, yet he has no root in himself, but endures for a while, and when tribulation or persecution arises on account of the word, immediately he falls away."* (13:20-21) Spiritual blindness does not mean that people can't or don't "respond" to the message of the Kingdom, only that they don't "understand" it in any meaningful sense. We see this reality played out here. These people, says Jesus, hear the word and "immediately" receive that word with joy. These people are excited about what they have heard and respond with enthusiasm. But there is a play on words at work here. The same people who "immediately" receive the message with joy, are the same people who "immediately" fall away. In other words, these people leave as quickly as they receive. Whatever their response involves, it is temporary, or as the Greek expresses it, they *"exist for a season."* Why? Because the seed has "no root" in this person. When the message of the Kingdom produces harsh winds of tribulation and persecution, these people are offended, "scandalized," by what is happening to them. As a result, they stumble and fall away.[115]

Thorns. *"As for what was sown among thorns, this is the one who hears the word, but the cares of the world and the deceitfulness of riches choke the word, and it proves unfruitful."* (13:22) Not only does spiritual blindness prevent the seed of the word from taking root in the life of the hearer, but other issues fight for their attention. Jesus refers to *"the cares of the world."* A more accurate translation would be *"the distractions of the age."* Like "Vanity Fair" of Bunyan's **The Pilgrim's Progress,** this present evil age possesses many distractions which fight for our attention and distract us from our primary purpose, which is to bear fruit for the Kingdom. In addition to distractions, Jesus refers to *"the deceitfulness of riches."* A better rendering of the Greek would be *"the delusion of wealth."* In addition to their spiritual blindness, people are both distracted by this present evil age and deluded by the pursuit of wealth and all its trappings. These distractions and delusions combine to "choke the word" in the life of the individual. The net result is that both the person and the word are rendered "unfruitful." And in the Kingdom of God, the only measure of either seed or soil that matters is its fruitfulness.

Good Soil, Fruitfulness And Ears

Fruit. *"As for what was sown on good soil, this is the one who hears the word and understands it. He indeed bears fruit and yields, in one case a hundredfold, in another sixty, and in another thirty."* (13:23) Having examined three types of bad soil, it is now time to examine the good soil. There simply is no way to say this differently. The mark of good soil is *fruitfulness.* In His description of this fourth soil, Jesus offers us a three-part description of a genuine disciple of the Kingdom. A disciple of the Kingdom is someone who 1) hears the word, 2) understands what he hears, and 3) bears fruit. Unlike the previous three soils, these disciples of the Kingdom are the ONLY ones in the parable who both hear AND understand what they have heard. No longer spiritually blind, their spiritual eyes have been opened to see what the others could not. They hear. They understand. And they are bearing fruit for the Kingdom, some a hundredfold, some sixty, and some thirty. But ALL bear fruit. Jesus concludes the parable with a declaration which masks a question, *"He who has ears, let him hear."* Do you have ears to hear what Jesus is saying?

What The Disciples Learned This Day

Standing alongside the disciples of Jesus we need to learn what they learned on this day. What they learned was that Jesus wasn't talking about soils or sowers or even seed. No. Jesus was talking about fruitfulness. On this day Jesus' disciples discovered that fruitfulness is a basic principle of discipleship in the Kingdom which must not be dismissed, ignored or taken lightly. In the Kingdom of God the only measure of either seed or soil that matters is its fruitfulness. And of the four soils represented in this parable, only one heard the word, understood what they heard, and bore fruit. On this day, the disciples learned that good soil is fruitful soil, and fruitful soil is good soil.

You and I cannot fix the spiritually blind soil of someone else's life any more than we can teach pigs to appreciate pearls or dogs to appreciate things which are holy.

In the Kingdom of God, you and I cannot fix the spiritually blind soil of someone else's life any more than we can teach pigs to appreciate pearls or dogs to

And They Dreamt Of A Kingdom

appreciate things which are holy. Only God can break through spiritual blindness and change the soil of someone's heart. The only soil you and I can cultivate and make more fruitful is our own, no one else's. For this reason, this parable, like so many of Jesus' parables, is designed and intended for reflection, not resolution.

Resolution asks, *"Were the people represented by the other three soils ever saved and part of the Kingdom?"*

Reflection asks, *"Which soil represents my life? Have I received the word of the Kingdom 'immediately,' only to fall away just as fast when trouble strikes? Have I allowed the distractions of this age and the delusions of wealth to choke the word in my life? Based upon the evidence of my own fruitfulness, am I part of the Kingdom? Am I a disciple of the Kingdom who bears fruit?"*

Jesus wasn't interested in resolution, but in reflection. Jesus wanted each of His disciples to reflect on their own fruitfulness. Indeed, Jesus wants each of us to reflect on our true spiritual condition and to examine the soil of our own life. If soil is measured by its fruitfulness for the Kingdom, what kind of soil am I? And what kind of soil are you? All other questions miss the point.

Questions For Reflection

Reflecting on this Lesson, what did you learn about discipleship and fruitfulness in the Kingdom of God that you did not know before?

How do Jesus' comments about the "distractions of the age" here in Matthew relate to what we learned earlier about God's plan for the Ages in Lesson 3? How have the "distractions of the age" had an impact on your own discipleship? What practical steps can you take to minimize the future impact of those "distractions of the age" on your life and ministry in order to be more fruitful for the Kingdom?

How do Jesus' comments about "the delusion of wealth" relate to what we learned earlier about the priority of the Kingdom in Lesson 29? How has the "delusion of wealth" impacted your own discipleship? What practical steps can you take to minimize the future impact of "the delusion of wealth" on your life and ministry in order to be more fruitful for the Kingdom?

What is the difference between spiritual blindness and spiritual immaturity? How does this truth help to explain the responses of people you know who have responded either positively our negatively to the gospel of the Kingdom and to spiritual truth you have shared with them?

How do you think Jesus defined "fruit" and "fruitfulness?" If Jesus defined "fruitfulness as "disciples how multiply themselves by making more disciples," how fruitful are you?

Key Thought

In the Kingdom of God, the only measure of either seed or soil that matters is its fruitfulness.

And They Dreamt Of A Kingdom

40 - False Wheat And Stumbling Blocks

"He put another parable before them, saying, 'The kingdom of heaven may be compared to a man who sowed good seed in his field, but while his men were sleeping, his enemy came and sowed weeds among the wheat and went away. So when the plants came up and bore grain, then the weeds appeared also. And the servants of the master of the house came and said to him, 'Master, did you not sow good seed in your field? How then does it have weeds?' He said to them, 'An enemy has done this.' So the servants said to him, 'Then do you want us to go and gather them?' But he said, 'No, lest in gathering the weeds you root up the wheat along with them. Let both grow together until the harvest, and at harvest time I will tell the reapers, Gather the weeds first and bind them in bundles to be burned, but gather the wheat into my barn.'"' (Matthew 13:24-30)

Discipleship Reading: Matthew 13:24-30, 36-43   **When:** Spring, A.D. 29
Contextual Reading: Matthew 13; Mark 4; Luke 8   **Where:** Galilee

       Throughout Matthew 13 Jesus describes the Kingdom of God in organic terms. Of the eight "Kingdom Parables" (i.e., *"the Kingdom of God is like . . ."*) which Jesus taught on this day (seven in Matthew and one in Mark), five of them used organic imagery to describe the growth of the Kingdom. The *"Parable of the Tares,"* as this parable is commonly known, is the second of those four organic parables. But what exactly does this parable mean?

The Interpretation
       "Then he left the crowds and went into the house. And his disciples came to him, saying, 'Explain to us the parable of the weeds of the field.' He answered, 'The one who sows the good seed is the Son of Man. The field is the world, and the good seed is the sons of the kingdom. The weeds are the sons of the evil one, and the enemy who sowed them is the devil. The harvest is the end of the age, and the reapers are angels. Just as the weeds are gathered and burned with fire, so will it be at the end of the age. The Son of Man will send his angels, and they will gather out of his kingdom all causes of sin and all law-breakers, and throw them into the fiery furnace. In that place there will be weeping and gnashing of teeth. Then the righteous will shine like the sun in the kingdom of their Father. He who has ears, let him hear.'" (Matthew 13:36-43)

       As we noted earlier, Jesus' disciples were no longer spiritually blind. But they were spiritually immature, and having a hard time wrapping their minds around this parable. Their new-found spiritual hunger motivated them to ask Jesus for an explanation, *"Explain to us the parable of the tares of the field."* In response to their question, Jesus interpreted the parable, and as a result much of the heavy lifting has been done, not only for the disciples, but for us.

       All of the participants in this parable are identified for us. The field is "the world," not the Church. The world is "the Kingdom" in the sense that the entire world is under God's rule, even though it is presently in rebellion against that rule. The good seed represents believers, the *"sons of the Kingdom,"* while the bad seed represents unbelievers the *"sons of the evil one."* Both grow side by side in the field of the world. When Jesus returns at the end of the age He will command His angels to separate the believers/wheat from the unbelievers/tares, with the wheat destined for life in the

And They Dreamt Of A Kingdom

Kingdom and the tares destined for *"the furnace of fire."*

As disciples of the Kingdom, the question which confronts us is, *"What are we supposed to learn from all of this?"* In order to answer this question we need to return to one of the principles which govern the purpose of parables: parables were designed and intended to make a specific point which the teller wanted to communicate, what Barclay described as *"one stabbing truth"* which would *"flash out at a man the moment he heard it."* [116] What is that "one stabbing truth" which seems to flash out from this parable? That the world we live in will be made up of both believers and unbelievers. They will grow alongside each other from now until Jesus returns, when He will separate and judge them. Until then, unbelievers/tares may give the appearance of being wheat. But we will be able to distinguish between believers/wheat and unbelievers/tares by the fruit they produce. And that is where we need to go next.

False Wheat

If we are going to fully understand this parable, one of the first things we need to learn concerns the nature of "tares." The Greek term translated "tares" (*zizanion*) refers to a specific weed which grows plentifully in the region around Israel. This weed is known as *"darnel."* But it is also known by another name: *"false wheat."* Its scientific name, *temulentus*, means "drunk." This weed closely resembles wheat in its early stages of growth, until its "fruit" appears. Its "fruit" consists of black seeds which, if consumed, act like a poison.

> *Wheat and tares are distinguished by their fruit.*

The symptoms of this poison include a form of drunkenness, inability to walk, hindered speech, vomiting and, in severe cases, even death. A tare resembles wheat, but produces bad fruit. Even in the world (remember, "the field" is the world, not the Church), there are those who resemble wheat, but are not. Early in our relationship with them we may be impressed because they seem to know the vocabulary and are able to go through the religious motions. But as time goes on, their fruit reveals their true nature. Wheat and tares are distinguished by their fruit.

Stumbling Blocks.

When Jesus describes the tares and their separation at "the end of the age," He uses two additional words or phrases to characterize this false wheat. *First,* Jesus describes the tares as "stumbling blocks" (Greek: *skandalon*). In Classical Greek, prior to the New Testament, this word originally referred to a stick to which bait was attached and was used to spring a trap. A *skandalon* was a snare. Over time it came to describe anything which causes a person to stumble or fall: a stumbling block. In this parable, a tare is a stumbling block that causes others to stumble or fall, particularly with regard their walk as a disciple of the Kingdom.

Stumbling Blocks In The New Testament. The New Testament has quite a bit to say about scandals and stumbling blocks. [117] In the previous Lesson we saw how the seed which sprang up "immediately" among the rocks also "immediately" fell away (*skandalidzo*) when the message of the Kingdom produced harsh winds of tribulation and persecution (Matthew 13:21). They were "scandalized" and stumbled over what it truly meant to be a disciple of Jesus.

But sometimes, even disciples can become stumbling blocks for others. And so Jesus would later warn Peter that Satan was using him as a stumbling block to thwart God's purposes (Matthew 16:23). This is why the Apostle Paul exhorted believers to guard themselves against becoming stumbling blocks for others (Romans 14:13; 21; 1 Corinthians 8:13), and to avoid people who are divisive and cause others to stumble (Romans 16:17). And the Apostle John taught his readers that our love for the brethren is our best protection against being a stumbling block for them (1 John 2:10). If we truly love God and one another we will think twice about doing something we know might cause a fellow-believer to stumble. But for those for whom love is not a sufficient motivation, Jesus warns us that God will judge all stumbling blocks harshly (Matthew 18:7; Luke 17:2).

Jesus Is A Stumbling Block. But perhaps the most important New Testament teaching concerning stumbling blocks involves Jesus, Himself. Scripture is clear that Jesus is God's appointed "stumbling block," and that needs some explanation. Jesus understood this truth about Himself. Late in His ministry Jesus expressed it in His encounter with the Jewish religious leaders in the Temple:

"But he looked directly at them and said, 'What then is this that is written: 'The stone that the builders rejected has become the cornerstone Everyone who falls on that stone will be broken to pieces, and when it falls on anyone, it will crush him.' The scribes and the chief priests sought to lay hands on him at that very hour, for they perceived that he had told this parable against them, but they feared the people." (Luke 20:17-19; see Matthew 21:42; Mark 12:10)

Jesus is the stone that the builders rejected. He has become The Cornerstone of everything God is doing on the Earth, in the Kingdom and in the Church (Ephesians 2:20). Everything depends upon how people respond to Jesus, The Cornerstone. In the passage above Jesus describes two basic responses. On the one hand, there are those who fall upon The Cornerstone and allow themselves to "be broken in pieces." These are believers and disciples of the Kingdom who allow themselves to be broken for God's Kingdom purposes. On the other hand, there are those upon who The Cornerstone falls and crushes them. These are those who reject the message of the Kingdom. One man's cornerstone is another man's stumbling block. The early church understood that Jesus (especially Jesus crucified) is foolishness and a stumbling block to some, but a Cornerstone, salvation and wisdom to those who believe:

> *Jesus is the stone that the builders rejected. He has become The Cornerstone of everything God is doing on the Earth, in the Kingdom and in the Church.*

"For Jews demand signs and Greeks seek wisdom, but we preach Christ crucified, a stumbling block to Jews and folly to Gentiles, but to those who are called, both Jews and Greeks, Christ the power of God and the wisdom of God" (1 Corinthians 1:22-24; see also Galatians 5:11).

"For it stands in Scripture: 'Behold, I am laying in Zion a stone, a cornerstone chosen and precious, and whoever believes in him will not be put to shame.' So the honor is for you who believe, but for those who do not believe, 'The stone that the builders rejected has become the cornerstone,' and 'A stone of stumbling, and a rock of offense.' They stumble because they disobey the word, as they were destined to do" (1 Peter 2:6-8; see also Romans 9:33).

Earlier in Lesson 32 we discovered that the pathway into the Kingdom of God is "restrictively narrow." And in the very center of that narrow path, blocking the way, stands Jesus - The Cornerstone. In order to enter the Kingdom of God, each of us must confront The Cornerstone. For those who choose to allow themselves to be broken by Him in repentance, faith and obedience, Jesus becomes their cornerstone, their doorway into the Kingdom, the foundation for everything we believe and do. For those who refuse to be broken by Him in repentance, faith and obedience, Jesus - The Cornerstone - becomes their stumbling block and rock of offense, barring their entrance to the Kingdom.

Lawlessness

But Jesus uses a second word to describe these tares and false disciples. In addition to being a stumbling block, a tare is someone whose life is characterized by "lawlessness." The Greek word (*anomia*) originally meant any violation of the Old Testament Law. But by Jesus' day the word had become a more general reference to sin, wickedness or iniquity. This is why the Apostle John could tell his readers, *"Everyone who makes a practice of sinning also practices lawlessness; sin is lawlessness"* (1 John 3:4). We see this meaning played out in Matthew 23:28 where Jesus rebukes the Scribes and Pharisees, accusing them of *anomia* or lawlessness, even though the Scribes and Pharisees were famous for their scrupulous observance of the Law. Lawlessness (or iniquity) is an internal condition

> *Lawlessness is the condition of any heart that is still in rebellion against God, refusing to allow itself to be broken upon The Cornerstone in repentance, faith and obedience.*

of the heart, as opposed to an outward breaking of the Law. Like the Scribes and Pharisees, you can be "lawless" while keeping the Law. Lawlessness is the condition of any heart that is still in rebellion against God, refusing to allow itself to be broken upon The Cornerstone in repentance, faith and obedience. Lawlessness is the condition of a tare, not a disciple of the Kingdom. The Apostle John, later in the passage we quoted above, explains it this way, *"No one born of God makes a practice of sinning, for God's seed abides in him, and he cannot keep on sinning because he has been born of God"* (1 John 3:9). Righteousness and lawlessness are both conditions of the heart, but one is the condition of a genuine disciple while the other is the condition of a tare.

The discipleship principle at work here is simple, but profound. There is a clear distinction between disciples of the Kingdom on the one hand, and the tares and false wheat on the other. A disciple of the Kingdom is known for practicing righteousness, whereas a tare practices "lawlessness." As disciples of the Kingdom we have come to The Cornerstone and have been broken

> *To be a disciple of the Kingdom is not to be perfect, but to be broken, redeemed and forgiven.*

upon it in repentance, faith and obedience. We have been redeemed from all our iniquities which God has graciously forgiven in Christ (Titus 2:14; Romans 4:7). And whereas we once gave ourselves willingly to sin in open rebellion against the King, we now yield ourselves to holiness and righteousness (Romans 6:19) as ambassadors on His behalf. God has shown mercy toward us and He no longer remembers our sins or iniquities (Hebrews 8:12; 10:17). To be a disciple of the Kingdom is not to be perfect, but to be broken, redeemed and forgiven.

Weeding And Separating

But how are we, as disciples of the Kingdom, supposed to respond to the tares in our midst? *First*, we are to recognize them by their fruit. False wheat produces bad fruit. *Second,* we should warn such people to guard themselves against becoming stumbling blocks for others (Romans 14:13; 21; 1 Corinthians 8:13), reminding them that, if they truly love God and their fellow believers, they will work hard not to cause others to stumble (1 John 2:10). *Third,* Paul would remind us to avoid such people (Romans 16:17) until they repent of their sin. *Fourth,* Jesus Himself has given us a process of admonishment by which to confront individuals in our midst in order to restore them to repentance (more about this in Lesson 18 of Volume 2 where we examine Matthew 18:15-20).

The good news here is that God has NOT called us to weed His field. There is a principle of "separating" in this parable, but it is God and His angels who do the separating at "the end of the age." False wheat may be able to fool people for a season, but God isn't fooled. Not for a moment. At "the end of the age" God will reap, separate and judge. He will separate the genuine wheat from the false wheat, the righteous from the wicked and will and judge all men according to their deeds (2 Corinthians 5:10). No one will escape His notice. Until that time, our calling as disciples of the Kingdom is to understand the importance of bearing good fruit, and of recognizing bad fruit when we see it manifested among people claiming discipleship in His Kingdom. [118]

The good news here is that God has NOT called us to weed His garden.

What The Disciples Learned This Day

Listening to Jesus teach on this day, the disciples must have experienced a sense of being overwhelmed. Each parable represented a lesson in Kingdom discipleship which would require a lifetime to unpack, understand and apply. And Jesus was just getting started.

A Lesson Concerning The Big Picture. Returning to the most basic principle for understanding parables, the disciples leaned a lesson concerning "the big picture." This world in which we live during "this present age" is divided into two groups of people: believers and unbelievers, wheat and tares, disciples of the Kingdom and everyone else. These two groups will grow side by side until Jesus returns. And some of those unbelievers have the ability to mimic wheat, until their fruit is revealed, reminding us, once again, that in the Kingdom of God, the only measure of genuine faith that matters is its fruitfulness.

A Lesson Concerning Two Wheats. Through this parable Jesus taught the disciples the difference between genuine and false wheat, between genuine disciples and false disciples. Genuine disciples are known by their good fruit. False disciples are known by their bad fruit. Genuine disciples are "wheat." The spiritual fruit of their lives is sufficient to feed others. False disciples are "tares." The fruit of their lives is poisonous, sufficient only to make others sick and to cause them to stumble. Genuine disciples have confronted The Cornerstone and have allowed themselves to be broken in repentance, faith and obedience. False disciples have confronted The

And They Dreamt Of A Kingdom

Cornerstone, only to find a stone of stumbling and a rock of offense. Genuine disciples practice righteousness. False disciples outwardly resemble genuine wheat, but they continue to *"keep on sinning"* and to practice "iniquity." But there was more. With Jesus, there always is.

A Lesson Concerning Three Challenges. Like so many of Jesus' lessons to His disciples, this lesson was intended for personal reflection. And on this day the disciples received at least three challenges to reflect on. *First,* if people are going to be offended and stumble over the good news of the Kingdom, our responsibility as disciples of that Kingdom is to make certain that they stumble over Jesus, The Cornerstone, not over us and our bad fruit. *Second,* it is not our responsibility to weed God's field. God is the one who separates and judges. Not us. *Third,* Jesus challenges every would-be disciple of the Kingdom to reflect upon a very basic question: *"Which am I? Am I genuine wheat, or am I a tare? What Kind of fruit am I producing? Are unbelievers stumbling over Jesus, The Cornerstone, or over me and my bad fruit?"*

Questions For Reflection

Reflecting on this Lesson, what did you learn about the difference between genuine wheat and false wheat that you did not know before?

What is the difference between Jesus as The Cornerstone and Jesus as a stumbling block? How does your discipleship reflect this truth?

If the people who know you were to judge you today on the basis of the fruit of your discipleship, would they conclude that you are genuine wheat or something else? Would they stumble over the fruit of your life, or would they conclude that Jesus is your Cornerstone?

If fruitfulness in the Kingdom of God is defined as disciples who multiply themselves by making more disciples, what is the potential danger that "tares" (false disciples) present to the life of the Kingdom and the ministry of the Church?

Key Thought

In the Kingdom of God, genuine disciples of the Kingdom are distinguished from false disciples, not by their outward appearance, but by their fruit.

And They Dreamt Of A Kingdom

41 - The Organic Growth Of The Kingdom

"And he said, 'The kingdom of God is as if a man should scatter seed on the ground. He sleeps and rises night and day, and the seed sprouts and grows; he knows not how. The earth produces by itself, first the blade, then the ear, then the full grain in the ear. But when the grain is ripe, at once he puts in the sickle, because the harvest has come.'" (Mark 4:26-29)

Discipleship Reading: Mark 4:26-35   **When:** Spring, A.D. 29
Contextual Reading: Mark 4; Matthew 13   **Where:** Galilee

As we noted in the previous lesson, five of the eight "Parables of the Kingdom" which Jesus taught on this day focused on a principle that is all too frequently overlooked today. Life in the Kingdom is organic as opposed to being organized or institutional. It is about good seed sown in productive soil which bears good fruit. It is about genuine wheat as opposed to false wheat. To borrow another metaphor from the Gospel of John (which we will examine later), life in the Kingdom is about abiding in the vine and bearing fruit, and bearing good fruit as opposed to bad fruit. In this third parable (which is found only in the Gospel of Mark), Jesus develops this theme by devoting the entire parable to the reality that the Kingdom of God is all about organic growth.

The Organic Mystery of The Kingdom

While the word "mystery" doesn't appear in this passage, the idea of "mystery" seems present in the statement, *"he knows not how."* Simply put, the organic growth of the Kingdom means that the Kingdom of God works and grows in ways we simply don't fully understand. In other words, it is a "mystery." And this presents a problem. Contemporary Western Christianity doesn't like a mystery. With roots which go deep into philosophical rationalism, we seem to believe that everything in the Kingdom of God should be reducible to processes and terms we can understand, and control. We want God to be big enough to run the universe, but small enough to fit into our carefully constructed boxes. Boxes which we control. When it comes to discipleship, we want a discipleship process which we can control toward a result which we can define, even pre-determine. While we claim to "trust God," the reality is that we trust ourselves and our methods more. After all, if we trust God He might not give us the end-product we desire, and that would throw a wrench into our plans. We want God to be Sovereign, so long as He obeys our formulas, blesses our organization and doesn't interfere with our plans. But a mystery means that God is in control, rather than us. A mystery means that God knows what He is doing, even if we don't.

> *. . . a mystery means that God is in control, rather than us. A mystery means that God knows what He is doing, even if we don't.*

The Steps Of Organic Growth

Although this parable is quite short (especially compared with the first two!), it is filled with truth laid out in six steps or phases. One way to understand these six steps or phases is to think of them as the six steps of organic evangelism in the

And They Dreamt Of A Kingdom

Kingdom of God, beginning with the sowing of the word (seed) and ending with a harvest.

Step 1: *A man sows seed.* *"The kingdom of God is like a man who casts seed upon the soil."* All evangelism - the proclamation of the good news of the Kingdom - begins by sowing seed. As we have already seen in the teachings of Jesus, sowing seed is an important metaphor in the Kingdom of God. The Kingdom of God grows where the seed of the Kingdom is sown. Without the sowing of spiritual seed there can be no spiritual crop to harvest. Even when we have the privilege of reaping where we have not sown, we can only do so because someone else has sown, just as Jesus told His disciples, *"I sent you to reap that for which you did not labor. Others have labored, and you have entered into their labor."* (John 4:38)   A s disciples of the Kingdom, to experience a greater spiritual harvest, we must sow more Kingdom seed. We sow that seed whenever we share the good news of the Kingdom with those around us, whether formally preached from a church pulpit or informally shared over a cup of coffee. We sow that seed whenever we cause our light to shine by engaging in good deeds and serving those in need in the name of Jesus and the Kingdom. We sow that seed through every Bible study or informal discussion about the Kingdom we have with those who are willing to listen. How we sow the seed of the Kingdom is not as important as the fact that we do.

> *The Kingdom of God grows where the seed of the Kingdom is sown.*

Step 2: *He goes about his normal life.* Our parable puts it this way, he *"goes to bed at night and gets up by day."* Those are the normal activities of life. Over the years there has been a great deal of chatter and talk about "lifestyle evangelism." This is the idea that we share the gospel by how we live. But as this parable and this passage makes clear, true "lifestyle evangelism" is more intentional. We intentionally sow the seed of the Kingdom by word and by deed, and then life goes on while we wait to see what will sprout up. Did our seed fall upon the path? Did it fall on rocky soil, or among the thorns? Often times, we simply don't know until much later. I have sown seed on soil I thought was receptive and would bear good fruit, only to be disappointed. And I have sown seed on what I thought was little more than rocks and thorns, later to be surprised by unexpected fruit and fruitfulness. It is out of our control.

> *In the Kingdom of God, organic spiritual growth is not about how much you know. It's about how much you sow.*

Step 3: *The seed sprouts up and grows.* *"The seed sprouts up and grows - how, he himself does not know."* Whether or not the seed we have sown into the soil of people's lives will germinate and sprout is beyond our control. But in the Kingdom of God sprouting seed and organic growth are the norm. The Apostle Paul understood this organic process and described it when he wrote to the believers in Corinth, saying, *"I planted, Apollos watered, but God gave the growth. So neither he who plants nor he who waters is anything, but only God who gives the growth. He who plants and he who waters are one, and each will receive his wages according to his labor. For we are God's fellow workers. You are God's field, God's building."* (1

Corinthians 3:6-9) Sometimes we are the ones who sow. Sometimes we are the ones who water. And sometimes we are the ones who reap. And while He gives us the privilege of laboring alongside Him, the organic growth belongs to God alone.

Step 4: The man does not know how it all works. *"The seed sprouts up and grows - how, he himself does not know."* In the Kingdom of God, organic spiritual growth is not about how much you know. It's about how much you sow. Organic spiritual growth in the Kingdom of God is a "mystery." Unfortunately, the organized church today spends an inordinate amount of time trying to analyze the "mystery" in the false hope of creating more effective formulas for "successful" evangelism or "church growth." In other words, we want to control the process toward our pre-determined outcomes (i.e., responses, indications of interest, prayers to receive Christ, etc.).

Step 5: The soil produces crops by itself through a gradual but certain process. *"The soil produces crops by itself; first the blade, then the head, then the mature grain in the head."* God does, indeed, have a process of organic growth. But it is a process, not a formula. It cannot be controlled or manipulated by us. People are not spiritually mature because they have completed our "program." They are mature when God has completed His work in their lives. Anyone who must be controlled and manipulated into the Kingdom will need to be continually controlled and manipulated all of their lives because they possess no organic life within themselves. Unfortunately, there will always be manipulative and controlling "leaders" willing to manipulate the compliant masses.

Step 6: The man recognizes when the harvest has come. *"But when the crop permits, he immediately puts in the sickle, because the harvest has come."* How does he know when the time for harvest has come? He can see the fruit, just as Jesus did (John 4:35). If gradual organic growth is the norm in the Kingdom of God, then so is reaping a harvest from what has been sown. Not a formula, but a divine process of organic growth in the Kingdom. All too often we want a harvest without a process. We want to reap without sowing or without allowing God's organic process to have its way in people's lives. Then, when the "fruit" of our reaping shows little or no genuine spiritual life - even falling away into a worse condition than where we found them - we quietly wonder why our fruit didn't abide like Jesus promised it would (John 15:16).

Two More Lessons In Organic Growth

Our passage from Mark 4 is not Jesus' only teaching on the principle of organic growth. Jesus taught two additional parables which illustrate and underscore this principle of organic growth. Let's briefly look at these parables and what we can glean from them.

The Mustard Seed. *"He presented another parable to them, saying, 'The kingdom of heaven is like a mustard seed, which a man took and sowed in his field; and this is smaller than all other seeds; but when it is full grown, it is larger than the garden plants, and becomes a tree, so that the birds of the air come and nest in its branches."* (Matthew 13:31-32)

This parable illustrates the principle of organic growth by emphasizing great growth from small beginnings - great trees from small seeds. The Kingdom of God begins small and inauspiciously, like sown seed, but it out-grows everything else. In

In the Kingdom God, small is big.

the Kingdom God, small is big. As disciples of the Kingdom, God isn't looking for us

245

to start something "big." Big is what He does, not what we do. In the Kingdom of God, our calling as disciples is to be faithful in sowing the seed of Kingdom. How "big" the yield of that seed will eventually be is not up to us, nor should it be our concern. The organic growth of the Kingdom is God's concern. But this parable reminds each of us that the organic growth of the Kingdom means that what God plants through us will grow to far exceed us.

The Leaven. *"He spoke another parable to them, 'The kingdom of heaven is like leaven, which a woman took, and hid in three pecks of meal, until it was all leavened.'"* (Matthew 13:33)

Contrary to much popular opinion among amateur commentators, leaven is not always evil. [119] This passage is a case-in-point, unless you think Jesus is comparing the Kingdom of God with something evil. Every Jewish listener in Jesus' audience used leaven on a daily basis to make bread dough (except during Passover), and would understand the principle at work here. Leaven describes uncontrolled organic growth which is powerful beyond its size or our expectation. That makes it powerful for either good or evil. Whereas the parable of the Mustard Seed emphasizes "size" (things which start very small but grow very big), the parable of the Leaven emphasizes the impact of uncontrolled organic growth, which is what Paul

> *. . . organic growth means that God desires us to have an impact that is far beyond our size or our expectations, and which is outside of our control.*

emphasized when he warned the Corinthians and the Galatians that *"A little leaven leavens the whole lump"* (1 Corinthians 5:6; Galatians 5:9). From a discipleship perspective, organic growth means that God desires us to have an impact that is far beyond our size or our expectations, and which is outside of our control.

Questions For Reflection

Reflecting on this Lesson, what did you learn about the organic growth of the Kingdom that you did not know before?

Spend some time reflecting on this statement: *"How we sow the seed of the Kingdom is not as important as the fact that we do."* Do you agree or disagree? Why? What are you currently doing to sow the seed of the Kingdom into the lives of those around you?

Key Thought

In the Kingdom of God, organic spiritual growth is not about how much you know. It's about how much you sow.

And They Dreamt Of A Kingdom

42 - Value And Discernment In The Kingdom

"The kingdom of heaven is like treasure hidden in a field, which a man found and covered up. Then in his joy he goes and sells all that he has and buys that field. Again, the kingdom of heaven is like a merchant in search of fine pearls, who, on finding one pearl of great value, went and sold all that he had and bought it." (Matthew 13:44-46)

Discipleship Reading: Matthew 13:44-52   **When:** Spring, A.D. 29
Contextual Reading: Matthew 13   **Where:** Galilee

In this final parable of this day Jesus changes the theme of His teaching concerning the Kingdom. Up to this point He has focused on the organic growth of the Kingdom. He now changes His focus from the organic growth of the Kingdom to the surpassing value of the Kingdom.

Throughout Scripture, Biblical values are established and understood by way of analogy - comparing one thing with another. Using analogies, the Scriptures compare earthly values with heavenly values. Starting with things we do understand (i.e., pearls), the Scriptures seek to communicate ideas and values we otherwise could never understand. And that is what Jesus does in this parable. We all understand the value of a pearl, even a *"pearl of great price."* But do we understand the value of the Kingdom? That's the analogy. The Kingdom of God challenges our sense of values and the worth of things. The Kingdom is a pearl of such great value that anyone discovering

The wealth of this world is little more than trinkets compared with the value of the Kingdom of God.

it would be willing to sell everything they possess in order to obtain it. For disciples of the Kingdom, the message is clear. The Kingdom of God is more valuable than any earthly treasure we might be called upon to give up in our pursuit of the Kingdom. The wealth of this world is little more than trinkets compared with the value of the Kingdom of God.

Value and Discernment

Like a surprisingly deep pond, this brief parable draws us in, overwhelms us and challenges us to respond to its truth, and to its unspoken questions, such as *"What is the Kingdom of God worth to you?"* But this parable is about more than the surpassing value of the Kingdom. It is also about the discernment required to recognize and appreciate what we have found. The parable confronts each of us with a question: *How discerning are we?* The merchant had the discernment required to distinguish between one special pearl and all others. And his discernment told him to sell everything he possessed to obtain it. Do we see it? Do we appreciate what we have discovered? Are we willing to give up everything in order to obtain it?

The Kingdom of God is a pearl of such great and surpassing value that the wise man would be willing to sell everything he possesses to obtain it, and would consider himself rich for having done so.

If any of this sounds vaguely familiar, it

And They Dreamt Of A Kingdom

should. The issue of discernment takes us back to an issue Jesus spent considerable time on in Lesson 38, namely, spiritual blindness. Spiritually blind people don't "get" it. They are not able to discern the value of the Kingdom. Why would anyone willingly give up the tangible treasures of this world in exchange for a life of serving the marginalized and a promise of intangible treasures in a coming Kingdom? Answer: They wouldn't. To see the surpassing value of the Kingdom requires faith, spiritual sight and discernment unlike anything known to the religion-shaped spirituality of 1st Century Judaism, or to the materialism-shaped spirituality of 21st Century American Christianity. Indeed, it requires a Jesus-shaped spirituality fit for a Kingdom.

On this day, Jesus' disciples learned a lesson required for every disciple of the Kingdom. They learned that you and I will never make the Kingdom of God our life's priority if we do not see, discern and appreciate its surpassing value. The Kingdom of God is a pearl of such great and surpassing value that the wise man would be willing to sell everything he possesses to obtain it, and would consider himself rich for having done so.

Every Disciple Of The Kingdom

"'Have you understood all these things?' They said to him, 'Yes.' And he said to them, 'Therefore every scribe who has been trained for the kingdom of heaven is like a master of a house, who brings out of his treasure what is new and what is old.'" (Matthew 13:51-52)

A long day of healing, confrontation and teaching was now drawing to a close. It had begun with Jesus performing a Messianic Miracle by healing a blind-deaf mute (back in Lesson 37). That miracle precipitated a confrontation with the Pharisees - the leaders of the local synagogues - who publicly rejected Jesus' messianic credentials and declared His power and His ministry to be from Satan. Jesus refuted their accusations, but He also changed the tone of His ministry. From this point on, for the remaining year of His public ministry, Jesus would only teach publicly in parables. Those in His audience with "ears to hear" would receive more truth in response to their questions (The concept of having "ears to hear" occurs some 12 times in the gospels, and is equivalent to having "spiritual sight"). But the

From this point forward, fruitfulness with what has been received would be the evidence which separates genuine discipleship from spiritual blindness.

spiritually blind and deaf would receive only more parables and more questions. Jesus would no longer cast the pearls of the Kingdom before people who either would not listen or could not appreciate them. Spiritual sight would be rewarded and spiritual immaturity would be given what it needed to grow. But from this point forward, Jesus would only give men as much truth as they were willing or able to receive and act upon. From this point forward, fruitfulness with what has been received would be the evidence which separates genuine discipleship from spiritual blindness.

It was a lot for twelve disciples to absorb. And so Jesus asked them a simple question: *"Have you understood all these things?"* The Greek word translated "understood" is the same word used to describe the seed upon the road (in Lesson 39). Many people heard the lessons Jesus offered on this day, but like seed sown on the road, they did not "understand" what they heard. The multitudes were unable to "put it all together." And so Jesus asked His disciples, *"Have you put it all together? Do you 'get it'?"*

"Yes," they replied. The disciples might be spiritually immature, but they were no longer spiritually blind. And they were growing quickly at the feet of Jesus. As genuine disciples of the Kingdom, they could see what others could not, and that included the Scribes. In the New Testament period the Scribes served as the professional interpreters of the Law in the synagogues. They were closely associated with the Pharisees, who ruled the Synagogues. If the Scribes had been willing to submit to Jesus and allow themselves to be "trained" in the Kingdom,[120] they would have gained spiritual sight and greater insight into the Law. They would have been able to "put it all together" by taking the old revelation of the Law, combining it with the new revelation which Jesus now offered and come to a true understanding of the Kingdom. But they and the Pharisees had rejected Jesus and His teaching. As a result, they would remain spiritually blind. The task of "putting it all together" and teaching the truths of the Kingdom would now fall to a group of marginalized fishermen, tax-collectors and zealots from Galilee who had believed the message of the Messiah-King, and had become disciples of His Kingdom.

Questions For Reflection

Reflecting on this Lesson, what did you learn about the surpassing value of the Kingdom that you did not know before?

How does the truth you learned apply to your own life and discipleship? Have you "put it all together?"

Key Thought

The Kingdom of God is a pearl of such surpassing value that anyone discovering it would be willing to sell everything they possess in order to obtain it, and would consider themselves rich for having done so.

And They Dreamt Of A Kingdom

43 - The Good News Of The Kingdom

Welcome to the good news of the Kingdom of God.

I'm curious as to how you arrived at this Lesson. I hope you're here because you read the entire book and have now arrived at the final Lesson. Having read the book, you should now have a fairly good grasp of what it means to be both a follower of Jesus and a disciple of the Kingdom of God. If this is true, then the purpose of this Lesson is to help you solidify what you have learned and to bring you to a point of personal commitment. What are you going to do with the call to faith and discipleship which Jesus has placed upon your life?

There is another reason why you may have come to this Lesson. Perhaps you began reading this book and somewhere along the way you realized that it was describing a faith in Jesus and a relationship with Him that seems to be missing in your own life. That's OK. This kind of realization can come to people who have been involved with a church all of their lives and have regarded themselves as Christians for many years. It can also come to people who have never attended a church or have never made any profession of "belief" in God or Jesus or the Kingdom. If this is true of you, then my guess is that you have skipped ahead to this Lesson in the hope of resolving the tension created by the absence of a genuine faith and a meaningful relationship with God in your own life. Be encouraged. There's good news ahead.

A Glorious Wreck

Unfortunately, the good news of the Kingdom begins with some bad news. You and I share a common heritage with everyone around us. We are a race of creatures in rebellion against our Creator and King. The human race is what the French theologian and reformer, John Calvin, once described as "a glorious wreck." Having been created by God in His Own image, we share a measure of God's glory. In the words of the Old Testament Psalmist, *"You have made him a little lower than the heavenly beings and crowned him with glory and honor"* (Psalm 8:5). Individually and collectively, we bear the divine imprint which marks us as uniquely His and sets us apart from the rest of Creation.

But man's willful rebellion and fall into sin, which began with Adam and Eve in the Garden, has brought about a moral and spiritual catastrophe which has spread to all men. As the Apostle explained it to believers in the city of Rome, *"Therefore, just as sin came into the world through one man, and death through sin, and so death spread to all men because all sinned."* (Romans 5:12) The entry of sin into the world has produced consequences which have been nothing less than a moral and spiritual catastrophe, for us individually and as a race of men, for *"all have sinned and fall short of the glory of God"* (Romans 3:23). As the great Old Testament Prophet, Isaiah, described it to the people of God some 700 years before Jesus, *"your iniquities have made a separation between you and your God, and your sins have hidden his face from you so that he does not hear"* (Isaiah 59:2).

The scope of our sin and rebellion against our God and King is so great that He would be perfectly just to condemn and punish us all on the spot, were it not for His great love and mercy toward us. As King David declared when God pointed out his sin of adultery with Bathsheba, *"Against you, you only, have I sinned and done what is evil in your sight, so that you may be justified in your words and blameless in your judgment"* (Psalm 51:4). Man's sin and rebellion - including yours and mine - have marred and effaced the divine image. Our sin has offended His holiness and our rebellion has offended His Kingly Majesty. Together they have rendered us rebellious subjects and "glorious wrecks," separated and alienated from the One in whom we live and move and have our being. Spiritually blind. Unable to save ourselves. In desperate need of redemption and restoration. This is our true, unvarnished spiritual condition. The relevant immediate question is this: do you understand that this describes your spiritual condition, too? This is a tough pill to swallow. But, then, good medicine often is.

Accepting Our True Spiritual Condition

This is important. The Kingdom of God does not allow for religious play acting by "hypocrites," people who pretend to be something they are not. For this reason, accepting the reality of our true spiritual condition is the necessary starting point for our journey into the Kingdom of God. There is no person more difficult to save than one who is firmly convinced that he (or she) is not lost. That's why it's important for you take a moment and reflect on your own spiritual condition. When your understanding of your true spiritual condition agrees with God's understanding of your spiritual condition as we have described it here, then you will be ready to move forward. Why? Because you will have reached a point known as "confession." And that deserves a little explanation.

In the New Testament, the Greek word translated "confess" (Greek: *homologeo* - *"to confess, to agree"*) literally means *"to say the same thing,"* hence, *"to agree."* In practical terms, to "confess" our sin means that we agree with God, that we "say the same thing" as God says, concerning our spiritual condition. It means that you agree with God that you are a sinner and a rebel against His Kingdom, and by your thoughts, your words and your deeds you have disobeyed His commands, offended His moral holiness and rebelled against His Kingly rule and authority over your life. It is only when you and I have come to terms with our true spiritual condition that we are ready to embrace the good news of the Kingdom of God. Are you ready?

Good News - At Last!

"Surely he has borne our griefs and carried our sorrows; yet we esteemed him stricken, smitten by God, and afflicted. But he was wounded for our transgressions; he was crushed for our iniquities; upon him was the chastisement that brought us peace, and with his stripes we are healed. All we like sheep have gone astray; we have turned--every one--to his own way; and the LORD has laid on him the iniquity of us all." (Isaiah 53:4-6)

Coming to terms with our true spiritual condition before God is a humbling journey. It brings us to a point of recognition - even despair - concerning our inability to heal and save ourselves. It leads us to an unavoidable conclusion. We need a savior who is able to save us from our fallen condition and to redeem us from the "slave market" of sin where we now find ourselves. We need someone greater than ourselves, someone able to deliver us from the "domain of darkness" and to bring us safely into the Kingdom of God.

The good news of the Kingdom is that God has provided just such a Savior. From the earliest days of biblical history His coming had been promised in the Old Testament Scriptures. His work of suffering on behalf of fallen, sinful humanity had been described in detail by the Prophet Isaiah 700 years before His arrival (see the above passage). He would be a suffering savior who would be wounded for our transgressions and crushed for our iniquities. Like a sacrificial lamb, God would place all of our sin and rebellion upon Him. He would be a Marvelous Counselor, a Mighty God and a Prince of Peace. He would come to serve, not to be served. He would seek and to save the lost, giving His own life as a ransom for many. He would be the Good Shepherd who would lay down His life for His sheep. His name would be Jesus, and He would fulfill all of the Old Testament promises by saving His people from their sins: *"'and you shall call his name Jesus, for he will save his people from their sins.' All this took place to fulfill what the Lord had spoken by the prophet: 'Behold, the virgin shall conceive and bear a son, and they shall call his name Immanuel' (which means, God with us)."* (Matthew 1:21-23)

Faith And A Heavenly Birth

"For God so loved the world, that he gave his only Son, that whoever believes in him should not perish but have eternal life. For God did not send his Son into the world to condemn the world, but in order that the world might be saved through him. Whoever believes in him is not condemned, but whoever does not believe is condemned already, because he has not believed in the name of the only Son of God." (John 3:16-18)

Do you remember Lesson 12 ("The New Birth")? It's the story of someone much like you and me. This person thought he "had it all together," and that His place in the Kingdom was fully assured. But in reality this person was spiritually blind to his true spiritual condition. He wasn't a religious hypocrite - a religious play actor pretending to be something he wasn't. No. He was very sincere and very knowledgeable. But he was also very blind, until Jesus spoke into His life.

When Jesus spoke into the life of Nicodemus, this religious leader of Israel who thought he "had it all together," Jesus told him three important realities concerning his true spiritual condition. *First,* Jesus told Nicodemus that all of his religious knowledge and experience of a lifetime was insufficient to obtain the Kingdom of God. Nicodemus - a teacher and leader of Israel - was as much a lost sinner and rebel as anyone else. Such a harsh dose of spiritual truth must have hurt. *Second,* Jesus informed Nicodemus that if he ever hoped to enter the Kingdom of God, he must experience the impossible - a new and heavenly birth by the Spirit of God. To enter the Kingdom of God, Nicodemus must be touched from above and transformed from within by the Holy Spirit. Such a heavenly birth was impossible by any means Nicodemus understood. *Third,* Jesus revealed to Nicodemus how the "impossible" was possible: by faith in Jesus. According to what is arguably the most famous verse in the Bible, the eternal life of the Kingdom is available to all those willing to believe in Jesus, the Son of God, *"For God so loved the world, that he gave his only Son, that whoever believes in him should not perish but have eternal life"* (John 3:16).

As we observed earlier, Nicodemus is much like you and me. In fact, we are so much alike that you and I must stand alongside Nicodemus and admit that all of our religious knowledge and experience is totally insufficient to obtain the eternal life of the Kingdom of God. We are as lost as he was, and he was as lost as we are. Like Nicodemus, we need the "impossible." We need a heavenly birth. We need to be touched from above and transformed from within by the Spirit of God. And as Jesus explained to him, the new birth and the eternal life of the Kingdom are available to *"whoever believes"* in Jesus.

And They Dreamt Of A Kingdom

Let's be clear on this point, because it's important. Entrance to the Kingdom of God isn't about what you know, or how much you know. It is about Who you know, and Who knows you. Entrance to the Kingdom of God and the eternal life it offers is personal. More specifically, it is a person - Jesus. As Jesus told His disciples, *"I am the way, and the truth, and the life. No one comes to the Father except through me"* (John 14:6). Our experience of the new and heavenly birth, along with our entrance to the Kingdom of God and the eternal life it offers, requires one thing on our part: faith in Jesus. It requires a genuine desire and willingness on our part to believe in Jesus, *"This is the work of God, that you believe in him whom he has sent."* (John 6:29) The key to eternal life and the Kingdom of God is faith in Jesus. The Apostle John summarized it this way:

"And this is the testimony, that God gave us eternal life, and this life is in his Son. Whoever has the Son has life; whoever does not have the Son of God does not have life. I write these things to you who believe in the name of the Son of God that you may know that you have eternal life." (1 John 5:11-13)

The Surest Signs of Genuine Faith

By now you might be asking yourself a very basic question: How do I know if I have the faith necessary to believe in Jesus, to experience the heavenly birth and to enter the Kingdom of God? That's a very good question. And there is a very good answer: Spiritually blind people don't ask those kind of questions! The very fact that you are wrestling with the question indicates that God is at work in your life. How do I know this? Because Scripture tells us that the very faith we need to believe and be saved is a gift from God. The Apostle Paul describes it this way:

"For by grace you have been saved through faith. And this (faith) is not your own doing; it is the gift of God, not a result of works, so that no one may boast. For we are his workmanship, created in Christ Jesus for good works, which God prepared beforehand, that we should walk in them." (Ephesians 2:8-10)

God in His love and grace illumines our spiritual darkness, enables us to see the reality of our true spiritual condition, and gives us the gift of faith to believe in Jesus and to embrace the good news of the Kingdom! And if you are wrestling with the issue of faith, that is one of the surest indicators that God is moving in your life to produce the genuine gift of faith. It doesn't mean that you're "in the Kingdom" yet, but it does mean that you've reached a critical turning point in your journey. There are two more sure signs of genuine faith that I want to mention, because, if your journey is true and your faith is genuine, they will soon apply to you. Both of them are mentioned in the following passage:

"Therefore, O King Agrippa, I was not disobedient to the heavenly vision, but declared first to those in Damascus, then in Jerusalem and throughout all the region of Judea, and also to the Gentiles, that they should repent and turn to God, performing deeds in keeping with their repentance." (Acts 26:19-20)

Fifteen years after His conversion encounter with the Risen Jesus on the Road to Damascus, while defending his faith before King Herod Agrippa II, the Apostle Paul mentioned two defining characteristics of His faith. Did you see them? Here they are: obedience and repentance. In biblical terms, to "repent" means that you and I not only agree with God concerning our true spiritual condition, but that we experience a profound change of heart which causes us to turn away from our sin and rebellion, and to turn toward God and His will. Obedience simply means that we take our faith and repentance seriously and desire to obey God in whatever He tells us to do, *"performing deeds in keeping with (our) repentance."* Obedience reveals whether or not the seed of the Kingdom has fallen on good soil in our lives. Our obedience to Jesus' commands represents the out-working of our faith and the fruit of our new life in Christ.

Taking The Next Step

There comes a point in our spiritual journey into the Kingdom of God when it is time to take "the next step," to make a conscious, personal commitment to Jesus and the Kingdom. Making such a commitment doesn't mean we know and understand everything there is to know about Jesus and the Kingdom. It simply means that we have reached a point where our desire for Jesus and the Kingdom exceeds the pull of those things which have held us back. Having read this book, you should have a pretty good idea of what such a commitment means. Spiritually speaking, you have arrived at the proverbial "fork in the road." It is time to choose between the spiritual light you have received thus far, or spiritual darkness. Those who choose light receive more light. Those who choose darkness plunge further into darkness. That's the way it works.

The good news is that because you have come this far without losing interest, God is apparently at work in your life, *"both to will and to work for his good pleasure."* (Philippians 2:13) He alone is the source of your desire to confess, to believe, to repent and to obey. But the next step is up to you. And one of the ways you can express your choice and your commitment is through prayer. "Prayer" is simply the term we use to refer to a conversation between us and God. Such "conversations" can be formal and written, or informal, spontaneous and personal. The important thing is that, whatever the form, they express the genuine condition, thought and desire of our hearts. Anything else is nothing more than religious play acting. The nature of a book like this pushes us toward a more formal written conversation, or prayer of commitment. To repeat-it-by-rote because the author told you to will accomplish absolutely nothing. Rather, let me encourage you to read the prayer below until you agree with it, make it your own and pray it back to God in the privacy of your own heart as a genuine expression of your own faith and commitment. At the conclusion of the prayer I have included an opportunity for you to sign and date it as a tangible reminder of the spiritual commitment to Jesus and the Kingdom which you made on this day.

Prayer Of Personal Commitment

"Heavenly Father, I seek your face in the name of Jesus, Your Son. I seek You in order to agree with You concerning my true spiritual condition. I confess and agree with You that I am a sinner against You and a rebel against Your Kingdom. I confess that by my thoughts, my words and my deeds I have ridiculed Your righteousness, rejected Your truth, disobeyed Your commands, offended Your moral holiness and rebelled against your Kingly rule and authority over my life. For all these things, and for many more which only You and I know, I ask your forgiveness. I acknowledge my need for a Savior, and I confess Jesus, Your Son, to be my only Savior, God and King. As the Scriptures promise, may the blood of Jesus, shed on my behalf, cleanse me from all of my sin. Create in me a clean heart, O God, and renew a right spirit

And They Dreamt Of A Kingdom

within me. Grant me the gift of faith to trust You, and the heavenly birth by Your Holy Spirit to enter Your Kingdom and to experience the eternal life you offer to all who believe. Grant me a spirit of genuine repentance, O God, to forsake the sin and rebellion I once loved. And in their place, enable me to love you with all of my heart, soul, mind and strength. Empower me to love my neighbor at least as much as I love myself, and to engage in such deeds of salt and light as would cause my neighbor to glorify You. Make me a disciple of Your Kingdom, Lord, for on this day I pledge to follow You wherever You may lead me. In Jesus' Name I pray. Amen."

_____

Signature

_____

Date

As a fellow pilgrim, allow me to welcome to the Kingdom of God and to the beginning of your journey of discipleship in that Kingdom. At this point, I would suggest that you start at the beginning and read through this book . . . again. I would encourage you to do this for two reasons. *First,* you'll be amazed at how "spiritual sight" changes your world. You'll find yourself suddenly seeing with a "clear eye" things which were right in front of you all along, but you never saw them. It's amazing what things spiritual blindness prevents us from seeing. *Second,* I would encourage you to re-read this book because, although you are no longer spiritually blind, you are still spiritually immature (a condition which requires a life-time in the Kingdom to correct). And by re-reading this book you'll discover more about discipleship in the Kingdom of God than the average professing Christian already knows. But always remember: discipleship in the Kingdom of God isn't about how much you know. It's about Who you know, and Who knows you.

Epilogue

We have come to the end of this book, but not to the end of Jesus' ministry or the discipleship lessons He wants to teach us. There's more. With Jesus, there always is. With the benefit of historical hindsight you and I know that much more lay ahead for these 12 men over the next 12-to-18 months than anything they could have imagined as they looked out over the Sea of Galilee on this day in the Winter of A.D. 29. Of the seven great miraculous signs recorded in the Gospel of John, four of them still lay ahead. They include the third and final "Messianic Miracle" (John 9), and one final miraculous sign so unexpected and profound that it would seal the decision by the religious leaders of Israel that, for the sake of the nation, Jesus must die (John 11). With Jesus, the lessons concerning our discipleship in the Kingdom become more challenging over time, not less. With Jesus, there is always more. But we'll save that for Volume 2. In this "Epilogue" I want to spend a few closing moments reflecting on where we have been with Jesus, over the course of this book. As we reflect on these two years of Jesus' public ministry we can discern that His ministry seemed to be characterized by four priorities, which we will briefly summarize.

1. Proclaiming The Good News Of The Kingdom. If we have learned anything about Jesus during these two years of ministry it is this: He was all about the Kingdom of God. Jesus proclaimed the Kingdom, manifested the Kingdom, modeled the Kingdom and taught the Kingdom. It is impossible to understand the ministry of Jesus apart from His commitment to the Kingdom of God. And we are forced to the unavoidable conclusions that Jesus expects that same commitment from every disciple of the Kingdom. If our message or ministry can be understood apart from the Kingdom of God, it isn't the message or ministry of Jesus.

2. Establishing His Messianic Credentials. Like the crowds which followed Him, we are often "wowed" by the miracles of Jesus without fully understanding why He performed them. Every miracle served two purposes. Every miracle embodied an act of genuine compassion by a Messiah-King who was genuinely moved by the brokenness of our fallen condition. From saving a young couple embarrassment on their wedding day by transforming water into wine, to healing a leper, a cripple or a blind deaf-mute, Jesus acted out of genuine compassion. The compassion shown a young couple at their wedding also brought His ever-watching disciples to genuine faith and began the process of establishing His Messianic credentials in their minds. Healing a paralytic on the Sabbath at the Pool of Bethesda established His credentials as Lord of the Sabbath, sharing equality with the Father. Healing a leper and a blind deaf-mute established His credentials as the Messiah, because only God's Messiah could perform such miracles (or so the Rabbis had taught). There was more, as we have seen, but the point is clear. By the time the Jewish religious authorities began their public rejection of Jesus (Lesson 37), they were without excuse. Their rejection was both knowledgeable and willful.

3. Building Depth In His Disciples. Throughout His first two years of public ministry Jesus was always more concerned with "depth" than He was with "breadth." While His ministry during this time was unquestionably characterized by a rising popularity among growing crowds, they represented the "backdrop" of His ministry, never His focus. He loved them, had compassion on them, frequently healed them and would soon die for them. But the focus of His ministry lay elsewhere. Jesus understood that "depth" in a few would eventually produce a more lasting "breadth," but that breadth pursued as an end-in-itself seldom - if ever - produces depth.

And They Dreamt Of A Kingdom

Breadth meant that seed might be widely sown on a variety of soil. Depth meant that only one of four soils would produce. But that one good soil would produce 40, 60 and even 100 fold. This is why it should come as no surprise that, for the first eighteen months of His public ministry, Jesus focused on no more than 7 disciples. He was willing to trade short-term success with the masses for long-term success with the disciples. He was always willing to sacrifice fickle "breadth" for a more mature "depth." And that alone is a lesson in Kingdom discipleship sufficient to guide each of us for a lifetime.

4. Challenging 1st Century Judaism To Repent And Acknowledge His Kingship. This challenge explains Jesus' sharp confrontations with Jewish religious leaders. Jesus made it clear that He had been sent first and foremost to *"the lost sheep of the house of Israel"* (Matthew 15:24). He was Israel's promised Messiah, and so He could tell the woman of Samaria that *"salvation is from the Jews"* (John 4:22). But the Kingdom of God and the salvation it promised was not a birthright to be claimed. It was a message requiring repentance and faith. It must be received on Jesus' terms, and no others. Judaism must submit to the Messiah-King, not the other way around. Jesus' message and His miracles challenged 1st Century Judaism to acknowledge His claims, repent of their religion-shaped rebellion, and to submit to His Kingship. Their rejection of Jesus as their Messiah-King would have two profound effects. It would produce a growing spiritual darkness in 1st Century Judaism, leading to the destruction of Judaism and the nation in 70 A.D. It would also open the door to the unhindered proclamation of the Kingdom to the Gentiles (i.e., all non-Jews).

Over the next 12-to-18 months of public ministry, we will watch Jesus build upon these four priorities and bring them to a fulfillment and a conclusion. In the process we will be challenged - as disciples of the Kingdom - to embrace Jesus' priorities as our own. We will be challenged to embrace Jesus' message of the Kingdom and to make it our own. We will be challenged to embrace Jesus' Messianic credentials and to call others to embrace them as well. We will be challenged to "make disciples" by building depth in a few, rather than pursuing "breadth" with the many. And we will be challenged to call all religious "pseudo" authorities to repent and to acknowledge the Kingship of Jesus alone.

But there is more. With Jesus, there always is.

Appendix

Table Of Scriptures, Lessons and Dates		
Passage	**Chapter Title**	**Chronos**
	Author's Preface	
	1 - October Tomatoes And The Kingdom of God	
	2 - The Kingdom	
	3 - The Kingdom As God Plan	
	4 - The Kingdom of God In Four Stages	
	5 - The Kingdom And The Church	
	6 - Disciples Of The Kingdom	
	7 - Believers Versus Disciples	
	8 - The Things That Shape Us	
John 1:35-51	9 - Beginnings	Summer, A.D. 26 Bethany, Beyond The Jordan
John 2:1-11	10 - A Wedding In Cana	Fall, A.D. 26 Galilee
John 2:13-25	11 - Zeal For Thy House	Spring, A.D.27 Jerusalem
John 3:1-21	12 - The New Birth	Spring, A.D. 27 Jerusalem
John 3:22-36	13 - He Must Increase	Summer, A.D. 27 Aenon/Salim
John 4:1-38	14 - With Jesus In Samaria	Summer, A.D. 27 Samaria, Sychar
Matthew 4:17 Mark 1:14-15	15 - Repent	Summer, A.D. 27 Galilee

Table Of Scriptures, Lessons and Dates		
John 4:46-54	16 - Healing A Nobleman's Son	Summer, A.D. 27 Galilee, Cana
Matthew 4:13-22 Mark 1:16-20	17 - Follow Me	Winter, A.D. 28 Galilee, Capernaum
Matthew 4:23-25; 8:14-17 Mark 1:21-39 Luke 4:31-43	18 - With Jesus On The Sabbath	Winter, A.D. 28 Galilee
Luke 5:1-11	19 - Do Not Be Afraid	Winter, A.D. 28 Galilee, Capernaum
Matthew 8:2-4; 9:1-8 Mark 1:40 - 2:12 Luke 5:12-26	20 - A Messianic Miracle and A Claim To Deity	Winter, A.D. 28 Galilee
Luke 5:27 - 32 Mark 2:13-17 Matthew 9:9-13	21 - The Call of Levi	Winter, A.D. 28 Galilee, Capernaum
Matthew 9:14-17 Mark 2:18-22 Luke 5:33-39	22 - Fasting, Garments And Wineskins	Winter, A.D. 28 Galilee
	Un-Recorded Passover	**Spring, A.D. 28**
John 5:1-18	23 - Healing At The Pool of Bethesda	Fall, A.D. 28 Jerusalem
John 5:19-47	24 - By What Authority?	Fall, A.D. 28 Jerusalem
Matthew 12:1-21 Mark 2:23-3:12 Luke 6:1-11	25 - Two Sabbath Healings	Spring, A.D. 29 Galilee
Luke 6:12-16 Mark 3:13-19	26 - And Then There Were Twelve	Spring, A.D. 29 Galilee
Matthew 5-7	27 - The Values of the Kingdom	Spring, A.D. 29 Galilee
Matthew 5:13 -15	28 - Salt, Light And Good Deeds	Spring, A.D. 29 Galilee
Matthew 6:19-34	29 - The Priority of the Kingdom	Spring, A.D. 29 Galilee

Table Of Scriptures, Lessons and Dates		
Matthew 7:1-5 Luke 6:37-42	30 - Specks, Logs And Measuring Cups	Spring, A.D. 29 Galilee
Matthew 7:6	31 - Dogs, Pigs And Pearls	Spring, A.D. 29 Galilee
Matthew 7:13-14 **18 Months Apart** Luke 13:23-30	32 - Broad Ways And Narrow Gates	Spring, A.D. 29 Galilee
Matthew 7:15-23 Luke 6:43-46	33 - False Prophets And Fruit	Spring, A.D. 29 Galilee
Matthew 7:24-27 Luke 6:47-49	34 - The Inverted Values of The Kingdom	Spring, A.D. 29 Galilee
Matthew 8:1-13 Luke 7:1-35 Matthew 11:1-30	35 - A Widespread Ministry	Spring, A.D. 29 Galilee
Luke 7:36-50	36 - She Who Loves Much	Spring, A.D. 29 Galilee
Matthew 12:22-50 Mark 3:20-35 Luke 8:1-3, 19-21	37 - The Peril Of Rejecting Jesus	Spring, A.D. 29 Galilee
Matthew 13:10-17 Mark 4:10-12 Luke 8:9-10	38 - Why Parables?	Spring, A.D. 29 Galilee
Matthew 13:1-9, 18-23 Mark 4:1-9; 13-25 Luke 8:4-8; 11-18	39 - Seed, Soil And Fruit	Spring, A.D. 29 Galilee
Matthew 13: 24-30, 36-43	40 - False Wheat & Stumbling Blocks	Spring, A.D. 29 Galilee
Matthew 13:31-33 Mark 4:26-35	41 - The Organic Growth of the Kingdom	Spring, A.D. 29 Galilee
Matt 13:44-52	42 - Value And Priority In The Kingdom	Spring, A.D. 29 Galilee
	43 - The Good News Of The Kingdom	
	Epilogue	

Endnotes

1. An "iconoclast" is a person who attacks cherished beliefs or traditional institutions because they see them as being "unbiblical" and based on error or superstition.

2. Ed Stetzer, *Subversive Kingdom: Living As Agents of Gospel Transformation* (Nashville: B&H Publishing Group, 2012).

3. Robert L. Thomas and Stanley N. Gundry, *A Harmony of the Gospels With Explanations and Essays* (New York: HarperOne, 1978).

4. For a more thorough argument in support of this chronology see W.R. Thompson's article *"Chronology (NT)"* in *The Zondervan Encyclopedia of the Bible*, Volume 1, Revised Full-Color Edition, Merril C. Tenney, General Editor, Moises Silva, Revision Editor (Grand Rapids: Zondervan, 2009), page 865ff. In my opinion, the classic work by Harold Hoerner, *Chronological Aspects of the Life of Christ* (Grand Rapids: Zondervan, 1977), relies too heavily on a Dispensational interpretation of Daniel 9 to establish its time line.

5. In the New Testament the concept of "this age" occurs no less than 12 times: Matthew 12:32; Mark 10:30; Luke 18:30; Luke 20:34-36; 1 Corinthians 1:20; 2:6 & 8; 3:18; Galatians 1:3-4; Ephesians 1:21; 1 Timothy 6:17; Hebrews 9:9

6. See Matthew 13:39, 40 & 49; 24:3; 28:20; Hebrews 9:26. This is what we frequently refer to as "the second coming."

7. Matthew 12:32; Mark 10:30; Luke 18:30; Ephesians 1:21; Hebrews 6:5.

8. The theological position presented here is commonly known as "Historic Premillennialism." Those wanting to explore this position in greater detail should read *"Chapter 55: The Millennium"* in Wayne Grudem's *Systematic Theology* (Grand Rapids: Zondervan, 1994). I am also deeply indebted to the excellent work of New Testament scholar George Eldon Ladd, *The Gospel of The Kingdom: Scriptural Studies in the Kingdom of God* (Grand Rapids: Wm. B. Eerdmans Publishing Company, 1990).

9. Lyotard, Jean-François, *The Postmodern Condition: A Report on Knowledge*, (1979) pp. xxiv - xxv.

10. Lyotard is asking: *"If we can't find 'truth' in meta-narratives, where can we find it?"* An excellent question. The challenge of exploring the Postmodern worldview is beyond the limited scope of this book. I would encourage the reader to see the treatment by James Sire, *The Universe Next Door: A Basic Worldview Catalogue*, 5th Edition (Downers Grove: IVP Academic, 2009). Specifically, see *"Chapter 9 The Vanished Horizon: Postmodernism."*

11. The Hebrew word translated "everlasting" is the word *'olam*. When applied to the affairs of men in "this present age" (such as Jonah spending three nights in the belly of the great fish), *'olam* can express various degrees of limited duration. But when applied to God and spiritual concepts, *'olam* expresses the duration of "eternity" (unless you think God's being and love will only last a short while - like "three days"). These two basic contexts (*"This Present Age"* of men and time, versus *"The Age To Come"* of God and eternal destinies) serve to distinguish between when *'olam* is being used in a temporal (i.e., time-bound and limited) sense, and when it is being used in an eternal sense of forever.

12. Ed Stetzer, *Subversive Kingdom: Living As Agents of Gospel Transformation* (Nashville: B&H Publishing Group, 2012), p. 5.

13. There are 300 Old Testament prophecies of a coming messiah which were fulfilled in the life, death and resurrection of Jesus. Dr. Peter Stoner (author of *"Science Speaks"*) calculated that the probability of only 48 of these prophecies being fulfilled by random chance in one person to be 1×10 to the 157th power. In comparison, the odds of winning the Powerball Lottery Jackpot are 1.75×10 to the 8th. Any would-be messiah would have better odds of winning the Powerball Jackpot once a year for the rest of his life than he would of fulfilling only 48 of the Old Testament prophecies which Jesus fulfilled. And Jesus fulfilled all 300.

14. Stetzer, *Subversive Kingdom*, 19.

15. The Greek word for "church" (*ekklesia*) comes from the Greek preposition "*ek*" meaning *"from"* or *"out of,"* and the Greek verb *kaleo* meaning *"to call."* Hence, the *ekklesia* was the *"the assembly of those who had been called out."*

16. You can read more about this project on the blog site of LifeWay Research at http://www.edstetzer.com/2012/10/new-research-obedience-not-eas.html

17. Outside of the Indicative mood the Aorist tense loses its force of past action, and simply denotes punctiliar action. The imperative mood in the Aorist (used here) denotes immediate punctiliar action. "Do it NOW!"

18. Flavius Josephus, *Antiquities*, Book 13: Chapter 14

19. Leon Morris, *The Gospel of John*, in *The New International Commentary On The New Testament*, F.F. Bruce, General Editor (Grand Rapids: Wm. B. Eerdman's Publishing Co., 1971), 206.

20. Morris, *The Gospel of John*, 454.

21. *"sine qua non"* (Latin: *"without which, not,"* hence, *"that which indispensable"*); Q.E.D. or *"quod erat demonstrandum"* (Latin: *"thus it is demonstrated or proved"*). The phrase *quod erat demonstrandum* is actually a Latin translation of a Greek phrase (*hoper edei deixai*, abbreviated OEΔ). The Greek reads, *"The very thing it was required to have shown"* which is closer to our Latin rendition of *"Thus it is proved."*

22. A. W. Tozer, *The Knowledge of the Holy* (New York: Harper & Row, 1961), 6.

23. Ibid., 7.

24. I want to express my profound thanks to the late Michael Spencer for challenging and clarifying my own thinking on the issue of a Jesus-shaped spirituality. See his excellent book, *Mere Churchianity: Finding Your Way Back to Jesus-Shaped Spirituality* (Colorado Springs: Waterbrook Press, 2010).

25. Source: National Congregations Study: American Congregations at the Beginning of the 21st Century available on-line at www.soc.duke.edu/natcong/

26. Using round numbers, this means taking a congregation of 360 people and dividing them into discipleship groups of 12, requiring 30 leaders, or a pastor who can disciple 30 groups of 12 on his (or her) own. In other words, a pastor who is 30 times more effective than Jesus.

27. A.B. Bruce, *The Training of the Twelve* (Grand Rapids: Kregel Publications, 1971), 1.

28. *"Strictly speaking there is no 'call' in this Gospel . . . Neither does Jesus call, nor John send. The disciples of John recognize the Messiah and spontaneously attach themselves to Him."* Morris, *The Gospel of John*, 155. See A.B. Bruce, *"For we have here to do not with any formal solemn call to the great office of the apostleship, or even with the commencement of an uninterrupted discipleship, but at the utmost with the beginnings of an acquaintance with and of faith in Jesus on the part of certain individuals. . .",* Bruce, 1. This invitation to "come and see" included staying with Him for the rest of that day and night, as it was already around 4:00pm in the afternoon (or "the tenth hour" by Jewish time-reckoning, which began at 6:00AM), and later to travel with Him back to Galilee. See Morris, 157ff.

29. Our understanding at this point is that the five included Andrew, Peter, Philip, Nathaniel, and John (the author of the Gospel). We regard John as the most likely candidate for the unnamed person who stood alongside Andrew (verses 35, 37 & 40). Scholars and writers of commentaries like to debate what they can't prove at this point. But A.B. Bruce sums it up best when he says, *"What if John were himself one of the five who on the present occasion became acquainted with Jesus? That would make a wide difference between him and the other evangelists, who could know of the incidents here related, if they knew of them as all, only at second hand. In the case supposed, it would not be surprising that to his latest hour John remembered with emotion the first time he saw the Incarnate Word, and deemed the minutest memorials of that time unspeakable precious."* A.B. Bruce, *The Training of the Twelve*, 2.

30. Forgive my shameless borrowing of Julius Caesar's message to the Roman Senate after defeating the Gauls and subduing the Province of Gaul for the Empire: *Veni Vidi Vici*, *"I came. I saw. I conquered."*

31. Known as "Bethany, Beyond-the-Jordan," in order to distinguish it from Bethany near the Mount of Olives.

32. The Gospel of John records seven (7) miraculous "signs" while alluding to many more. We will discuss the issue of miraculous signs in greater detail in Lesson 16 as we move forward.

33. Because the Romans forbade the Jews from minting their own coinage, Jewish leaders chose Tyrian silver didrachms and tetradrachms, which approximated by weight the Jewish half-shekels and shekels, as the official Temple coinage for all transactions.

34. The Greek word *polloi*, translated in 2:23 as "many" is the word commonly used in Classical Greek in a negative or pejorative sense with reference to "the unwashed masses."

35. F.F. Bruce, *The Gospel of John* (Grand Rapids: William B. Eerdmans Publishing Company, 1993), 78.

36. There is a different Greek word (*anagennao* - *"to be begotten or born again"*) which is more limited and specific in its meaning. Jesus could have used this word, but chose *anothen* in stead. Peter uses *anagennao* in 1 Peter 1:3 and 1:22-23.

37.Morris, *The Gospel of John*, 212.

38. F.F. Bruce, *The Gospel of John*, 86.

39.See Malachi 4:5-6. Although John himself denied this identification, Jesus affirmed it. See Matthew 11:14 & 17:10-13.

40.Morris, *The Gospel of John*, 256.

41.Ibid., 274.

42.Ibid., 279, particularly foot note 85 in which he relates the story of H.V. Morton at Jacob's well.

43. A.W. Tozer, *"Miracles Follow The Plow"* excerpted in Warren Wiersbe, *The Best of A.W. Tozer* (Camphill: Christian Publications, 1992; Copyright Baker Book House Company 1978), 243

44.Repentance in the Old Testament was expressed by two Hebrew words: _nacham_ describes a "grieving" which produces a change of attitude, heart or mind. _shuwb_ carries the basic meaning of *"movement back to the point of departure,"* hence, *"to turn and go in a different direction."*

45.See Morris, *The Gospel of John*, 289 and note 110 for more.

46.Sign # 1: The Wedding At Cana (John 2:1-11); Sign # 2: Healing A Nobleman's Son (John 4:46-54); Sign # 3: Healing the Lame Man At The Pool of Bethesda (John 5:1-18); Sign # 4: The Feeding of The Multitude (John 6:1-15); Sign # 5: Walking On The Water (John 6:16-21); Sign # 6 - Healing The Man Born Blind (John 9:1-41); Sign # 7: The Raising of Lazarus (John 11:1-57)

47.Morris, *The Gospel of John*, 290. Morris has an excellent extended treatment of "signs" in "Additional Note G" on page 684ff.

48.The standard Greek word for "son" is _huios_, but here John uses the Greek word _paidion_. In Classical Greek _paidion_ referred to a child up to seven years of age. It is formed by using the Greek root for child (_paid-_), and adding secondary suffix (_-ion_) which serves to "diminish" the root concept. It is best described as an "affectionate diminutive" and should be translated "little child" or "little boy."

49.Ibid., 291.

50.Leon Morris sums it up well,*"Previously the man had known enough about Jesus to regard Him as a talented wonder-worker. But the 'sign' pointed him beyond that. He plainly saw the hand of God in it, and his whole attitude was modified accordingly. He became a believer. The 'sign' transformed his faith into a greater faith."* Morris, 292.

51. A chronology note is perhaps in order at this point. As firm chronology markers are scarce in the Gospels (see our basic chronology outline on page 10), we have attempted to use certain "guidelines" such as the time of the year best suited to the narrative. The absence of significant public ministry activity during the winter months (basically three months between the winter solstice and the spring solstice) is appropriate to conditions. The

same is true concerning the significant amount of ministry activity from Spring to late Fall. According to our chronology, Lessons 17 thru 24 occur in the Spring-Summer-Fall of A.D. 28, including an unrecorded Passover in the Spring of A.D. 28. Lessons 25 thru 42 take place in the Spring of A.D. 29, prior to the Passover mentioned in John 6:4 (which we treat in Volume 2).

52. For the sake of clarity, the original five consisted of John (unnamed), Peter, Andrew, Philip, and Nathaniel. Only 3 of the five are present in Matthew 4:18-22. James - brother of John - has been added. All total, this would make six, half of the eventual twelve, and roughly 18 months have elapsed since Jesus met the first five disciples at the River Jordan.

53. This type of construction suggests an *"Introductory action which highlights the involvement of the subject(s) in an action which is important to the subsequent narrative."* On the use and meaning of the Greek periphrastic construction in the Gospel of Luke see Carl E. Johnson, *"A Discourse Analysis of the Periphrastic Imperfect in the Greek New Testament Writings of Luke,"* a Ph.D. Dissertation, The University of Texas at Arlington, 2010. ISBN 978-1-1240-5558-9

54. A similar point is made by Joel B. Green, *"We may follow throughout this section an interest in Jesus' identity. The townspeople are ignorant on this score, though they marvel at him and acclaim his authoritative status. Not knowing who he is, they fail to understand the nature of his mission (vv42-44). Demons, on the other hand, recognize him as 'Jesus of Nazareth,' 'the Holy One of God,' 'Son of God,' and 'Messiah.'"* Green, **The Gospel of Luke**, in **The New International Commentary On The New Testament**, Joel B. Green, General Editor (Grand Rapids: Wm. B. Eerdman's Publishing Co., 1997), 221.

55. Green makes a similar point when he says, *"Additionally, Jesus' command may be an attempt to avoid further acclamation by an agent of evil, lest Jesus thus be seen as working in league with an unclean spirit."* Green, 224.

56. Green's observation concerning Luke's use of these terms is helpful, *"Usually for Luke, 'power' is the inherent capacity to perform, while 'authority' is the attribution of the right to act."* Green, 242.

57. John White, **When The Spirit Comes With Power: Signs And Wonders Among God's People** (Downers Grove: InterVarsity Press, 1988), 141.

58. Ibid., 141.

59. Some commentators combine the events of Luke 5:1-11 with those of Matthew 4:13-22 and Mark 1:16-20, treating them as a single event. We disagree and believe that the details are sufficiently different to recognize them as two separate events in the life of Jesus and the twelve.

60. Green offers an excellent comparison between Luke 5:1-11 and Isaiah 6:1-10, and breaks both passages into four steps: 1) epiphany, 2) reaction, 3) reassurance, and 4) commission. See Green, **The Gospel of Luke**, 233.

61. The simple phrase *"Do not be afraid"* occurs no less than 33 times in Scripture, mostly in passages where God is encouraging people to not be afraid (the same is true of the phrase "fear not" which also occurs some 33 times).

62. Green's Excursus *"§11 Faith and Possessions In Luke"* offers this excellent observation, which is in keeping with what we have said in this Lesson, *"Discipleship demands that one no longer be a slave to wealth or cling to possessions as though they were one's source of security or social position, and that one give precedence to the family of God and especially to those in need."* Green, *The Gospel of Luke*, 229.

63. Ibid., 237-238.

64. The three "Messianic Miracles" were: 1) the healing of a leper, 2) The casting out of a mute/dumb demon, and 3) healing someone who was blind from birth.

65. Robert L. Thomas and Stanley N. Gundry, *A Harmony of the Gospels With Explanations and Essays* (HarperOne: New York, 1978), page 53, note "k." Later in His ministry, as if to add an exclamation point to this lesson, Jesus would heal ten lepers with a word. Jesus didn't just heal a leper. All totaled, He healed at least 11 lepers.

66. Jesus' "authority" to forgive sin is not something which has been delegated to Him, but is that authority which is rightfully His as the second person of the trinity.

67. See also Matthew 9:10-13; 11:19; Mark 2:15-16; Luke 6:32-33; 7:34-37; 15:1-7; 19:7

68. R.T. France, *The Gospel of Matthew,* in *The New International Commentary On The New Testament*, Joel B. Green, General Editor (Grand Rapids: Wm. B. Eerdman's Publishing Co., 2007), 351.

69. Joel Green, *The Gospel of Luke*, 245.

70. *Tractate Toharot 7:6* says, *"If tax gatherers entered a house (all that is within it) becomes unclean"*; people *"may not be believed if they say 'We entered but we touched nought.'"* Quoted by Leon Morris, *The Gospel According To Matthew* (Grand Rapids: Wm B. Eerdmans Publishing Company, 1992), 221, note 26.

71. Some ancient manuscripts do not include the part about the angel stirring the water (basically, verse 4, which we've placed in brackets). In the opinion of your author, the passage seems to make more sense when the section is included, but the best manuscript evidence excludes it. Assuming the verses to be original, it would appear that John is relating local legend or lore without passing judgment pro or con. He is simply describing the local circumstances to His readers, explaining what people believed and why the lame man was there. It is simply the background to the incident he is about to relate to us.

72. Leon Morris, *The Gospel According To John*, 301, note 13.

73. The Greek word <u>krabbatos</u> describes a small pallet or cot which could be rolled up and carried on one's shoulder.

74. This transition from "type" to "substance" can be seen in the use of the words "Passover" and "Sabbath." The word Passover occurs 50 times in the Old Testament, 26 times in the Gospels, but only 3 times in the rest of the NT, reflecting the decline of its importance in the spiritual life of the Church. A similar pattern is seen in the use of the word "Sabbath" which occurs 77 times in the Old Testament, 50 times in the Gospels, but only 11 times in the rest of the NT (9 of those in the book of Acts and only 2 in the Epistles). In both instances it is clear that the Church had moved from the"type and shadow" of the Law to the substance

and fulfillment of Christ.

75.The use of two imperfect tense verbs in verse 16 (*edokon* and *epoiei*), communicates the idea that the religious leaders were "continually persecuting" Jesus because He was "continually doing these things" on the Sabbath. Jesus' Sabbath activities have been noticed and the conflict with the religious authorities which begins here will grow and will eventually culminate in His death at their hands. See Leon Morris, *The Gospel According To John*, 209 and 308.

76.The importance of this episode in the Gospels, in the ministry of Jesus and in His work of discipleship cannot be overstated. Jesus' claim to equality and deity is the foundation upon which everything which follows rests. As Leon Morris observes, "*. . . His claim to be the living bread, the Good Shepherd and much more beside depends on the truth here set forth,*" Morris, 312. This reality alone makes the truth shared here the dividing line between faith and unbelief.

77. Leon Morris, *The Gospel According to John*, 323ff.

78. *quod erat demonstrandum*; Latin: *"thus it is demonstrated or proved"*

79. Leon Morris, *The Gospel According To Matthew*, 299.

80. France notes, *"The basis for this exception is in who they are (the priests, appointed for this divine service) and the institution which requires it (the temple, as the focal point of God's presence among his people)."* R.T. France, *The Gospel of Matthew*, 460.

81. Ibid.

82.The Greek word used for Jesus' "anger" is the word *orge*, the most common New Testament word for the "wrath" of God. See John 3:36; Romans 1:18; 5:9; Ephesians 5:6; Revelation :16-17; 19:15.

83.This decline can be observed in the New Testament, where the word "Sabbath" occurs 59 times in the Gospels and Acts, but only 2 times in the Epistles. The understanding of the early church concerning the Sabbath can be seen in the one place where the Apostle Paul addresses it. Writing to the Gentile believers in Colossae, Paul encourages the disciples not to allow others (i.e., Judaizers) to criticize or judge them for not keeping Jewish observances, including the Sabbath, *"Therefore let no one pass judgment on you in questions of food and drink, or with regard to a festival or a new moon or a Sabbath."* (Colossians 2:16) This is in keeping with the instructions given by the Apostles and Elders in Jerusalem to Gentile believers in Acts 15. In the early church, a "Judaizer" was someone who insisted that their "fellow-believers" should follow the Law of Moses. The term originates from a confrontation between Paul and Peter, recorded in the book of Galatians, *"But when I saw that their conduct was not in step with the truth of the gospel, I said to Cephas [Peter] before them all, 'If you, though a Jew, live like a Gentile and not like a Jew, how can you force the Gentiles to live like Jews?'"* (Galatians 2:14) The Greek word translated "live like Jews" (*Ioudaizo*) means exactly that: *"to adopt Jewish customs and to live like a Jew."* To "Judaize" means to force Christians to live like Jews.

84.This would be an on-going issue in the life of the Church. For example Canon 29 from the Council of Laodicea (ca. A.D. 365) decreed, *"Christians must not judaize by resting on the Sabbath, but must work on that day, rather honouring the Lord's Day; and, if they can, resting then as Christians. But if any shall be found to be judaizers, let them be anathema* from Christ." (Percival Translation). A comment on this Canon by Theodore Balsamon, a 12-century canonist of the Eastern Orthodox Church and the Orthodox Patriarch of Antioch, reads, *"Here the Fathers order that no one of the faithful shall stop work on the Sabbath as do the Jews, but that they should honour the Lord's Day, on account of the Lord's resurrection, and that on that day they should abstain from manual labour and go to church. But thus abstaining from work on Sunday they do not lay down as a necessity, but they add, 'if they can.' For if through need or any other necessity any one worked on the Lord's day this was not reckoned against him."* See, **Nicene and Post Nicene Fathers**, 2-14. **The Seven Ecumenical Councils,** Philip Schaff, Editor, Edinburgh: T&T Clark. Public Domain. Published online by Christian Classics Ethereal Library at CCEL.org/.

85. Jesus' public ministry began in the Spring of A.D. 27 (see Lesson 11), and it is now the Spring of A.D. 29. Five of the disciples began their association with Jesus earlier, in the Summer of A.D. 26. Two more, James and Levi, joined the disciples in the Spring of A.D. 28. The remaining five were officially recognized (named) in the Spring of A.D. 29. Prior to this moment we have no record of any other disciples being called or named. In this passage we discover that there were other followers of Jesus whom the Gospel writers describe as "disciples." Apparently, it is from this larger pool of followers or disciples that Jesus chooses the remaining five disciples for a total of twelve.

86. Biblical head counts are always challenging. Counting the number of disciples is no exception. Our guesstimate begins conservatively with the 72 disciples sent out by Jesus in Luke 10:1, includes the 120 "brothers" who gathered in the Upper Room in Acts 1:15 and ends on the numerical high side with Jesus' post-resurrection appearance to *"more than five hundred brothers at one time"* recorded by Paul in 1 Corinthians 15:6. Again, those committed to Jesus as "disciples" were numbered in the hundreds, not multitudes.

87.The idea that the five now joined the seven as disciples of Jesus seems to be suggested by the lists given by both Gospel writers. Both lists name the seven first (ending with Matthew, the last of the seven called), followed by the five.

88.Thayer - παιδαγωγός (*paidagogos - a leader, or escort*; Latin - *paedagogus*), from the time of Herodotus (8, 75) on down, a tutor, a guide and guardian of boys. Among the Greeks and Romans the name was applied to trustworthy slaves who were charged with the duty of supervising the life and morals of boys belonging to the better classes. The boys were not allowed so much as to step out of the house without them before arriving at the age of manhood .

89.The early Church instructed three behaviors on the part of gentile believers to avoid offending their Jewish brethren: abstain from idolatry (i.e., things sacrificed to idols), abstain from sexual immorality, and abstain from meats which have been improperly handled ("blood" and "strangled"). These instructions are consistent with Paul's teaching on this subject 1 Corinthians 8.

90.The concept of good deeds or "good works" occurs some 32 times in the New Testament. Those 32 occurrences are almost equally divided between two Greek phrases (*agathos ergon* and *kalos ergon*), which are so similar in use and meaning as to be interchangeable.

91.The root word *zeteo*, meaning "to seek" has been intensified by the addition of the preposition *epi* .

92. *"The Epistle of Mathetes to Diognetus"* from **The Apostolic Fathers,** translation by Lightfoot & Harmer, 1891.

93. W. Gunther, ʹυποκρινο in **The New International Dictionary of New Testament Theology**, Vol. 2, Colin Brown, General Editor (Grand Rapids: Zondervan Publishing House, 1976), 468.

94. Greek: *plateia*, meaning "broad" from which we get "plateau"; Greek: *euruchoros*, from *eurus* meaning "broad" or "spacious" and *chora* meaning "place"; Greek: *apoleia*, "destruction," is a primary New Testament word for eternal punishment; Greek: *polloi*, frequently used in Greek to refer to "the masses."

95. The Greek word *stenos* (translated "small") comes from a root suggesting "groaning." *Stenos* describes a "narrow, restrictive way." The Greek word *thlibo* (translated "narrow") is a verb meaning *"to press hard"* or *"to oppress"* or *"to afflict."* As a passive perfect participle it is being used to refer to something "narrow" or "restrictive." See "Narrow," in W. E. Vine, **Expository Dictionary of New Testament Words**.

96. The two Greek verbs are *eiserchomai* meaning simply *"to enter into,"* and *eurisko* meaning *"to find, to discover, to obtain."*

97. In 1 Corinthians 4:20 the Apostle Paul states, *"For the kingdom of God does not consist in talk but in power."* There, Paul is confronting false teachers, not false prophets.

98. The Greek word is *phronismos*, meaning *"intelligent, thoughtful, prudent and mindful of their own best interests."*

99. Jim Elliott, journal entry for October 28, 1949.

100. It is important to note that this is when a good harmony or chronology of the gospels helps our understanding of events. At this point Matthew's account becomes more "topical" after verse 11, while Luke's account is the more chronologically consistent.

101. Greek: *splagchnizomai* - *"to be moved as to one's bowels, hence to be moved with compassion, have compassion (for the bowels were thought to be the seat of love and pity.)"* - Thayer

102. The Greek word translated "offended" is the verb *skandalidzo*, from which we get our English verb "to be scandalized." See our extended treatment of this word in Lesson 40.

103. Jesus "prophecy" here has a dual fulfillment. First, it was fulfilled in the destruction of Jerusalem in A.D. 70 at the hands of the Romans. Like the destruction of Jerusalem by the Babylonians in 586 B.C. as God's judgment for Israel's continued disobedience, the destruction of Jerusalem by the Romans in A.D. 70 represented God's judgment upon 1st Century Judaism for their rejection of Jesus, the Messiah-King. Second, Jesus' prophecy will find its ultimate fulfillment on the great Day of Judgment when God calls all men to account for their response to the good news of the Kingdom.

104. Since classical times, the Greek verb *brecho* meant "to rain" or "to send rain" or "to fall like rain." It occurs 7 times in the New Testament, twice in this passage and five times elsewhere describing literal rain.

105. The Greek word *daimonidzomai* is what's known as a middle deponent verb, best rendered *"to be demonized"* rather than *"to be demon possessed."*

106. Specifically, the use of the Greek particle *meti*, used in questions where a negative answer is expected.

107. The sin of "blasphemy against the Holy Spirit" means to knowingly and willfully attribute the work of the Holy Spirit to Satan. The Pharisees knew that Jesus was the Messiah-King, based upon His own testimony AND the two Messianic Miracles He had already performed. Their rejection was conscious and willful.

108. The biblical doctrine of the Trinity(one God in three persons) is discernable at this point. Jesus the Son shares "equality" with the Father and performs the miraculous work of the Kingdom by the power of the Holy Spirit. The Jews would accuse Jesus of "blasphemy" for claiming equality with God (John 10:33). Now Jesus accuses the Pharisees of "blasphemy" for assigning His deeds, done in the power of the Holy Spirit, to Satan.

109. Thomas and Gundry's footnote on Matthew 13:1-3 is helpful here. They point out that 1) the parables of this chapter were taught on the same day as the Pharisees' rejection of Jesus, and 2) the parables enabled Jesus to instruct His disciples without giving His opponents unnecessary opportunities to catch Him with His own words. Jesus would no longer cast pearls before swine.

110. C.H. Dodd defines a parable as *"a metaphor or simile drawn from nature or common life, arresting the hearer by its vividness or strangeness, and leaving the mind in sufficient doubt about its precise application to tease it into active thought."* (**The Parables of the Kingdom** [London, 1936], 16), quoted by Morris, **The Gospel According To John**, 333, note 1.

111. William Barclay, **Matthew**, Volume 2, in **The New Daily Study Bible** (Louisville: Westminster John Know Press, 2001), 66.

112. The Greek phrase translated *"this"* (*dia touto*) is a grammatical idiom which carries the sense of *"on account of what has just been said."*

113. *"The parable is a powerful method of teaching, but perhaps some measure of commitment is required in hearers if they are really to understand what a parable is saying. It is a fallacy that everyone can understand a parable."* Morris, **The Gospel According To Matthew**, 339.

114. The Greek word *suniemi* means *"to put it all together,"* hence, *"to understand."*

115. Greek: *skandalidzo*. Literally, to stumble. See our extended treatment in Lesson 40.

116. William Barclay, **Matthew**, Volume 2, 66.

117. This word group, consisting of the verb *skandalidzo* and the noun *skandalon*, occurs some 32 times in the Gospels (19 in Matthew alone) and 13 times in the Epistles.

118. This principle of God separating the wicked and the righteous is important enough for Jesus to repeat it in the parable of the Dragnet in Matthew 13:47-50.

119.See R.T. France and his discussion of verse 33, page 528. Leaven should more properly be more properly understood as "sourdough starter" than as yeast. France's point is the same as ours here, ". . . *the point is that a little leaven has a great effect."* That is the organic growth of the Kingdom.

120. The word "trained" is the Greek word _matheteuo_, "to disciple"; in the passive voice here it means "to be discipled"

www.ingramcontent.com/pod-product-compliance
Lightning Source LLC
Chambersburg PA
CBHW070344090426
42733CB00009B/1277